Successful Glossary of Common Library Terms

Successful Glossary of Common Library Terms

Bhagwan Das

CYBER TECH PUBLICATIONS
4264/3, Ansari Road, Daryaganj, New Delhi-110002 (India)
Ph.: 011-23244078. Fax: 011-23280028
E-Mail: cyberpublicationsdelhi@yahoo.com

SUCCESSFUL GLOSSARY OF COMMON LIBRARY TERMS

Bhagwan Das

First Edition 2009

Published by :

G.S. Rawat for **Cyber Tech Publications**
4264/3, Ansari Road, Daryaganj, New Delhi-110002 (India)
Ph.: 011-23244078. Fax: 011-23280028
E-Mail: cyberpublicationsdelhi@yahoo.com

Printed at : **Amit Enterprises**, Maujpur, Delhi, (9810878184)

Preface

Although numerous books, both theoretical and practical, have been published on the subject of library terminology and the conservation of archival materials, there would seem to be a need for one that approaches the subject by examining the meaning and usage of the many terms, expressions, and names pertaining to the various subjects.

Although this dictionary is intended first and foremost for those actively involved in one or more aspects of the overall field of library terminology and book conservation, including bookbinders, conservators of library and archival materials, and the like, it is perhaps no less intended for those working in related fields, such as bibliography and librarianship, where the many terms and expressions relating to the overall field may be less familiar and even more confusing.

The compilers accept full responsibility for the selection of terms for inclusion, as well as for the even more difficult task of rejection. The definitions themselves, although herein the responsibility of the same persons, were, whenever possible, drawn from the most authoritative sources available (as indicated by the number in parentheses at the end of a definition, which refers to the Sources and Bibliography section) and supplemented by the experience of the authors.

Where a term has more than one definition, each is numbered and arranged in its descending order of significance in relation to library terminology.

—Author

Glossary of Common Library Terms

AB bookman's weekly : A trade publication used mainly by antiquarian booksellers to locate rare, out of print, and difficult to find titles, *AB Bookman's Weekly* began as a section of *Publisher's Weekly* under the title *Antiquarian Bookman*. In 1948 it became an independent weekly of the same title published by R.R. Bowker. Publication under the current title began in 1967.

abandoned property law : A statute of particular interest to archivists, describing the procedures by which an individual or organization may obtain clear, legal title to material that it holds but does not own. In the United States, federal statutory law does not address abandoned property; such statutes are enacted state by state, with less than half of the 50 states having taken the step. Click here to learn about New Hampshire's Abandoned Property Law, courtesy of the New Hampshire State Treasurer. Synonymous with *unclaimed property law*.

ABC : See Activity Based Costing

abebooks : A leading online market place for used, rare, and out of print books, Abebooks provides a list of over 40 million titles available from a network of over 10,000 booksellers. The company provides additional services to librarians, such as consolidated billing and purchase orders. Click here to connect to the Abebooks.com homepage. *See also*: Alibris.

abecedary : A book containing the letters of the alphabet and basic rules of spelling and grammar, used in Europe as a primer before the invention of the printing press. Early printed examples (sometimes in the form of a broadsheet) displayed the alphabet in uppercase and lowercase letters in both roman and gothic type, with separate lists of vowels, dipthongs, and consonants. By 1700, some ABC books included children's rhymes. Synonymous with *abecedarium* (plural: *abecedarii*). *See also*: horn book.

aberrant copy : A copy of a book containing obvious printing and/or binding errors that are more serious than minor defects.

aberrant date : In archives, a date that falls outside the chronological sequence of dates pertaining to the majority of the documents in the record unit described (Richard Pearce-Moses, *A Glossary of Archival and Records Terminology*, Society of American Archives).

ABM : See Activity Based Management

above the fold : The printed half of a broadsheet newspaper that appears higher on the page than the horizontal fold. Articles placed near the top have greater prominence because most languages are read from top to bottom of the writing surface.

Abridged Decimal Classification (ADC) : A logical truncation of the notational and structural hierarchy of the full edition of Dewey Decimal Classification, developed for general collections of 20,000 titles or less. Click here for more information, courtesy of OCLC.

abridgment : A shortened version or edition of a written work that preserves the overall meaning and manner of presentation of the original but omits the less important passages of text and usually any illustrations, notes, and appendices. Often prepared by a person other than the original author or editor, an *abridged edition* is generally intended for readers unlikely to purchase the unabridged version because of its length, complexity, or price (*example*: The New Shorter Oxford English Dictionary). Also spelled *abridgement*. Abbreviated *abr*. Synonymous with *condensation*. Compare with simplified edition. *See also*: abstract, brief, digest, epitome, summary, and synopsis.

absenteeism : The failure of an employee to report for work, usually due to illness, accident, family responsibilities, or personal business. A persistently high rate of absenteeism may be a sign of low morale among the staff of a library or library system. *See also*: burnout.

absorbency : The capacity of paper to absorb and retain moisture, which varies with type of paper and is of particular importance in printing processes that use liquid ink. *See also*: water-damaged.

absorption : The incorporation of one serial by another. The note *Absorbed:* followed by the title of the assimilated serial is added to the bibliographic record representing the assimilating publication, and the corresponding note *Absorbed by:* followed by the title of the assimilating serial is added to the record for the assimilated publication. The absorbed title usually assumes the title and numbering of the assimilating publication. Compare with merger.

abstract : A brief, objective representation of the essential content of a book, article, speech, report, dissertation, patent, standard, or other work, presenting the main points in the same order as the original.but having no independent literary value. A well-prepared abstract enables the reader to 1) quickly identify the basic content of the document, 2) determine its relevance to their interests, and 3) decide whether it is worth their time to read the entire document. An abstract can be informative, indicative, critical, or written from a particular point of view (slanted). Examples of the various types of abstracts can be seen in the Appendix of the ANSI/NISO Z39.14 *Guidelines for Abstracts*. Length depends on the type of document abstracted and the intended use of the abstract. As a general rule, abstracts of long documents, such as monographs and theses, are limited to a single page (about 300 words); abstracts of papers, articles, and portions of monographs are no longer than 250 words; abstracts of notes and other brief communications are limited to 100 words; and abstracts of very short documents, such as editorials and letters to the editor, are about 30 words long. In a scholarly journal article, the abstract should appear on the first page, following the title and name(s) of author(s) and preceding the text. In a separately published document, the abstract should be placed between the title page and the text. In an entry in a printed indexing and abstracting service or bibliographic database, the abstract accompanies the citation. Because the abstract is a searchable field in most bibliographic databases, attention must be paid by the abstractor to the keywords included in it. Authorship of an abstract can be unattributed or indicated by name or initials. Compare with summary. *See also*: abstracting journal, author abstract, and structured abstract.

abstract resource : Imaginary resource introduced so that its availability and activity requirement gives an extra means of control. For example, two jobs not being worked upon simultaneously in order to obviate an accident hazard. [D04377]

abstracting : The preparation of a brief, objective statement (abstract) of the content of a written work to enable the researcher to quickly determine whether reading the entire text might satisfy the specific information need. Abstracting is usually limited to the literature of a specific discipline or group of related disciplines and is performed by an individual or commercial entity, such as an indexing and abstracting service, that provides abstracts regularly to a list of subscribers.

abstracting and indexing (A&I) : A category of database that provides bibliographic citations and abstracts of the literature of a discipline or subject area, as distinct from a retrieval service that provides information sources in full-text.

abstracting journal : A journal that specializes in providing summaries (called abstracts) of articles and other documents published within the scope of a specific academic discipline or field of study (*example*: **Peace Research Abstracts Journal**). Synonymous with *abstract journal*. Compare with abstracting service.

abstracting service : A commercial indexing service that provides both a citation and a brief summary or abstract of the content of each document indexed (*example*: *Information Science & Technology Abstracts*). Numbered consecutively in order of addition, entries are issued serially in print, usually in monthly or quarterly supplements, or in a regularly updated bibliographic database available by subscription. Abstracting services can be comprehensive or selective within a specific academic discipline or subdiscipline. Compare with abstracting journal.

abstraction : The creation of a view or model that suppresses unnecessary details to focus on a specific set of details of interest. [D04796]

academic freedom: The principle that faculty members employed at institutions of higher education (including librarians with faculty status) should remain free to express their views and teach in the manner of their own choosing, without pressure or interference from administration, government, or any outside organization.

academic library : A library that is an integral part of a college, university, or other institution of postsecondary education, administered to meet the information and research needs of its students, faculty, and staff. In the United States, the professional association for academic libraries and librarians is the Association of College and Research Libraries (ACRL), which publishes *Standards for Libraries in Higher Education*. For more information on academic libraries in the United States, see *E.D. TAB: Academic Libraries: 2000*, a report published in November 2003 by the National Center for Education Statistics (NCES). *Libweb* provides a list of links to academic libraries in the United States by region and state. Compare with research library. *See also*: college library, departmental library, graduate library, undergraduate library, and university library.

academic status : Recognition given by an institution of higher education that the librarians in its employ are considered members of the teaching or research staff but are *not* entitled to ranks, titles, rights, and benefits equivalent to those of faculty. The Association of College and Research Libraries (ACRL) has published *Guidelines for Academic Status for College and University Librarians* (June 2002). Compare with faculty status.

academy award : An award given annually in the United States by the voting membership of the Academy of Motion Picture Arts and Sciences for excellence in motion picture performance and production. To qualify, a film must have opened in Los Angeles during the preceding calendar year. Nominees are announced in advance and the ceremony, hosted by a celebrity, is televised nationally. Awards are given in seven major categories: best picture (feature length), best director, best actor, best actress, best supporting actor, best supporting actress, and best foreign-language film. Awards are also given for animated and short films. Also called an "Oscar" for the nickname given to the golden trophy statuette received by each winner. See *HowStuffWorks* for more information about the Academy Awards. *The Internet Movie Database* provides a summary of past award winners. Click here to connect to the official Academy Awards Web site.

academy file : In archives, a series, often found in Congressional records, that includes applications for admission to one of the United States service academies, often accompanied by letters of recommendation from appropriate members of Congress. The academies include the Military Academy at West Point, the Naval Academy at Annapolis, the Air Force Academy at Colorado Springs, the Coast Guard Academy at Groton, and the Merchant Marine Academy at King's Point.

academy format : The moving image format chosen by representatives of the Academy of Motion Picture Arts and Sciences, American Society of Cinematographers (ASC), Society of Motion Picture and Television Engineers (SMPTE), and American Projection Society to be the standard for 35mm film. Academy format for silent film had an aspect ratio of 4:3 or 1.33:1 (width to height of image). When sound film was introduced, the format changed to 1.37:1, which remained the international standard for about 25 years until widescreen was introduced (the image ratio remained 1.33:1 with an added area on one side for the sound track). Synonymous with *Academy aperture*.

Academy of Certified Archivists (ACA) : Founded in 1989 at the annual meeting of the Society of American Archivists, ACA is an independent, nonprofit professional organization that certifies individuals who meet specific standards and requirements for archival education, knowledge, and experience. To become a Certified Archivist, applicants must pass an examination given annually in conjunction with the annual meeting of the SAA and simultaneously at several announced sites and petitioned sites in the United States and Canada. Click here to connect to the ACA homepage.

acanthus : A stylized representation of the elegantly scalloped leaf-form of *Acanthus spinosus*, a species of Mediterranean herbaceous plant with thick, fleshy leaves, used in Antiquity to ornament Corinthian capitals and later as a decorative motif in medieval art, especially in the borders and initial letters of illuminated manuscripts where it usually appears painted in unrealistic colors (red, yellow, blue, purple), often in combination with small images of flowers, birds, insects, and animals. Click here to view acanthus borders in a 15th-century Flemish Book of Hours (Getty Museum, MS Ludwig IX 8) or see this example in a 15th-century French translation of Saint Augustine's *De Civitate Dei* (Koninklijke Bibliotheek). Another variation on the style can be seen in this 15th-century version of *Saint George and the Dragon* (Getty, MS 2). Compare with *rinceaux*.

accelerated aging test : A laboratory procedure used by archivists and special collections librarians to estimate the rate at which a material (film, paper, ink, etc.) will deteriorate in storage, to facilitate prediction of its life expectancy. According to the Society of American Archivists, such tests are often based on the Arrhenius function, which assumes that materials age in a predictable manner relative to temperature. However, such tests may be of limited usefulness because degree of permanence is influenced by conditions of storage, which vary widely. Also, empirical verification of the accuracy of accelerated aging tests requires experiments conducted over a number of years.

acceleration : The use of methods for completing work in a shorter time than previously planned or required by the contract.

acceptability criteria : A limit or limits placed upon the degree of non-conformance permitted in material expressed in definitive operational terms.

acceptable quality level ("AQL") : The maximum percent defective (or the maximum number of defects per hundred units) that, for the purpose of sampling inspection, can be considered satisfactory as a process average.

acceptable use policy (AUP) : Guidelines established by a library or library system concerning the manner in which its computer systems and equipment may be used by patrons and staff; for example, most public and academic libraries prohibit the use of library computers for private commercial or unlawful activities. In most libraries, a printed copy of acceptable use policy is posted near the workstations to which restrictions apply. Some libraries make their policy statement available electronically, and users may be required to assent to it by clicking on a small box or icon before access is granted. Synonymous with *Internet use policy*.

acceptance : The act of taking custody based on satisfactory verification.

acceptance criteria : Performance requirements and essential conditions that have to be achieved before project deliverables are accepted.

acceptance letters : Four (or more) formal letters written during the final Stage(s) of a project, i.e. Systems, Operations, Security, User and Business Acceptance Letters.

acceptance number : The maximum number of defects or defective units in the sample that will permit acceptance of the inspection lot or batch.

acceptance review : A specification compliance control gate or check point at which adherence to expectations of the service or deliverables is verified. Performed at any level of the system or process.

acceptance test : A predefined test to prove an equipment will perform the allotted task.

acceptance test procedure ("ATP") : Detailed step-by-step instructions for the setup, operation, and evaluation of tests. The procedure includes the approach to sampling and statistical quality control.

acceptance testing : Formal testing conducted to determine whether or not a system satisfies its acceptance criteria and to enable the customer to determine whether or not to accept the system.

access : Ability to enter the site of the project works and/or the necessary project data.

access code : An identification code, such as a username, password, or PIN, which a user must enter correctly to gain access to a computer system or network. In most proprietary systems, access codes are tightly controlled to exclude unauthorized users. Synonymous with *authorization code*.

access policy : A formal written statement issued by the person(s) or body responsible for managing archives or special collections, specifying which materials are available for access and by whom, including any conditions or restrictions on use, usually posted or distributed by some method to users.

access services : The provision of access to a library's resources and collections, which includes the circulation of materials (general circulation, reserves, interlibrary loan, document delivery), reshelving, stack maintenance, security, and signage. Large libraries employ an *access services librarian* to manage these activities.

access time : The amount of time it takes a computer system to provide stored data to a person who logs on and follows correct procedures for retrieval. Access time is often slower during periods of peak use.

accession : The act and procedures involved in taking records or papers into physical and legal custody by an archival agency or manuscript repository. The purpose is to extend basic control over a collection as quickly as possible to prevent its being confused or mixed with other material in custody. 2. The materials involved in such a transfer of custody.

accession number : A unique number assigned to a bibliographic item in the order in which it is added to a library collection, recorded in an accession record maintained by the technical services department. Most libraries assign accession numbers in continuous numerical sequence, but some use a code system to indicate type of material and/or year of accession in addition to order of accession. *See also*: Library of Congress Control Number and OCLC control number.

accession order : The arrangement of books or other documents on shelves in the chronological and numerical order of their addition to a specific category or class, as opposed to an arrangement based entirely on a classification system.

accession record : A list of the bibliographic items added to a library collection in the order of their addition. Normally such a list includes the accession number, brief bibliographic identification, source, and price paid for each item. Synonymous with *accession catalog*, *accession list*, and *accession register*.

acclimatization : The process of allowing archival records and other materials to adapt to environmental changes (in temperature, humidity, etc.), especially when removed from cold storage for use at room temperature. Because materials can take hours to adapt to normal room temperature, the Society of American Archivists does not recommend cold storage as a practical solution for preserving frequently consulted items. Click here to learn about acclimatization of film, courtesy of the National Film and Sound Archive of Australia. Also spelled *acclimatisation*.

accommodation : The provision of suitable space and/or arrange to include additional requirements without processing a scope change.

accompanying material : Related but physically distinct material issued with an item, for example, a floppy disk, CD-ROM, slide set, answer book, teacher's manual, atlas, or portfolio of prints or plates, intended by the publisher to be used and stored with it, often in a pocket inside the cover or loose inside the container. In *AACR2*, the presence of accompanying material is indicated in the physical description area of the bibliographic record. *See also*: dashed-on entry.

accordion fold : A method of folding a piece of paper (or several pieces pasted together edge to edge) in which each successive fold is parallel with, but in the opposite direction to, the preceding one. Click here to see a 14th-century Korean accordion-style manuscript of the *Lotus Sutra* on indigo-dyed mulberry paper (Metropolitan Museum of Art) and here to view an untitled early 19th-century example from Nepal (Library of Congress). See also this early 20th-century Thai manuscript in a lacquered cover (Cornell University Library). Synonymous with *fan fold* and *z-fold*. *See also*: Chinese style and concertina.

account : A listing or statement of fiscal, corporate or project cost data.

account book : A blankbook, ruled or unruled, in which the details of transactions, usually financial, are recorded, often in the form of a ledger with columns tallied at the end of each day, week, month, or year to show the profitability of the enterprise. Account books can be a valuable source of historical information. Click here to see the manuscript account book of the 18th-century Philadelphia joiner, John Head, courtesy of the American Philosophical Society, and here to see a page from a 19th-century household account book (National Museum of American History). Compare with cash book.

accountability : The extent to which persons in government and the workplace are held answerable for their conduct in office and for the quality of their performance of assigned duties, particularly when incompetence, dereliction, or malfeasance is at issue. *See also*: performance evaluation.

accountability/responsibility matrix : A structure which relates the project organization structure to the work breakdown structure; assures that each element of the project scope of work is assigned to a responsible individual.

accountable : Responsible, answerable.

accountant : A person responsible for maintaining fiscal or corporate accounts.

accounts : In project accounting, a set of cost statements that display the current status of the project and future status upon completion.

accreditation : The voluntary nongovernmental evaluation process by which an educational or service organization regularly establishes that its programs, or the institution as a whole (or one of its schools or units), meets pre-established standards of quality and integrity. In higher education, accreditation is a collegial process based on self-assessment and peer evaluation for the improvement of academic quality and public accountability. In the United States, institutions of higher learning are evaluated by regional accrediting bodies. Evaluation of academic libraries is included in the institutional process. Graduate programs of library and information science are evaluated by the Committee on Accreditation (COA) of the American Library Association (ALA). Formal evaluation of individual competence is called certification. *See also*: accredited program and credential.

accreditation action : One of seven possible decisions by the Committee on Accreditation (COA) of the American Library Association (ALA) affecting the accreditation status of a library and information studies program under the *Standards for Accreditation of Master's Programs in Library and Information Studies* (1992), conveyed to the dean of the program and to the institution's chief executive officer in a formal Decision Document. The actions are:

accredited program : In the United States, a professional degree program in library and information science, regularly evaluated by the Committee on Accreditation (COA) of the American Library Association (ALA) and found to meet or exceed pre-established standards of quality, as distinct from an approved program recognized or certified by a state board or educational agency as meeting its standards. Some approved programs are also ALA-accredited. *See also*: accreditation action and retroactive period of accreditation.

accrual : An unpaid liability (debt) incurred from the receipt of materials or services, e.g. unpaid invoices, deliveries, contractor's time sheets, progress payments due and payables.

accrual accounting : A system of accounting in which expenses are recognized when incurred, and revenues are recognized when they are known, regardless of the time when actual payment of cash is made or received.

accrual method : A method that determines when the cost for a resource is incurred, the fixed costs for tasks, and when actual costs are charged to a project.

accrued cost : A cost that is incurred all at once at a certain time in a project or gradually, for instance, over the entire time a task is being worked on.

accumulation : In library collection development, the policy of acquiring as much of the published literature as possible on a subject, or in an academic discipline, usually in support of primary research in the field. The collections of large academic and research libraries typically reflect this priority, in contrast to public libraries, where weeding is done regularly on the basis of usage, and special libraries operating under constraints that require maintenance of the collection in a steady state. In archives, the accumulation of recurring records is often governed by a disposition schedule.

accuracy : A degree of exactness. In project work, usually expressed as a range particularly in connection with estimates of cost and time.

acetate decay : The chemical deterioration of film that has an acetate plastic base, an autocatalytic process caused by moisture, heat, and high relative humidity. According to *The Film Preservation Guide* (National Film Preservation Foundation, 2004), decay occurs in five stages, accelerating at it progresses: (1) the film releases acetic acid, emitting a characteristic vinegar odor; (2) the film base begins to shrink, curling and warping along both dimensions (length and width); (3) the film loses flexibility; (4) the emulsion begins to crack (see crazing) and flake off; and (5) a white powder appears along the edges and surface of the film. Acetate decay cannot be reversed, only slowed by cold storage. The Image Permanence Institute (IPI) recommends freezing film in an advanced state of decay until the content can be evaluated for transfer to new film stock or copying in another medium. Synonymous with *vinegar syndrome*. Compare with nitrate decay. *See also*: A-D strip and molecular sieve.

achievement : A measure of performance or accomplishment to date.

acid : A substance capable of forming hydrogen ions when dissolved in water. Acids can weaken cellulose in paper, board, and cloth, leading to embrittlement. Acids may be introduced in the manufacture of library or archival material. Acids may also be introduced by migration from other materials or from atmospheric pollution.

acid barrier : A sheet of acid-free or buffered paper, or polyester film, placed loose between an acidic component of a book, such as a bookplate, and the adjacent leaf or board to prevent acid migration.

acid migration : The movement of acid from a material containing acid to one that is less acidic, pH neutral, or alkaline. The process can occur through direct contact or vapor transfer. One of the most common problems in document preservation is the migration of acid from the boards, endpapers, or paper covers of a book to the less acidic paper of the text block (or vice versa). Acid can also migrate from bookplates, inserts, tissues used in interleaving, and labels that are not acid-free. The result may be discoloration and eventual embrittlement (click here to see an example of acid migration from a newspaper clipping to the pages of a book). The process can be arrested by removing the contaminating material and subjecting the sheet(s) or volume to deacidification. Synonymous with *acid transfer*. *See also*: buffered paper.

acid-free : Materials with a pH value of 7.0 (neutral) or higher (alkaline), preferred in printing and binding to prevent deterioration caused by acid over time. Acid-free papers are often buffered to counteract acids that may develop with age as a result of bleaching and sizing or be introduced through acid migration or atmospheric pollution. Synonymous with *nonacidic*.

acid-free paper : Paper that has a neutral or alkaline pH level (7.0 or higher) at the time of manufacture, commonly used for fine art prints, limited edition printing, and photo albums, and in the preservation of library materials. Lignin contained in wood pulp is the primary source of acid in paper and board. Acid-free paper is not necessarily permanent, but permanent papers are acid-free. *See also*: buffering.

acidic : Substances that have a pH value less than 7.0 (neutral). The main source of acid in paper products is lignin contained in wood used for pulp. Because acid causes the paper and board used in printing and binding to deteriorate over time, lignin is removed in all but the lowest-grade papers. A buffer such as calcium carbonate or magnesium carbonate may be added in papermaking to neutralize acids that develop or are introduced after the manufacture of paper. The opposite of alkaline. Compare with acid-free.

acquisition : The obtaining under contract of supplies and services to meet the needs of a project.

acquisition control : A system for acquiring project equipment, material and services in a uniform and orderly fashion.

acquisition evaluation : Review and analysis of responses to determine supplier's ability to perform the work as requested. This activity may include an evaluation of suppliers financial resources, ability to comply with technical criteria and delivery schedules, satisfactory record of performance and eligibility for award.

acquisition methods : The various ways by which goods/ services are acquired from suppliers.

acquisition negotiations : Contracting without formal advertising. This method offers flexible procedures, permits bargaining and provides an opportunity to prospective suppliers to revise their offers before the award.

acquisition number : A unique number used by the acquisitions department of a library to identify a specific bibliographic item on a purchase order. Some libraries use a standard number such as the ISBN (International Standard Book

Number) or ISSN (International Standard Serial Number) as the acquisition number.

acquisition plan : The document that describes the approach for acquisition. It defines competitive or sole source, schedule, funding, manpower, facilities, risk, etc. Also called the System Acquisition Plan.

acquisition plan review ("APR") : The control gate to approve the Acquisition Plan. The APR is the decision point to initiate the project and commit funding, personnel, and other resources to the acquisition.

acquisition planning : The process by which the efforts of all personnel responsible for an acquisition are coordinated and integrated through a comprehensive plan for fulfilling the organization's need in a timely manner and at a reasonable cost. It includes developing the overall strategy for managing the acquisition.

acquisition process : The process of acquiring personnel/goods/services for new or existing work within the general definitions of contracts requiring an offer and acceptance, consideration, lawful subject matter and competent parties.

acquisition strategy : Determining the most appropriate means of procuring the component parts or services of a project

acquisitions : The process of selecting, ordering, and receiving materials for library or archival collections by purchase, exchange, or gift, which may include budgeting and negotiating with outside agencies, such as publishers, dealers, and vendors, to obtain resources to meet the needs of the institution's clientele in the most economical and expeditious manner.

acquisitions section (AS) : Created in 1991, AS is the section of the Association for Library Collections and Technical Services (ALCTS) within the American Library Association (ALA) charged with (1) promoting the effective acquisition of information resources in all formats, through purchase, lease, and other methods, in all types of institutions; (2) developing sound ethical, fiscal, and legal policies and procedures in acquisitions management, including relationships with suppliers; and (3) assessing and advancing awareness of the organization and role of the acquisitions function within the library and in relationships with other functional areas (purchasing, accounting, collection management, etc.). Click here to connect to the AS homepage.

acronym : A new name or word (neologism) that is pronounceable and hence memorable, coined from the first or first few letters or parts of a phrase or compound term (*example*: **ERIC** for **E**ducational **R**esources **I**nformation **C**enter). Click here to connect to the *Yahoo!* list of online acronym and abbreviation finders. Compare with abbreviation and initialism.

act : One of the major divisions in the action of a play, usually marked by the dropping of the curtain and followed by an intermission. In modern drama, most plays are divided into three acts, which may be further subdivided into *scenes*. *See also*: one-act play.

acting edition : An edition of a play intended for the use of actors and others directly involved in theater production, which includes fuller stage directions (entrances, exits, stage properties, etc.) than one intended for reading, usually published in limp paper covers and priced lower than other editions of the work. Compare with script.

action : A measure intended to influence the course of the project.

action item : Something agreed to be done as a result of a discussion at a meeting and usually recorded in the minutes of that meeting.

action item flags : A symbol or other form of alert to warn project team members of things to be done usually at or by a specified date and time.

action plan : A description of what needs to be done, when and by whom.

activation : The process of getting something started, typically a project activity of some importance and often dependent upon some prior condition such as completion of a milestone.

active listening : Paying careful attention to what is being said, then rephrasing that information and feeding it back to the originator to ensure that what you think you heard is what they meant.

active records : Records required by an agency or individual to function effectively on a daily basis, usually kept close at hand, organized to render them readily accessible. Synonymous with *current records*. The opposite of inactive records. *See also*: intermediate records.

activity : A task or set of tasks that are carried out in order to create a deliverable

activity arrow net : Project plan in the form of a structural network where the activities are denoted graphically by nodes.

activity based costing ("ABC") : A methodology that measures the cost and performance of activities, resources, and cost objects. Resources are assigned to activities, then activities are assigned to cost objects based on their use. Activity based costing recognizes the causal relationships of cost drivers to activities.

activity based management ("ABM") : The broad discipline that focuses on achieving customer value and company profit by way of the management of activities. It draws on activity-based costing as a major source of information.

activity book : A book designed to engage the user in a pursuit other than (or in addition to) reading, for example, an instruction manual for science or craft projects, or a volume containing puzzles or word games. Some children's activity books are oversize. Libraries select judiciously, avoiding formats that require the reader to fill in the blanks or otherwise alter the physical state of the item. When an activity book is part of a kit, its presence is indicated in the physical description area of the bibliographic record.

activity calendar : In computer scheduling, calendar that defines the working and non-working patterns applicable to an activity. The Activity Calendar is normally overridden by the Project Calendar. See also Resource Calendars.

activity card : A card or set of cards printed with symbols, words, numerals, and/or pictures intended for use by an individual or group in performing a specific action (or set of actions) or in following a pursuit. Compare with flash card. *See also*: game and kit.

activity code : A set of numeric or alpha-numeric characters that uniquely identifies a particular activity.

activity definition : Identification of the specific activities that must be performed in order to produce project deliverables.

activity description : A statement specifying what must be done to achieve a desired result.

activity duration : The best estimate of the time (hours, days, weeks, months, etc.) necessary for the accomplishment of the work involved in an activity, considering the nature of the work and resources needed for it.

activity duration estimating : The estimation of the number of work periods that will be needed to complete the activity.

activity elaboration : A more detailed explanation of the work involved in the Activity, possibly by describing a series of tasks.

activity file : A file containing all data related to the definition of activities on a particular project.

activity ID : A unique code identifying each activity in a project.

activity list : List of project activities.

activity node net : Project plan in the form of a structural network where the activities are denoted graphically by arrows.

Activity on Arc ("AOA") : In documenting and drawing a network one may place the activities on the arcs or on the nodes (Activity on Node)

Activity on Arrow ("AOA") : See Arrow Diagramming Method.

Activity on Node : A network where activities are represented by a box or a node linked by dependencies.

Activity Oriented : A planning approach focused primarily on activities rather than events.

Activity Oriented Schedule : Schedule which presents information in terms of activities (i.e. periods of time, as opposed to points in time, e.g. milestone dates). See also Precedence Diagramming.

Activity Properties : A description of the attributes of the activity such as start and finish times, resources required and anticipated cost, etc.

Activity Quantities : Units of consumption or production associated with an Activity.

Activity Status : The state of completion of an activity. A planned activity has not yet started. A started activity is in progress. A finished activity is complete.

Activity Timing : The time parameters within which the Activity is expected or required to take place.

Actor : Someone or something, outside the system that interacts with the system.

Actual : Information that shows what has actually occurred. For example, the actual start date for a task is the day on which the task actually started, and its actual cost is the amount spent up to the present.

Actual and Scheduled Progress : A comparison of the observable work done at a given time with the work planned up to that time.

Actual Cost : Incurred costs that are charged to the project budget and for which payment has been made, or accrued.

Actual Cost Data Collection : The assembly of recorded expenditures for an Activity, set of Activities, and/or within a given time frame in the past.

Actual Cost of Work Performed ("ACWP") : Total costs incurred (direct and indirect) in accomplishing work during a given time period. ACWP is used in the earned value method of progress measurement. See also earned value analysis.

Actual Costs : The costs actually incurred and recorded for work performed.

Actual Dates : The dates that activities really started and finished as opposed to planned or projected dates.

Actual Direct Costs : Those costs specifically identified with a contract or project, based upon the contractor's cost identification and accumulation system. See also Direct Costs.

Actual Expenditures : See Actual Costs.

Actual Finish : Date on which an activity was completed.

Actual Finish Date : The calendar date that work actually ended on an activity. It must be prior to or equal to the data date. The remaining duration of this activity is zero.

Actual Start : Date on which an activity was started.

actual start date : The calendar date work actually began on an activity. It must be prior to or equal to the data date. [D00063]

actuality : A nonfiction motion picture (documentary), usually of very short length, made prior to 1910 to demonstrate the technological advance of moving images over still photography. Most examples capture familiar scenes of everyday life (people, places, and events) with authenticity but, in some instances, a bit of manipulation. Exotic novelties borrowed from 19th-century commercial photography were also popular. The earliest public venues were *nickelodeons*—peep show parlors with machines that played short film loops. By the turn of the century, "movies" were being shown in store-front theaters and traveling carnivals. During the first decade of the 20th century, when they also began to be projected in vaudeville and burlesque theaters, the growing popularity of the fiction film eclipsed the actuality, which peaked in 1903. Click here to learn more about actualities and view examples, courtesy of the *American Memory* project of the Library of Congress.

ACWP : See Actual Cost of Work Performed

ad hoc : Latin for "to this," used to indicate that something was created or exists for the particular purpose in view at the moment. Also refers to something organized for a specific purpose, for example, an *ad hoc committee* elected or appointed to address a specific issue or handle an unanticipated contingency, usually dissolved once the need has been met.

ad loc. : An abbreviation of the Latin phrase *ad locum*, meaning "at the place [cited]."

Adaptation : Something that has been made to fit.

adaptive technology : Systems, devices, and software specifically designed to make library materials and services more accessible to people with physical and/or cognitive disabilities, including large print books, closed captioned videorecordings, Braille signage, voice amplification devices, screen magnification and screen reading software, voice recognition software, etc. Some libraries have found focus groups helpful in selecting adaptive technologies. Synonymous with *assistive technology*. *See also*: alt tag.

add note : A brief note in the Dewey Decimal Classification schedules instructing the cataloger to append to a given base number one or more numerals found elsewhere in the classification in order to build a class number. For example, the instruction to "add to base number 027.1 (private and family libraries) notation from 1-9 from Table 2, e.g., family libraries in the United Kingdom 027.141."

added charge : A further charge made by a publisher or vendor against a subscriber's account after initial payment has been received, usually to cover (1) an increase in the subscription price that occurs after billing, before the order is processed; (2) publication of additional volumes; or (3) fluctuations in currency exchange rates. The charge is made in the form of a supplemental invoice.

added copy : A copy of an item already owned by a library, added to the collection usually when demand warrants. Compare with duplicate.

added edition : An edition of a work added to a library collection, which is not the same as editions of the same title already owned by the library.

added entry : A secondary entry, additional to the main entry, usually under a heading for a joint author, illustrator, translator, series, or subject, by which an item is represented in a library catalog (*AACR2*). *See also*: name-title added entry and tracings.

added title page : A title page preceding or following the one used by the cataloger as the chief source of information in creating the bibliographic description of an item. It may be more general, as in a series title page, or of equivalent generality, as in a title page in another language (*AACR2*).

Added Value : The addition of some worthwhile quality or performance improvement as a result of some action taken, which may or may not have been part of the original understanding, agreement or contract.

addendum : Brief printed matter, less extensive than a supplement or appendix, included in a book or other publication after the work has been typeset because it is considered essential to the meaning or completeness of the text, usually printed separately on a slip of paper tipped in at the beginning or end of the text. Plural: *addenda.* Compare with errata.

additional volume : An extra volume issued by the publisher of a serial, not included in the original publication schedule for the title, for which an added charge may be made against the customer's account, on a supplemental invoice.

Address : An identifier that specifies the source or destination of IP packets and that is assigned at the IP layer to an interface or set of interfaces.

Adequacy : The extent that an item or action is sufficient for the purpose.

adhesive : A substance applied to a material to make it stick to another surface by chemical or mechanical action. Gummed adhesives require moisture to be effective. Solid at room temperatures, hot-melt adhesives liquefy when heated and set up quickly as they cool. Some types of adhesive are pressure-sensitive. Various kinds of adhesives are used extensively in binding and by libraries in technical processing. In document conservation, adhesives are often selected for their reversibility. *See also*: adhesive binding, glair, glue, paste, and polyvinyl acetate.

adhesive binding : A generic term for binding methods in which the leaves are held together by a strong adhesive applied directly to the back of the text block, usually done after the binding edge is milled but sometimes after the sections are sewn. The most commonly used adhesives are animal glues, hot-melts, and polyvinyl acetate (PVA).

Click here to see examples of adhesive binding. Synonymous with *threadless binding* and *unsewn binding*. Compare with non-adhesive binding. *See also*: caoutchouc binding, double-fan adhesive binding, notched binding, Otabind, and perfect binding.

adhesive tape : Tape manufactured with a sticky backing. Its use should be avoided in mending paper because the adhesives used on most brands stain with age, and the tape can be difficult to remove, causing permanent damage to library materials (see this example).

Adjourning : The last stage of Team Building where the team disbands.

adjunct : A librarian employed part-time in an academic library at an institution that grants librarians faculty status. At some institutions, an adjunct employed less than half-time may not be eligible for benefits. Synonymous with *part-time faculty*.

Adjustment : An action to make something fit a predetermined requirement or condition. An adjustment may apply to physical parts or to data such as a cost estimate.

ADM Project : Non-hierarchical project that uses the arrow diagramming method.

Administration : That part of the organization responsible for, or the act of, directing and managing the activities of the organization, program, project or major work package.

administration : The range of activities normally associated with the management of a government agency, organization, or institution, such as a library or library system. Also refers collectively to the persons responsible for such activity, from director to secretary. *See also*: library administration.

Administrative Change : A unilateral contract modification, in writing, that does not affect the substantive rights of the parties (e.g., a change in the paying office or the appropriation data).

administrative history : In archives, the part of a finding aid that provides pertinent information concerning the records it lists and describes, such as the history and organizational structure of the agency (or group of related agencies) that generated them, or significant details of the life and career of the individual or family with which they are associated, usually in the form of a biographical note.

Administrative Management : Management that operates in the public trust, such as national, regional or local government administrations. Designed to survive indefinitely, the intended goal is to provide an environment acceptable to its constituents for their survival, prosperity and comfort.

adopt a book : A library program in which a person, often a library patron, agrees to donate a modest sum (usually a fixed amount) to help cover the cost of conserving a book or other bibliographic item that is deteriorating from age or overuse. Click here to learn about the British Library's Adopt a Book program. The University of Leeds Library uses a commemorative bookplate to record the adoption. At some public libraries in the United States, the program is designed to supplement funding for collection development (click here to see an example). Also spelled *adopt-a-book*.

adult : A fully grown, mentally competent person of sufficient age to be considered capable of making mature decisions and held legally accountable for the consequences of his (or her) actions. Libraries operate on the assumption that adult patrons are capable of deciding independently what they wish to read and borrow. Although the parent is responsible for supervising the actions of his or her child, it is appropriate for a librarian to provide guidance to users of all ages in the selection of materials suitable to their age level and interests, if asked to do so. Older adults often have special needs that must be met through outreach. *See also*: readers' advisory.

adult content : Material in digital or print format, considered by some to be unsuitable for children, usually because it contains sexually explicit text and/or images, graphic depictions of violence, or frank discussions of gender identity or sexual preference. In August 2005, *American Libraries* reported that a state statute was enacted in Utah on March 21, 2005 establishing an Adult Content

Registry of legal Web sites deemed harmful to minors, to be compiled and maintained by the Utah State Attorney General's Office. Internet users may request that a service provider block sites on the Registry or offer filtering software. ISPs that do not comply face criminal misdemeanor charges and a fine of up to $10,000 for each day that listed material is not blocked. On June 9, 2005, a group of 14 Utah bookstores, Internet service providers, and free-speech groups filed suit in the U.S. District Court in Salt Lake City challenging the constitutionality of the new law. Among the plaintiffs are the American Civil Liberties Union (ACLU) of Utah, the Freedom to Read Foundation (FTRF), and the American Booksellers Foundation for Free Expression. *See also*: adult content filter.

adult content filter : Software designed to block retrieval over on the Internet of material considered unsuitable for children (violence, sexually explicit text and images, etc.). The constitutionality of laws requiring the use of such filters in libraries is a subject of debate in the United States. Most image search engines include a default adult content filter that the user can turn off. Synonymous with *mature content filter*. *See also*: *Children's Internet Protection Act*.

adult education : Courses designed specifically for adults who have spent their lives outside the system of formal higher education. Because nontraditional students often lack the library skills of students who follow a traditional course of study, they may require more assistance at the reference desk and a more basic level of bibliographic instruction.

adult learner : A person older than traditional college age who pursues an independent, organized course of study, usually without the benefit of formal instruction at an established educational institution. When enrolled as a nontraditional student at a college or university, such a person may require reference services and bibliographic instruction at a more basic level than traditional students.

adult services : Materials, services, and programs intended to meet the needs of the adult users of a public library, as opposed to those designed for children and young adults, for example, information on tax or resume preparation. *See also*: readers' advisory.

advance copy : A copy of a book or other publication bound in advance of the normal press run to enable the publisher to check that all is in order before binding of the edition proceeds. Advance copies are also sent to booksellers, book club selection committees, and reviewers before the announced publication date, sometimes unbound or in a binding other than the publisher's binding, often with a review slip laid in. Copies sent unbound are known as *advance sheets*. Synonymous with *early copy*. Compare with reading copy and review copy.

advance on royalty : An amount paid to the author(s) of a new book prior to its publication against the royalties it is expected to earn, usually offered as an inducement to sign a book contract with the publisher. Synonymous with *author's advance*. *See also*: publisher's agreement.

advance order : An order placed for a new book prior to its date of publication, usually in response to prepublication promotion. The number of copies ordered in advance may assist the publisher in determining the size of the first printing, the price, and how much to spend on advertising.

Advanced Material Release ("AMR") : A document used by organizations to initiate the purchase of long-lead-time or time-critical materials prior to the final release of a design.

adventure : A fiction genre in which the hero undertakes a difficult venture of uncertain issue, usually in an exotic setting, often culminating in a hazardous chase or decisive struggle. Adventure appeals to a predominantly male audience. Subgenres include the spy/espionage novel, tale of political intrigue and/or terrorism, technothriller, survival story, and male romance (*example*: Kim by Rudyard Kipling). Adventure stories are often published in series featuring a series hero (*example*: the Horatio Hornblower novels of C.S. Forester). If the hero is a swaggering ruffian, the tale is known as a *swashbuckler*. To learn more about the genre, see the adventure/suspense section of *Genreflecting*. *See also*: romance and western.

advertisement : A public notice of the availability of goods or services through purchase, subscription, or other commercial means, commonly appearing in newspapers and magazines and on broadsides, handbills, posters, etc. In magazines, the word "Advertisement" may appear at the head of the page to distinguish advertising from editorial content. In binding, stacked advertising in issues of a periodical may be removed to reduce bulk. *See also*: advertorial.

advertorial : Advertising text written in editorial style and format. To avoid confusion, most magazine publishers add the word "Advertisement" to the running head. *See also*: infomercial.

adverts : Advertisements bound into a book, usually at the end of the back matter. Click here to see an example following the title page in a late 18th-century edition (University of Pittsburgh Libraries). Abbreviated *ads* or *advrts*.

advice book : A form of literature for women that provided practical and philosophical guidance on the domestic skills required in everyday life, such as etiquette, household management, cooking, gardening, childcare, family health and recreation, and female employment, often written from the perspective of a parent, Christian minister, or other authority, rather than from a feminist point of view. Beginning with *The English Housewife* by Gervase Markham, published in 1615, such works conveyed the code of behavior considered appropriate for women in society up to the early 20th century. Examples can be seen in the online exhibitions *Defining Her Life: Advice Books for Women* (University of Delaware Library) and *The Making of a Homemaker* (Smithsonian Institution Libraries). A precursor of the how-to book and self-help book. Synonymous with *conduct book*.

advisory service : A periodical publication, usually issued weekly, biweekly, or monthly in print or online, providing research, statistical analysis, and guidance on financial investments (stocks, bonds, options, mutual funds, etc.), for example, *The Value Line Investment Survey*, published weekly since 1936 by Value Line, Inc. Libraries often store current issues of a print advisory service in loose-leaf bindings to facilitate updating.

advocacy : Concerted action taken in support of libraries, particularly political action aimed at securing adequate funding for library operations and capital improvements, which may include lobbying legislators and government officials, organizing voter rallies, securing media coverage, etc. The most effective advocacy campaigns are often based on an action plan. Thomas J. Hennen, Jr., recommends "10 Rules for Local Advocacy" in the article *Stand Up for Libraries* in the June/July 2005 issue of *American Libraries*. The American Library Association (ALA) maintains an Issues and Advocacy Web site that includes a section on Best Practices. The Advocacy Institute offers workshops at ALA annual and midwinter conferences to help train participants in advocacy skills and strategies. *See also*: Americans for Libraries Council and library advocate.

aeronautical chart : A chart prepared specifically for aerial navigation, showing essential topographic features, known obstructions, navigational aids, and other information of interest to aircraft pilots, such as airport name and 3-letter designator, control tower radio frequency, field elevation, length of longest runway, etc. Aeronautical charts are generally produced in several series, each on a specified map projection and differing in scale, format, and content, for use as dictated by type of aircraft and whether the flight is to be conducted under visual or instrument flight rules (*Glossary of Cartographic Terms*, Perry-Castañeda Library). Click here and here and here to see examples at various scales.

Affect : To make happen, or to cause an effect or change to occur, or has or will result. Typically used to identify secondary impacts as a result of a primary change.

Affected Parties : Those who have been, or will be, impacted by a change.

affiliate : A separately administered organization closely connected with another by formal agreement and mutual interest, for example, the various organizations affiliated with American Library Association (ALA). Also refers to the process of forming such a link. *See also*: affiliated library.

affiliated library : A library that is, by formal agreement, part of a larger library system but administered independently by its own board or management structure. Medical and law libraries at large universities often fall into this category. Compare with branch library.

affirmative action : An active effort, begun in the late 1960s, to enhance opportunities in the United States for minority groups and women, through federal regulations and programs intended to counteract bias and discrimination in government employment and contracting and in admissions to state-supported educational institutions. Most publicly supported libraries in the United States are affirmative action employers. The legality of affirmative action has been called into question by individuals and political groups who believe that legislating equality discourages initiative and results in reverse discrimination. *See also*: diversity.

afterword : A brief passage or essay, usually written by the author, appearing at the end of a work as explanation or, in a special edition, as commentary on the work's reception. In a collection, the editor(s) may include an afterword to tie together or sum up the main themes developed in the selected works. Compare with epilogue.

against the grain : A popular expression meaning "contrary to natural inclination" originally used in the printing trade to refer to machine-made paper folded across the grain of its fibers. In book production, sheets are printed with the grain running from top to bottom of the leaves, allowing them to flex easily lengthwise after they are bound. When folded *with* the grain, paper tears easily and cleanly along the fold. When folded *across* the grain, it cracks and leaves a ragged edge when torn.

agate : A naturally occurring stone, composed of a form of silica similar to chalcedony, usually light in color with darker bands of brown, purple, or pink, shaped and polished for use as a burnishing tool, to impart a reflective sheen to gold and other metal leaf in the edge gilding of books, raised gilding in manuscripts, and gilding of paintings and picture frames. When mounted in a handle, such a tool is known as a "dog tooth" (see these modern examples in various shapes). Click here to see an agate burnisher in use.

Agency : A legal relationship by which one party is empowered to act on behalf of another party.

agency : For archival purposes, any commercial enterprise, organization, institution, or other corporate body that creates and manages records of its business, activities, or affairs. In very large organizations, subordinate units (sections, departments, offices) may function as separate agencies. In a more general sense, any person (agent) or organization that has the authority to perform a specific function, for example, the National Endowment for the Humanities (NEH). *See also*: government agency.

agency-assigned data element : In library cataloging, a data element in the MARC record whose content is determined by a designated agency and is the responsibility of that agency, for example, field 222 (Key Title) which is the responsibility of an ISSN Center. Although this type of data element is usually input by the designated agency, it may be transcribed by another organization. (*MARC 21 Concise Formats*)

agenda : A list of topics or issues to be discussed at a meeting, sometimes solicited from prospective attendees in advance by the person who calls or chairs the meeting. It is customary to distribute the agenda before the meeting begins, to allow attendees time to prepare. A *hidden agenda* is a goal or intention consciously or unconsciously concealed, usually to gain the advantage of surprise, a tactic that often backfires when unsuspecting persons discover that they have been manipulated.

agent : An individual or company that acts as middleman between a library or library system and a publisher in the purchase of materials, for example, a subscription service such as EBSCO that manages periodical subscriptions for client libraries. *See also*: literary agent.

Aggregation : Summation of parts. Typically used in reference to estimating.

aggregator : A bibliographic service that provides online access to the digital full-text of periodicals published by different publishers. Because aggregator databases can be very large, tracking their coverage is not an easy task for serials librarians. A task group of the Program for Cooperative Cataloging (PCC) is working on standards for analytic catalog records for serials titles available electronically from aggregator services. Currently, the top three journal aggregators in the United States are EBSCO, the Gale Group, and ProQuest. Recently, EBSCO has been building market share by offering higher up-front payments to secure exclusivity from the publishers of certain journals. The effects of this competitive practice on libraries and the end-user are as yet unclear.

aggregator-neutral record : A bibliographic record describing the online version of a serial publication, containing information applicable to all versions distributed by all providers, regardless of whether the serial has a print counterpart or was born digital. In July 2003, CONSER abandoned its earlier policy of creating a separate record for each aggregation, focusing instead on providing a single bibliographic description for an electronic serial issued in multiple aggregations. Although nothing in the record specifically indicates that it is aggregator-neutral, multiple URLs may be included in the record for packages containing the complete serial. OCLC is engaged in converting existing bibliographic records for electronic serials to the new practice. Click here to learn more about CONSER policy on aggregator-neutral records.

Agility : The ability of an organization to adapt and react expeditiously and appropriately to changes in its environment and to demands imposed by the environment.

Agreement : Harmony of opinion or feeling; a contract or promise.

Agreement, legal : A legal document that sets out the terms of a contract between two parties.

aisle : The space left unoccupied between two parallel bookcases or shelf ranges, or at right angles to a bank of ranges, to allow library patrons and staff to access the stacks. Minimum aisle width is 36 inches for fixed shelving in libraries open to the public in the United States. Some types of compact shelving allow staff or users to shift movable ranges, usually along tracks in the floor, opening aisles as needed. *See also*: cross aisle and range aisle.

album : A bound or loose-leaf book containing blank pages for mounting stamps, photographs, poems, quotations, newspaper clippings, or other memorabilia or for collecting autographs. Also, a book containing a collection of pictures, with or without accompanying text. Click here to view a leaf from a 17th-century Ottoman album containing drawings done in ink on paper, courtesy of the Metropolitan Museum of Art. *See also*: *album amicorum* and record album.

album amicorum : Latin for "book of friends." A personal album containing memorabilia contributed by the owner's family and close friends (inscriptions, original poems and songs, allegorical emblems, heraldic devices, sketches of contemporary scenes, etc.). Precursor of the modern autograph book, this type of volume originated in Germany in the 16th century and was fashionable among university students and scholars who traveled from place to place in the course of their careers. Some contain illustrations contributed by the signatories and occasionally more professional artwork commissioned in a manner similar to the illumination of preceding centuries. Click here to view a page of illustration from a late 16th-century Dutch example, courtesy of the Koninklijke Bibliotheek. The 195 contributions in the *album amicorum* of Egbert Philip van Visvliet (1736-1799) make it one of the most extensive 18th-century examples (Koninklijke Bibliotheek). To see other examples, try a keywords search on the term in *Google Image Search*. Synonymous with *liber amicorum*.

albumen print : An early photographic process in which a paper support was floated on an emulsion of egg white (albumen) and salt, then coated with a light-sensitive solution of silver nitrate, dried in the dark, and exposed in the camera or under a collodion negative. Although the process was capable of producing a high definition image, print quality often depended on the particular egg-white recipe used by the photographer and fading was a common problem. Invented in 1850 by Louis-Désiré Blanquart-Evrard, the albumen print replaced the earlier salted paper print and was the dominant photographic medium of the 19th century, especially for cartes-de-visite and early cabinet cards, superseded in about 1890 by faster and more standardized gelatin silver papers. Click here to see examples (Getty Museum). To learn more about albumen prints try *The Albumen Site*, courtesy of *Conservtion OnLine* (*CoOL*), Stanford University.

alcove : A semiprivate recessed area within a library formed when two free-standing shelving units are placed at right angles to one or more units of wall shelving, usually large enough to provide access to materials on the shelves and to accommodate a small number of readers, seated at desks or around a study table. The architect Sir Christopher Wren is credited with originating this style of seating in his design of the library at Trinity College, Cambridge, in 1676. Synonymous with *cell*. *See also*: carrel.

Alexandrian Library : Founded by Ptolemy I in about 300 B.C., the great library at Alexandria in Egypt became the most important center of Hellenistic culture in Antiquity. At its peak, it contained over 500,000 manuscripts, mostly papyrus scrolls, some of which were translated into Greek from other languages. The collection was cataloged in the "Pinakes" of Callimachus, which included the author's name and a summary of the content of each item. The main library was part of a museum that functioned as an academy, attracting scholars from all parts of the Mediterranean world. A smaller library was established in the Temple of Serapis by Ptolemy III in about 235 B.C.

Algorithm : A particular mathematical model used for running calculations, typically computerized. For example, different project management scheduling software programs use different Algorithms for calculating Resource Leveling.

alignment : In typography, the arrangement of characters in a line of type in such a way that the tops and bottoms form a straight line across the page, parallel with other lines. Also, the setting of type in lines that are even at both right and left margins. Compare in this sense with justification. In a more general sense, the lining up of type or graphic matter in relation to any common horizontal or vertical line for printing on a page or display on a computer screen.

alkaline : Substances with a pH exceeding 7.0 (neutral), for example, calcium carbonate or magnesium carbonate added to paper in manufacture as a reserve or buffer to neutralize any acids that might develop with age. Alkaline substances are also used in the deacidification of materials made from acid paper or board. The opposite of acidic. *See also*: alkaline reserve.

Alkaline Buffer : Alkaline substances, which have a pH of over 7.0, may be added to materials to neutralize acids or as an alkaline reserve or buffer for the purpose of counteracting acids that may form in the future. A buffer may be added during manufacture or during the process of deacidification. A number of chemicals may be used as buffers, but the most common are magnesium carbonate and calcium carbonate.

alkaline reserve : A compound such as calcium carbonate added to pulped fiber in the manufacture of paper (a process called buffering) to neutralize any acid that might be generated by natural aging or introduced through acid migration or exposure to atmospheric pollution. Alkaline reserve is usually expressed as a percentage of paper weight. The ANSI/NISO Z39.48-1992 (R2002) standard for *Permanence of Paper for Publications and Documents in Libraries and Archives* calls for a minimum alkaline reserve equivalent to 2% calcium carbonate based on the oven dry weight of coated or uncoated paper. Synonymous with *alkali reserve.*

all along : A sewing method used in hand-binding in which each section of the text block is sewn separately to cords or tapes, from kettle stitch to kettle stitch inside the fold. For the sake of economy or to reduce swell, sections may be hand sewn two on. Synonymous with *all across* and *all on.*

all firsts : An expression used in the antiquarian book trade and in library cataloging to indicate that all the items in a group of publications are known to be first editions.

all over : A style of binding in which the entire surface of both covers is decorated, as opposed to design appearing on the front or back cover only, in the centers and/or corners, or around the edges. Click here to view a 17th-century gold-tooled example (Glasgow University Library: Special Collections, BD14-i.23) and here to see the style used on an early 20th-century deluxe edition of *Paradise Lost* (Metropolitan Museum of Art). To see other examples, try a keywords search on the phrase "all over" in the British Library's *Database of Bookbindings.*

all published : A note in the bibliographic record describing a publication originally proposed in more than one part or volume but never completed, usually because it was discontinued by the publisher. Similarly, a note describing all the issues of a periodical for which publication has ceased. In bookselling, a serially published work for which all issued parts are present.

all rights reserved : A phrase printed in or on a published work, usually on the verso of the title page of a book, giving formal notice that all rights granted under existing copyright law are retained by the copyright holder and that legal action may be taken against infringement.

alla rustica : Binding a book in a plain but sturdy paper case, a technique used from the 17th to the 19th century in Italy and Spain on remaindered books. According to former Yale University conservator Jane Greenfield, the sections were sewn on supports laced into paper covers with wide turn-ins (*ABC of Bookbinding*, Oak Knoll/ Lyons Press, 1998). In modern conservation binding, vellum or paper cases are sometimes used without adhesive.

allegory : A narrative that can be interpreted literally but that also has at least one symbolic meaning, usually expressing or elucidating an abstract idea or moral principle. Also, a form of extended metaphor used primarily in works of fiction and poetry in which an event, idea, thing, or person stands for itself and simultaneously for something else. A *dream allegory* is a medieval poem or story about a dream that has allegorical significance, for example, King René's **Book of Love** (*Le Cueur d'Amours Espris*). Allegory is a common theme in medieval manuscript illumination, as in this image of Fortuna turning a symbolic wheel from a 15th-century French version of Boccaccio's *Fall of Princes* (Glasgow University Library: Special Collections, MS Hunter 371). Click here to learn more about allegory in the Middle Ages, courtesy of *Wikipedia*. *See also*: beast epic, fable, morality play, and parable.

Alliance : An agreement to act jointly. See Partnering.

alligator : Leather made from the skin of a reptile, not as widely used in bookbinding as it once was for shoes and fashion accessories. In England, the material is known in the binding trade as *crocodile*. Click here to see a 20th-century alligator binding, courtesy of the Otto G. Richter Library, University of Miami, Florida.

Allocated Baseline : Requirements allocated to lower level system elements that are controlled by formal change control.

Allocated Requirements : Requirements apportioned to the elements of a system by applying applicable knowledge and experience. Determination of allocated requirements is not as scientifically rigorous as determination of derived requirements.

Allocation : The process of allocating work on an activity to specific Resources.

allocation : A quantity of time, money, materials, or other resources reserved by an organization for a specific purpose, usually to meet a need essential to realizing its goals and objectives. In most libraries and library systems, funds are *allocated* in accordance with an annual or biennial budget determined by the availability of funds.

allonym : The name of a person known to have existed, assumed as a pen name by another writer, as opposed to a fictional pseudonym, for example, the name "Publius" for the Roman tribune Publius Clodius Pulcher, used by Alexander

Hamilton, John Jay, and James Madison in writing *The Federalist*.

Allowance : An amount set aside, usually time or money.

allusion : A brief figurative or symbolic reference in a literary text usually made indirectly to a familiar person, place, thing, or event outside the text or to another literary work or passage in it. Allusions are sometimes indexed and published in collections (*example*: Allusions—Cultural, Literary, Biblical, and Historical: A Thematic Dictionary by Laurence Urdang and Frederick Ruffner). In a more general sense, any implied indication, indirect reference, or casual mention, as opposed to an explicit reference.

alpha test : The first full-scale test of a newly designed computer software system or hardware device, or of existing software or hardware that has undergone a major upgrade, usually conducted by the designer in a laboratory environment. Compare with beta test.

alphabet : The complete set of characters used to write or indicate the speech sounds of a language, usually arranged in traditional order. The roman alphabet used in writing the English language contains 26 letters (5 vowels and 21 consonants), each with an uppercase and lowercase form. The roman alphabets used for other languages may contain fewer or additional letters, with diacritical marks used to indicate specific sounds. Click here to find out more about the *Evolution of Alphabets*, courtesy of Professor Robert Fradkin at University of Maryland, or try *Omniglot: A Guide to Writing Systems*. Compare with syllabary. *See also*: alphabetical, alphabetization, and exotics.

alphabet book : A picture book for preschool children with illustrations designed to teach the letters and sequence of the alphabet by showing on each page, or double spread, one or more objects, animals, etc., belonging to a class whose name begins with the letter displayed (**a** for **apple**, etc.). Click here to see an early lithographed alphabet of wild animals, here to see a 19th-century French example (Thomas Parry Library, University of Wales), and here to see a page from a 19th-century alphabet illustrated by Walter Crane. Library and Archives

Canada provides the online exhibition *Beyond the Letters: A Retrospective of Canadian Alphabet Books*. Compare with counting book. *See also*: abecedary and horn book.

alphabetical : In the customary order of the letters of the alphabet of a given language. Alphabetization can be letter-by-letter, ignoring punctuation and divisions between words, or word-by-word, with entries beginning with the same word alphabetized by the next word, and so on. The terms in this dictionary are listed alphabetically letter-by-letter.

alphanumeric : A contraction of *alphabetic-numeric*, referring to a character set containing letters of the alphabet, numerals, and/or special characters. The access codes used in computer systems are often alphanumeric (*example*: the username **smith003**). Also spelled *alpha-numeric*. Synonymous with *alphameric*.

Alpha-Numeric System for Classification of Recordings (ANSCR) : A scheme for classifying sound recordings of all types, based on a set of 23 major subject categories represented by letters of the Latin alphabet (*example*: **M** for popular music), with some categories subdivided and represented by double letters (**MJ** for jazz). To the alphabetic category is added a three-or four-letter code representing type of subarrangement (by title of work; name of composer, performer, or author; name of skill, language, or sound; etc.). The third part of the classification number is composed of the first letter of each of the first three keywords in the title of the work or album, or a number if the work is known by form and numbered. The fourth part is composed of a letter representing the name of an individual closely associated with the performance on the recording, followed by the last two digits of the commercial recording number:

alt tag : When a computer user manipulates the mouse to pass the cursor over an image in a Web page, holding it on the image for several seconds, a text message is often displayed, serving as a replacement for the information content of the image, a feature intended for visually impaired Internet users who would otherwise perceive only a hole or gap at the location of the image. Coded as an attribute of the IMG tag in HTML, the alt tag provides an "alternate text" message for viewers who cannot see graphics, an important component in the design of Web sites for compliance with the *Americans with Disabilities Act,* especially sites using graphic menu systems for navigation. Click here to learn more about the use of alt text in HTML documents, courtesy of A.J. Flavell and the Web Design Group.

alternate delivery : Shipment by a publisher or vendor of materials ordered by a library via a commercial delivery service rather than the U.S. Postal Service.

Alternate Resource : A resource that may be substituted as the requirement for an activity if the requested resource is not available.

alternate title : A title found in or on a bibliographic item, that varies from the one given in or on the chief source of information, for example, a title appearing on the label or container of a videocassette that differs from the one given in the videorecording itself. In library cataloging, any alternate titles are entered in the note area of the bibliographic record. Compare with alternative title.

Alternative Analysis : Breaking down a complex scope situation for the purpose of generating and evaluating different solutions and approaches.

Alternative Dispute Resolution ("ADR") : Any procedure or combination of procedures voluntarily used to resolve issues in controversy without the need to resort to litigation. These procedures may include, but are not limited to, assisted settlement negotiations, conciliation, facilitation, mediation, fact-finding, mini-trials, and arbitration.

alternative press : A small, politically progressive publisher not controlled by the handful of giant multinational corporations that dominate the publishing industry worldwide. Alternative press publications often address important social issues and publish innovative and experimental works largely ignored or covered superficially in the mainstream press. For the past 30 years, the Alternative Press Center (APC), an affiliate of the Social Responsibilities Round Table (SRRT) of the American

Library Association, has provided access to such publications through the *Alternative Press Index*, available in the reference section of large academic and public libraries.

alternative title : The second part of a title proper consisting of two parts, each a title in itself, connected by the word "or" or its equivalent in another language (*example*: The Female Quixote, or, The Adventures of Arabella), not to be confused with alternate title. Compare with subtitle.

Alternatives : Review of the means available and the impact of trade-offs to attain the objectives.

alum : An acidic substance used in papermaking to adjust the pH level of water in pulp and to fix rosin (a sizing agent first used in the 18th century) to cellulose fibers, giving paper a less permeable surface to prevent bleeding. In medieval book production, alum salts were also used to prepare animal skins for use in binding. Creamy white in color, alum-tawed skins are supple and more permanent than leather produced by tanning.

alum rosin : An acidic size, consisting of rosin precipitated by alum (aluminium sulfate or potassium sulfate), used in the manufacture of paper in the 18th and 19th century to produce a less absorbent writing surface. In his article *The Need for a Re-evaluation of the Use of Alum in Book Conservation and the Book Arts* published in the 1989 issue of *The Book and Paper Group Annual*, Tom Conroy questions the conclusion that use of alum in small amounts in binding and papermaking is detrimental to book conservation.

amateur : A term used in cataloging moving images to indicate the form of a work created for private rather than commercial viewing, for example, a "home movie" made by someone not professionally associated with the film/video industry, intended to be shown within a circle of family and friends, rather than exhibited publicly.

ambient conditions : The prevailing characteristics of the environment within the room or building in which library or archival materials are stored or used, including temperature, humidity, natural and artificial light, air pollution, dust, etc., important considerations for long-term preservation. *See also*: microclimate.

ambient light : The level of illumination in an enclosed space, from both natural and artificial sources, an important consideration in the preservation of materials that deteriorate when exposed to light, especially the ultraviolet radiation (UV) in direct sunlight. Former Yale University conservator Jane Greenfield recommends that in libraries and archives visible radiation be kept below 200 lux, and UV radiation below 75 lux because the damage it causes continues to a lesser extent even after the light source is removed (*The Care of Fine Books*, Nick Lyons Books, 1988). Incandescent light is the least damaging, but it emits more heat and is more costly than fluorescent light, which is higher in UV radiation. UV filters are available for fluorescent fixtures. As a general rule, the lights in a library should be turned off when not needed. *See also*: blue scale.

ambigram : A term coined by Douglas Hofstadter (see *Metamagical Themas* [Basic Books, 1985]) and friends for a graphic figure that spells a word or group of words that can be read in at least two different ways, usually symmetric when rotated 180 degrees (upside down) or when reflected along the vertical axis, as in a mirror. Click here to see the inversions of Scott Kim. Other examples can be seen in *Gef's Ambigram Gallery*. Compare with palindrome.

Ambiguity : Something that is likely to be interpreted in more than one way.

ambrotype : A photographic process in widespread use for about a decade beginning in 1852, in which an under-exposed wet-collodion glass negative is made to appear positive when placed against a dark background (usually black fabric or paper) or by coating the back with black lacquer or varnish, causing the clear areas of the negative to appear dark and the opaque silver areas bright in reflected ambient light. Although the ambrotype lacked the tonal range of the daguerreotype, the process required less exposure time and production was faster and less expensive. The image is not laterally reversed, as in a daguerreotype, and can be viewed from any angle. Ambrotypes were usually preserved in a lined leather case under a stamped metal mat to conceal the uneven edges of the negative, and some were hand-colored (click here to see examples). Due to the fragility of glass, the process was largely replaced by the tintype and paper prints by the mid-1860s. Click here to see examples (Getty Museum) and here to learn more about the process. Synonymous with *collodion positive.*

Amendment : A change in a solicitation prior to contract award.

amendment : A change made in a document by addition, deletion, or revision, usually to correct errors or make improvements. Also, a change proposed or made in a bill or law, for example, the first ten amendments to the Constitution of the United States, known as the "Bill of Rights." *See also*: First Amendment.

American Antiquarian Society (AAS) : An independent national research library founded in 1812 in Worcester, Massachusetts, to document the history of the American people from the colonial period through the Civil War and Reconstruction. The collections of the AAS include books, pamphlets, newspapers, periodicals, manuscripts, broadsides, juvenile literature, music, graphic arts, genealogy, and local history. The AAS publishes the semiannual *Proceedings of the American Antiquarian Society* and is currently is in the midst of producing the five-volume work of collaborative scholarship, *A History of the Book in America*, jointly with Cambridge University Press. Click here to connect to the AAS homepage.

American Association of Law Libraries (AALL) : Founded in 1906, AALL has a membership of librarians and related information professionals who serve the legal profession in bar associations, courts, law schools, law societies, private law firms, businesses, and government. AALL seeks to promote and enhance the value of law libraries to the legal community and general public, fosters the profession of law librarianship, and provides leadership in the field of legal information. An affiliate of the American Library Association, AALL has published the quarterly *Law Library Journal* since 1908. Click here to connect to the AALLNET Web page.

American Association of School Librarians (AASL) : Founded in 1951, AASL is a division of the American Library Association with a membership of elementary and secondary school library media specialists and others interested in the improvement and extension of services for children and young adults. AASL publishes the quarterly journal *School Library Media Research* and its bimonthly online companion *Knowledge Quest*. Click here to connect to the AASL homepage.

American Association of University Professors (AAUP) : A professional association founded in 1915 to represent college and university faculty, the AAUP is also open to administrators, graduate students, and the general public. The organization is dedicated to defending academic freedom and tenure, advocating collegial governance, developing policies to ensure due process in the workplace, lobbying government in the interests of higher education, and providing statistics and analysis of trends in academic employment. Library faculty members at colleges and universities in the United States who are members of the AAUP may be covered by a collective bargaining agreement negotiated by their chapter. Click here to connect to the AAUP homepage.

American Book Trade Directory (ABTD) : Published annually by R.R. Bowker, the *ABTD* provides basic directory information on booksellers, jobbers, dealers, and antiquarians in the United States and Canada, listed geographically by state/province and indexed by name and type of store, as well as information about auctioneers of literary property, appraisers of library collections, book exporters and importers, and national and regional associations involved in the book trade.

American Booksellers Association (ABA) : Founded in 1900, the ABA is the oldest trade association of independent bookstores with store front locations in the United States. Its mission is to meet the needs of its members through advocacy, education, research, and the dissemination of information. The ABA actively supports fee speech, literacy, and programs that encourage children to read. The organization also publishes an annual handbook for book buyers and maintains the BookWeb.org Web site.

American Film Institute (AFI) : Established in 1967 at the recommendation of a Stanford Research Institute report funded by the National Endowment for the Arts and with initial funding from the NEA, the Motion Picture Association of America, and the Ford Foundation, AFI is a nonprofit organization devoted to (1) training the next generation of filmmakers, (2) presenting the moving image in its many forms to a national and international public, (3) preserving the motion picture heritage of the United States, and (4) redefining the moving image in the digital era. AFI maintains a Conservatory in Los Angeles, coordinates film preservation through the AFI Film Collection held at the Library of Congress and in other archives, and publishes the *American Film Institute Catalog of Motion Pictures Produced in the United States: Feature Films* and the *AFI Silent Film Database*. AFI sponsors an extensive nonprofit exhibition program of over 3,000 film events throughout the year and gives an annual Lifetime Achievement Award to an outstanding performer or director. Click here to connect to the AFI homepage. *See also*: British Film Institute.

American Folklife Center : Created by Congress in 1976, the American Folklife Center is an agency within the Library of Congress dedicated to preserving and presenting the American folk tradition. It incorporates the Archive of Folk Culture, established in 1928 as a repository of American folk music. Click here to connect to the homepage of the American Folklife Center.

American Indian Library Association (AILA) : Founded in 1979, AILA is an affiliate of the American Library Association with a membership of individuals and institutions committed to promoting the development, maintenance, and improvement of library services and collections for Native Americans, particularly cultural and information resources needed on reservations and in communities of Native Americans and Native Alaskans. AILA publishes the quarterly *AILA Newsletter*. Click here to connect to the AILA homepage. *See also*: tribal library.

American Institute for Conservation of Historic and Artistic Works (AIC) : Formerly the American Group within the International Institute for Conservation of Historic and Artistic Works (IIC), AIC is a national membership organization of conservation professionals dedicated to preserving for future generations the art and historic artifacts that constitute the cultural heritage of the United States. Founded in 1972, AIC provides a forum for the exchange of ideas on conservation, seeks to advance the practice of conservation, and promotes the importance of preserving cultural property by facilitating the exchange of knowledge, research, and publications. Its membership includes practicing conservators, conservation scientists, educators, administrators, collections care professionals, technicians, and students; archivists, curators, and other museum and library professionals; and architects and art historians. AIC publishes the *Journal of the American Institute of Conservation* and the bimonthly newsletter *AIC News*. Click here to connect to the AIC homepage.

American Institute of Graphic Arts (AIGA) : Founded in 1914 in New York, AIGA is a nonprofit organization that fosters excellence in graphic design as an academic discipline, communication medium, business tool, and cultural force by providing a forum for graphic designers, art directors, illustrators, and craftsmen involved in printing and allied graphic arts to exchange ideas and information, participate in research and critical analysis, and enhance education and ethical practice. AIGA publishes *Trace: AIGA Journal of Design* thrice yearly. Click here to connect to the AIGA homepage.

American Libraries (AL) : A professional magazine for librarians published since 1907 by the American Library Association, *AL* provides news and announcements, analysis of trends, feature articles, job postings, and advertising by library-related businesses in 11 issues per year. ISSN: 0002-9769. Click here to connect to the online version of *AL*. For reviews of books and other categories of materials collected by libraries, see *Booklist*, also published by the ALA.

American Library Association (ALA) : The leading professional association of public and academic libraries and librarians in the United States, the ALA was founded in Philadelphia in October 1876 by a group of library leaders (90 men and 13 women) that included Melvil Dewey. An "association of associations," the ALA is organized in divisions, each with its own officers, budget, and programs, and is closely tied to over 50 state and regional chapters. The Association also sponsors round tables on specific issues and topics and is affiliated with other independent library-related organizations. Its imprint is ALA Editions. The most widely read periodicals published by the ALA are the professional journal *American Libraries* and the review publication *Booklist*. The ALA is a member of the International Federation of Library Associations and Institutions (IFLA). Click here to see a complete list of periodicals published by the various branches of the ALA. Click here to connect to the ALA homepage. *See also*: ALA Allied Professional Association, Association des Bibliothécaires Français, Australian Library and Information Association, Canadian Library Association, Chartered Institute of Library and Information Professionals, and Deutscher Bibliogtheksverband e.V.

American Library Directory (ALD) : A serial published annually by R.R. Bowker since 1923, available in the reference section of most libraries, providing directory information (name, location, phone and fax number[s], department heads, budget, collection size, special collections, electronic resources, network participation, etc.) for over 30,000 academic, public, research, county, provincial, regional, medical, law, and other special libraries in the United States, Canada, and Mexico. *ALD* also includes separate sections listing library networks and consortia, library systems, libraries for persons with special needs, and state and federal library agencies. It also contains an alphabetically arranged *Personnel Index* of all the individuals named in the entries for libraries, library systems, and library consortia, with contact information. ISSN: 0065-910X.

American Literary Translators Association (ALTA) : Founded in 1978, ALTA provides essential services to literary translators from all languages and serves as a professional forum for the exchange of ideas on the art and craft of literary translation. From its headquarters at the Center for Translation Studies at the University of Texas, Dallas, ALTA also seeks to enhance the quality and status of literary translation and to improve the market for its publication. The organization is currently supported by members, occasional grants from the National Endowment for the Arts, and the University of Texas, Dallas. ALTA sponsors an annual conference and publishes the semiannual journal *Translation Review*. Click here to connect to the ALTA homepage. *See also*: American Translators Association.

American National Standards Institute (ANSI) : A nonprofit national clearinghouse founded in 1918 to facilitate standardization by voluntary consensus in the United States in both the public and private sectors and to coordinate and administer standards of all types. ANSI membership includes over 1,400 companies, organizations, government agencies, and other institutions. The United States is represented by ANSI in the International Organization for Standardization (ISO). Standards for library and information science are developed by the National Information Standards Organization (NISO), a nonprofit association accredited by ANSI. The Institute publishes the quarterly newsmagazine *ANSI Reporter* and the biweekly e-newsletter *What's New?* Click here to connect to the ANSI homepage.

American Printing History Association (APHA) : Founded in 1974, APHA encourages study and research in printing history and related arts and skills, including calligraphy, type founding, papermaking, bookbinding, illustration, and publishing. From its headquarters in New York City, APHA publishes the *APHA Newsletter* and the semiannual journal *Printing History*. Click here to connect to the APHA homepage.

American Reference Books Annual (ARBA) : A reference serial published annually by Libraries Unlimited since

1970, *ARBA* provides comprehensive coverage of English-language reference books and electronic reference works published in the United States and Canada during the previous year, listing reviews in a classified arrangement, indexed by author/title and subject. The reviews are usually 100 to 300 words long, written by scholars, librarians, and library educators who are asked to examine new works as they are published and provide well-documented critical comments, both positive and negative. All reviews are signed. *ARBA* is usually shelved in the reference section of large academic and public libraries. In *ARBAonline*, reviews are provided in a searchable database that is available on subscription. ISSN: 0065-9959.

American Society of Composers, Authors and Publishers (ASCAP) : Established in 1914, ASCAP is a membership association of over 160,000 American composers, songwriters, lyricists, and music publishers of every kind of music, dedicated to protecting the rights of its members by licensing and distributing royalties for nondramatic public performances of their copyrighted works. Through agreements with international affiliates, ASCAP also represents hundreds of thousands of music creators worldwide. Click here to connect to the ASCAP homepage.

American Society of Indexers (ASI) : Founded in 1968, ASI is an affiliate of the American Library Association that seeks to promote indexing, abstracting, and database construction. Its members are professional indexers, librarians, editors, publishers, and organizations that employ indexers. ASI publishes the semiannual journal *The Indexer* and the bimonthly bulletin *Key Words*. Click here to connect to the ASI homepage.

American Society of Picture Professionals (ASPP) : Founded in 1966, ASPP is a national organization of persons who produce, sell, edit, catalog, and use photographic imagery. Open to professionals with at least four years experience in the picture field, ASPP provides a forum for the open exchange of information on industry ethics and standards, business practices, and new technology. The organization also provides opportunities for professional networking; seeks to inform and educate those interested in photography and visual communications; promotes a Code of Fair Practice for picture research, usage, and handling; and offers knowledge and support to persons interested in choosing a career as a picture professional. ASPP sponsors a conference and publishes the quarterly magazine *The Picture Professional*. Click here to connect to the ASPP homepage.

American Theological Library Association (ATLA) : Founded in 1947, ATLA is an affiliate of the American Library Association with an ecumenical membership that includes theological librarians, persons interested in theological librarianship, and theological institutions dedicated to providing programs, products, and services in support of theological and religious studies libraries and librarians. ATLA publishes the quarterly *ATLA Newsletter*. Click here to connect to the ATLA homepage.

American Translators Association (ATA) : Founded in 1959, ATA is the largest professional association of translators and interpreters in the United States, with over 8,500 members from over 60 countries. The primary goals of ATA are to foster and support the professional development of translators and interpreters and to promote the translation and interpreting professions. ATA sponsors an annual conference and publishes the monthly professional journal *ATA Chronicle*. Click here to connect to the ATA homepage. *See also*: American Literary Translators Association.

americanize : To convert to American English the style and spelling of a work written in (or translated into) British English. Compare with briticize.

Americans for Libraries Council (ALC) : A newly established nonprofit organization that advocates for libraries at the national level and develops and promotes programs aimed at realizing the potential of libraries in the 21st century. Comprised of business, civic, educational, philanthropic, and library leaders, ALC is committed to developing a national agenda to: 1) focus attention on libraries as national assets essential for a healthy economy and vital democracy, 2) provide effective models for library services and library support, 3) establish a new base of financial support for library preservation and innovation, and 4) increase advocacy for libraries in the corporate, philanthropic, and civic sectors. Click here to connect to the ALC homepage.

Americans with Disabilities Act (ADA) : Legislation passed by Congress in 1990 guaranteeing right of access to public facilities and resources to persons with physical disabilities and prohibiting discrimination against them in employment. The *ADA* has had a profound effect on the delivery of library services in the United States, from architectural planning (ramps, elevators, automatic door-openers, signage in Braille, etc.) to the design and placement of furniture, equipment, and shelving and even the design of computer interfaces. Click here to learn more or see the print publication *How Libraries Must Comply with the Americans with Disabilities Act (ADA)* by Donald Foos and Nancy Pack (Oryx, 1992)..*See also*: adaptive technology.

amicus curiae : A Latin term meaning "friend of the court." An individual, group, or organization seeking to advise the court on a point of law or fact in a legal case to which the amicus is neither party nor counsel but that may set a legal precedent affecting its interests. Although it is not required, the amicus is usually an attorney. Permission must be obtained from the court but is usually given if the parties consent. Such appearances occur most frequently at the appellate level in cases involving civil rights and issues of public interest, by formal brief or, in rare cases, oral argument. The American Library Association sometimes files an amicus curiae brief, as in the case of *New York Times Co. v. Tasini*. Plural: *amici curiae*.

Amount at Stake : The severity or extent of adverse consequences which could occur to the project. For example, the cost of recovery from lost production, plus the cost of recovering from the delay, etc.

ampersand : The symbol & derived from a fusion of the letters of the Latin word *et*, meaning "and." Under *AACR2*, when the title proper contains an ampersand (*example*: Notes & Queries), it is transcribed in the title and statement of responsibility area of the bibliographic description exactly as it appears on the chief source of information, and an added entry is made under the title with "and" spelled out.

anaglyph : A composite stereographic image produced by printing the same image twice, in complementary colors slightly displaced laterally, rather than superimposed exactly. In cartography, red is normally used for the right component and green or blue for the left. Although the image appears to be out of register when seen with the naked eye, a three-dimensional effect is produced by viewing it through a pair of eyeglasses equipped with filters of corresponding colors. Click here to see a cartographic example (courtesy of North Dakota State University). To see other examples, try a keyword search on the term in *Google Image Search*.

anagram : A word, phrase, sentence, name, or title made from another by the rearrangement of its letters. The basic rule of anagramming is that all the letters must be used once and only once, as in "cone" made from the letters of the word "once." The best anagrams are meaningful and related in some way to the original subject. Anagrams are often humorous (*example*: Adolf Hitler = Heil, old fart). Click here to see an anagram in the dedication of a 17th-century volume to Frederik III of Denmark (Royal Library of Denmark). and here to learn more about anagrams.

analects : From the Greek *analekta*, meaning "things gathered up." A collection or "gleaning" of miscellaneous literary excerpts or fragments (*example*: the teachings of the Chinese philosopher Confucius).

analog : A representation of an object, physical condition, or process that closely replicates the original, reflecting any variations in its state. In technology, analog devices are designed to monitor conditions such as sound, movement, or temperature and convert the resulting measurements into electrical signals or mechanical patterns representing the fluctuations of the actual phenomenon, for example, sounds recorded on a phonograph record. Analog data is encoded in signals that are continuous over a range or interval of values, for example, data transmitted over a telephone line that must be converted by a modem into the discrete values of digital code in order to be processed by a digital computer.

Analysis : The study and examination of something complex and separation into its more simple components. Analysis typically includes discovering not only what are the parts of the thing being studied, but also how they fit together and why they are arranged in this particular way. A study of schedule variances for cause, impact, and corrective action.

Analysis and Design : A discipline in the Unified Process, whose purpose is to show how the system's use cases will be realized in implementation; (general) activities during which strategic and tactical decisions are made to meet the required functional and quality requirements of a system. For the result of analysis and design activities, see Design Model.

Analysis Time : Refers to something that occurs during an analysis phase of the software development process. See design time, modeling time.

analytical entry : An entry in a library catalog for a part of a work (chapter in a book) or an entire work (story, play, essay, or poem) contained in an item, such as an anthology or collection, for which a comprehensive entry is also made. Analytical entries are made under the author, title, and subject of the part and include a reference to the title of the work containing the part. Because preparation of analytical entries is time-consuming, the level of bibliographic description provided in a catalog depends on the administrative policy of the library and its assessment of local needs. Synonymous with *analytics*. *See also*: analytical note.

Anecdotal : Based on hearsay rather than on demonstrated facts, hard data or personal experience.

annotation : Annotations are critical evaluations of works, often found in bibliographies. Do not confuse an annotation with an abstract, which is a noncritical summary of the work.

Annotation : Unlike an abstract, which is an objective description or summary of a work, an annotation is a critical or subjective evaluation of a piece of work, usually included in a bibliography or citation.

anthology : A collection of extracts or complete works by various authors, selected by an editor for publication in a single volume or multivolume set. Anthologies are often limited to a specific literary form or genre (short stories, poetry, plays) or to a national literature, theme, time period, or category of author (click here to see a 19th-century example, courtesy of the Glasgow University Library). The works *anthologized* are listed in the table of contents by title in order of appearance in the text. In the card catalog, analytical entries may be prepared for works published in anthologies. In the online catalog, the individual works contained in an anthology are listed in the bibliographic record in a contents note searchable by keyword(s) in most catalog software. Compare with compilation. *See also*: garland and miscellany.

Anticipated Award Cost : The most probable contract price at time of tender and award. It forms part of the forecast to complete. See Cost Types.

antitrust : Federal laws prohibiting businesses from monopolizing the market for a product or service, price-fixing, and other collaborations in restraint of free trade, enforced by the Antitrust Division of the U.S. Department of Justice. On February 11, 2005, more than 50 lawyers and law professors, antitrust experts, federal and state regulators, economists, professors, librarians, and international delegates met at the Georgetown University Law School in Washington, D.C., to explore the effect of unconstrained mergers in the publishing industry on legal and scholarly communication, spurred by the spiraling costs of journal subscriptions. The symposium was sponsored by the American Antitrust Institute (AAI) and the Information Access Alliance (IAA), an advocacy group formed by the Association of Research Libraries (ARL), the American Association of Law Libraries (AALL), the Medical Library

Association (MLA), the Special Libraries Association (SLA), and the Scholarly Publishing and Academic Resources Coalition (SPARC). Although there is, as yet, insufficient data to establish a connection between mergers and price escalation under current antitrust law, the group compiled a list of strategies for future action. For more information, see Lee Van Orsdel's report on *Antitrust Issues in Scholarly and Legal Publishing* in the May 2005 issue of *C&RL News*.

anti-virus software : A computer program designed to periodically check the hard drive of a computer (or all the computers attached to a network) for the presence of man-made computer viruses and eliminate them if found. The anti-virus software used on computer networks usually includes an update feature that automatically downloads profiles of newly created viruses soon after they are detected.

antonym : A word or phrase that is the *opposite* in meaning of another term. Dictionaries of antonyms are available in the reference section of larger libraries. In some indexing languages, one of the terms in a pair of opposites may be selected to represent both, with a cross-reference made from the other. The opposite of synonym.

APIPA : See Automatic Private IP Addressing.

apocryphal : Writings that scholars consider to be of dubious authorship or authenticity (not genuine), for example, the 14 to 15 books of the Greek translations of the Old Testament (Septuagint), known as the *Apocrypha*, accepted as authoritative by the Roman Catholic and Greek Orthodox churches but rejected in Judaism and not considered canonical in Protestantism. Compare with anonymous. *See also*: spurious work.

Apparent Low Bidder : The contractor who has submitted the lowest compliant bid for all or part of a project as described in a set of bid documents.

application : Computer software that allows the user to process data or perform calculations necessary to achieve a desired result, as opposed to the operating system designed to control the computer's hardware and run all other programs. Common microcomputer applications include word processing, spreadsheets, e-mail, presentation graphics, desktop publishing, database management systems, and Web browsers. *See also*: multitasking.

Application Area : A category of projects that have common elements not present in all projects. Application areas are usually defined in terms of either the product of the project (i.e., by similar technologies or industry sectors) or the type of customer (e.g., internal vs. external, government vs. commercial, etc.). Application areas often overlap.

Application for Expenditure ("AFE") : A formal document presented to management to permit the expenditure of funds, typically supported by appropriate justification documentation. See also Application for Expenditure Justification.

Application for Expenditure Justification : The formal documentation required to support an Application for Expenditure. Typically a submission requesting funding to undertake the ïImplementationÍ and ïCommissioning, Startup & CompletionÍ Phases of a capital project. It reprcsents complete summary documentation of the project up to that point and is required by management to enable an appropriate decision to be made concerning continuation of the project and to ensure that a proper basis has been established for the conduct of the project during those ensuing phases.

Application Programmers : Those programmers responsible for the development of function and industry relevant software that is determined by their employer's particular business (for example, banking, aerospace, stock brokerage, insurance, accounting, inventory).

Applied Direct Costs : The actual direct costs recognized in the time period associated with the consumption of labor, material, and other direct resources, without regard to their date of commitment or the date of payment.

Apportioned Effort : Effort directly related to some other measured effort.

Apportioned Task : A task that is dependent on or related to the performance of another task.

Appraisal : An impartial evaluation of information concerning a system, service or product to determine its measure of effectiveness and efficiency for purposes of making recommendations for acceptance, correction, or preventive action.

Appraise : To evaluate the worth, significance, or status of. Baseline-A specification or product that has been formally reviewed and agreed upon, that thereafter serves as the basis for further development, and that can be changed only through formal change control procedures.

Approach : A way of doing things. For example, project planning may require different approaches, or different approaches may be considered as a way of reducing Project Risks

Appropriation : An allocation of funds to a project by the owner or sponsor in response to a Capital Appropriation Request (CAR) or a Request For Appropriation (RFA). In a structured organization, a commitment cannot be made until an appropriation has been obtained. However, a lower threshold value may be set below which a formal appropriation is not required. Prefeasibility and similar studies are such examples.

Appropriation Estimate : An estimate prepared to establish a budget to be included in an application for project funding (i.e. for an "appropriation" of funds from corporate sources). Prepared from the best available, but not necessarily complete, information. Also known as a Budget Estimate.

Approval : A process for sanctioning a proposed course of action usually following some form of review. It should involve the transfer of the necessary supporting Authority and Responsibility with the expectation of Reliability and Accountability.

Approval to Proceed : The term used when an individual accepts a deliverable as fit for purpose so that the project can continue. Approval given to the project at initiation or prior to the beginning of the next stage.

Approve : To accept as satisfactory. Approval implies that the thing approved has the endorsement of the approving agency-, however, the approval may still require confirmation by somebody else. In management use, the important distinction is between approve and authorize. Persons who approve something are willing to accept it as satisfactory for their purposes, but this decision is not final. Approval may be by several persons. The person who authorizes has final organization authority. This authorization is final approval.

Approved Bidders List : A list of contractors that have been prequalified for purposes of submitting competitive bids

Approved Changes : Changes that have been approved by higher authority.

Approved Project Requirements : A statement of realistic requirements, approved and signed off by the Stakeholder(s).

arabesque initial : From the Italian *arabesco* meaning Arabian in style. An initial letter in a medieval manuscript, decorated with a complex, often interlaced, design of abstract or geometric and highly stylized foliate curvilinear forms. Adapted in about 1,000 A.D. by Muslim artisans from Hellenistic precursors, the decorative style eventually became formalized, with animal and human forms excluded for religious reasons. Click here to see examples in a 12th-century English manuscript (British Library, Arundel 74).

Arbitrary : Something done without apparent logic.

Arbitration : A formalized system for dealing with grievances and administering corrective justice as part of collective bargaining agreements.

Arc : The line connecting two nodes or representing precedence in a PERT or CPM network.

Architectural Baseline : The baseline at the end of the Elaboration phase, at which time the foundation structure and behavior of the system is stabilized.

Architectural View : A view of a software system architecture from a given perspective focusing primarily on structure, modularity, essential components, and the main control flows.

Architecture : The design and interconnection of the main components of a hardware/software system.

Architecture, executable : See Executable Architecture.

archival box : A strong cardboard container specifically designed for the long-term storage of archival materials (manuscripts, papers, letters, periodicals, maps, prints, mounted photographs, etc.), made from strong acid-and lignin-free board, usually lined with buffered paper and fastened on the exterior with metal-edged corners, without the use of adhesive or staples. Containers made of inert polypropylene plastic are also used for this purpose. Archival boxes are available from library suppliers in a variety of sizes and designs (clamshell-hinged, drop-fronted, with telescoping lids, etc.), shipped flat or pre-assembled. They are usually neutral in color. Click here to see examples, courtesy of the Heritage Collections Council, Australia. Synonymous with *archives box. See also*: box list.

archive : The building, facility, or area that houses an archival collection (the term *repository* is preferred by most archivists). Also, to place documents in storage, usually to preserve them as a historical, informational, legal, or evidential record, permanently or for a finite or indefinite period of time. *See also*: digital archive.

Archive Plan : A function of some computer programs that allows versions of a plan to be archived.

archives : Archives are special collections of materials, such as personal papers, photographs, manuscripts, rare books, etc. The South Texas Archives of Texas A&M University Kingsville was established to make available to the public materials about the history and natural history of South Texas. The Archives are housed in Baugh Hall on Richard Street.

archives policy : A formal written statement defining the authority under which an archives operates, the scope of its activities (mission, objectives, conditions/restrictions, etc.), and the range of services it provides. Compare with access policy.

archivist : The person responsible for managing and maintaining an archival collection, usually a librarian with special training in archival practices and methods, including the identification and appraisal of records of archival value, authentication, accessioning, description and documentation, facilitation of access and use, preservation and conservation, and exhibition and publication to benefit scholarship and satisfy public interest. Archivists are organized in the Society of American Archivists. *See also*: Academy of Certified Archivists.

Area of Project Application : See Area of Project Management Application

Area of Project Management Application ("APMA") : The environment in which a project takes place, with its own particular nomenclature and accepted practices e.g. facilities, products or systems development projects (to name a few.)

aristonym : A surname used as, or derived from, a formal title of nobility (*example*: **Louis Aimé Augustin Le Prince**).

armorial : A book containing illustrations of coats of arms, and sometimes other heraldic devices, usually accompanied by explanatory text. Click here to view a 15th-century manuscript treatise on heraldry (Bodelian Library, University of Oxford, MS Lat. misc.e.86).

armorial binding : A binding, usually in leather, decorated with a coat of arms or other heraldic device to signify the royal or noble lineage of its original owner. Click here to view a 16th-century Bible with an armorial design blind tooled on the back cover (Glasgow University Library Special Collections, Da-i.35) and here to see the royal arms of King James I as a gilt-tooled centerpiece on a 17th-century presentation copy (Princeton University Library). The category also includes bindings with arms fashioned in metal affixed to the cover. Click here to see a 16th-century example (British Library, Burney 38). To view other examples, try a search on the keyword "armorial" in the British Library's *Database of Bookbindings*. *See also*: royal binding.

armorial initial : An illuminated initial letter in a medieval manuscript or early printed book, decorated with a coat of arms, sometimes that of the person or family for whom the book was made. Click here to see an example in a

16th-century Italian manuscript. Armorial motifs are also found in the ornamental borders of medieval manuscripts (see this opening page of the 15th-century *Chroniques de Hainaut*, courtesy of the Getty Museum).

ARP Cache : A table for each interface of static or dynamically resolved IPv4 addresses and their corresponding MAC addresses.

Arrow : The graphic presentation of an activity. The tail (see I-Node) of the arrow represents the start of the activity. The head (see J-Node) of the arrow represents the finish. Unless a time scale is used, the length of the arrow stem has no relation to the duration of the activity. Length and direction of the activity are usually a matter of convenience and clarity.

Arrow Diagram Method ("ADM") : One of two conventions used to represent an activity in a project. Also known as Activity on Arrow method.

Arrow Diagramming : A technique that may be used in both CPM and PERT to display the network sequence and timing of activities. The technique is event oriented in that the connecting arrows represent the activities. It is simple to understand and display straight forward networks. Its flexibility is limited in comparison with precedence diagramming.

Arrow Diagramming Method : A network diagramming technique in which activities are represented by arrows. The tail of the arrow represents the start and the head represents the finish of the activity (the length of the arrow does not represent the expected duration of the activity). Activities are connected at points called nodes (usually drawn as small circles) to illustrate the sequence in which the activities are expected to be performed. See also precedence diagramming method.

Art & Architecture Thesaurus (AAT) : A structured vocabulary for describing and indexing works of visual art and architecture. Initially developed by the Getty Information Institute, the *AAT* is made available through the Getty Research Institute.

art : A general term used in publishing and printing for the illustrative matter in a book or other publication for which no setting of type is required, including any hand lettering, photographs, reproductions of drawings, prints, and paintings, etc. Compare with artwork.

art book : A volume, usually of relatively large size, containing high-quality reproductions of works of visual art (paintings, drawings, prints, etc.) or photographs of sculpture, architecture, or other three-dimensional works of art, usually with accompanying text. In an exhibition catalog, the text may be minimal. Because art books are expensive to produce, they are sometimes co-published to achieve economies of scale. For examples, see the books section of the Met Store at the Metropolitan Museum of Art in New York City. Compare with artist's book. *See also*: coffee table book.

Art Libraries Society/North America (ARLIS/NA) : Founded in 1972, ARLIS is an organization of librarians, institutions, and individuals with an interest in art librarianship and the curatorship of visual art resources in public and academic libraries, museums, galleries, art institutes, and publishing houses. An affiliate of the American Library Association, ARLIS publishes the bulletin *Art Documentation* twice a year. Click here to connect to the ARLIS/NA homepage. *See also*: art library.

art library : A library charged with acquiring, organizing, preserving, and providing access to information and resources in the diverse fields constituting the visual arts (architecture, drawing, graphic design, painting, photography, sculpture, etc.). An art library usually functions as a unit within a larger academic or public library, or as a special library maintained by a host organization such as a gallery, museum, art institute, or publishing house (*example*: National Art Library at the Victoria & Albert Museum, London). The first modern art library in the United States was founded in 1871 by the San Francisco Art Association (now the San Francisco Art Institute). The International Federation of Library Associations and Institutions (IFLA) maintains the *International Directory of Art Libraries*. *See also*: art book and Art Libraries Society/North America.

Article : Sometimes referred to as a paper, an article is a brief composition on a subject, usually appearing in a magazine or journal.

article : An essay or research report on a subject. Articles appear in MAGAZINES, JOURNALS, newspapers and other sources such as encyclopedias.

Artificial : Not genuine or real, as in conditions created for running tests, or in postulating possible risk scenarios.

artificial collection : A collection of archival materials accumulated unsystematically around a person, subject, event, activity, etc., from diverse (sometimes unknown) sources, without regard to archival integrity (*respect des fonds*) or provenance. Richard Pearce-Moses notes in *A Glossary of Archival and Records Terminology* (Society of American Archivists, 2005) that "artificial collections, as distinguished from organic collections, typically do not grow out of a single, specific function, and are often arranged for the convenience of description or retrieval rather than in an order originally established by the creator" of the records. In archival description, such a collection is entered under the name of the person chiefly responsible for its assemblage, with the term *collector* added following the name. If the collector is unknown, entry is made under the title.

artist's book : A book created as a form of visual and/or tactile artistic expression, often of unusual shape or form and incorporating materials not normally used in printing and binding. Artist's books created for exhibition may be one-of-a-kind. Examples can be seen in *Personal Visions: Artists' Books at the Millennium* (University of Delaware Library) and in the gallery of *The Book Arts Web*. The Canadian Bookbinders and Book Artists Guild (CBBAG) also provides an Online Gallery. For more information, see *Structure of the Visual Book* (1994) by Keith A. Smith. Synonymous with *livre d'artiste*. Compare with art book. *See also*: book art and novelty binding.

artist's proof : An impression taken in the process of printmaking to allow the artist to examine the current state of the plate, stone, woodblock, etc., while it is still possible to make alterations (some artists pull every tenth print to examine it for quality). Reserved for the artist's use and often distinguished by the artist's signature, such a print is accepted as belonging to the edition but left unnumbered or numbered separately. Some artists destroy them as competing works but to art historians, curators, and collectors, they are evidence of the development of the image, each serving as a snapshot of the work in progress. Because of their uniqueness and possible differences from the "standard" print of the edition, artist's proofs often command a higher price when available in the market place. Click here to see an artist's proof of an etching by Wilkie Collins.

artwork : A general term used in publishing and printing to refer to illustration originals in any medium, as opposed to reproductions of art originals. Such works may have artistic and monetary value independent of the publication for which they were created. Compare with art.

As-built Design : The documentation that describes the ultimate "As-built" configuration to provide for future replication. It includes design changes implemented for manufacturing improvements and integration and verification corrective actions. The "As-built" baseline becomes the "Build-to" baseline for new builds. In construction, "As-built" drawings are referred to as the "record" drawings.

As-built Documentation : Drawings and diagrams that provide an accurate representation of how the product or facility is actually built.

As-Built Schedule : A reconstruction of the Project Schedule to reflect the sequence and durations in which the project work was actually accomplished. A process frequently used in developing or analyzing contractor claims for extra money by high-lighting delays to progress.

ASCII (American Standard Code for Information Interchange) : A standard code designed by the American National Standards Institute (ANSI) to facilitate information interchange between unstandardized data processing and communications equipment. The code, consisting of eight bits including a parity bit, can represent a character set of 128 alphabetic, numeric, and special symbols.

ASK 24/7 : This is live chat reference service that is available round the clock throughout the year. The ASK 24/7 service is provided by the Boston Library Consortium and is available as a link from the Tisch Library webpage.

As-Late-As-Possible ("ALAP") : An activity for which the application sets the early dates as late as possible without delaying the early dates of any successor.

As-Needed : Delivery or consumption of resources or information just as and when required.

aspect : In Dewey Decimal Classification, an approach to a subject from a discipline other than the one in which the subject is classified, for example, the *economic* or *sociological* aspects of health care delivery.

aspect ratio (AR) : The relationship of width to height of a frame of motion picture film, projected or printed. The normal range of vision of the human eye is an ellipse with proportions of approximately 1.85:1. The aspect ratio of silent film was 1.33:1, but the image was later squared to accommodate a sound track along the edge of the film. In 1932, the Academy of Motion Picture Arts and Sciences returned the aspect ratio of 35mm film to 1.33:1 by masking the top and bottom of the frame and *Academy aperture* became the international standard for theatrical releases and the source of the standardized aspect ratio for television screens. CinemaScope introduced in 1953 by Twentieth Century-Fox had an original aspect ratio of 2.55:1, later changed to 2.35:1 to accommodate an optical sound track. Standard widescreen at 1.85:1 was achieved at the expense of the image by masking the top and bottom of the frame. 70mm films are projected with an aspect ratio of 2.2:1. Click here to see a table of aspect ratios and here to see them illustrated. *Wikipedia* provides additonal information about aspect ratio.

As-Performed Schedule : The final project schedule which depicts actual completion (finish) dates, actual durations, and start dates.

Assembly : A functional unit designed and managed as an entity. Examples include electronic boxes, mechanical assemblies, and software components. Level 5 of the system hierarchy.

Assembly Sequence : Two or more parts or subassemblies joined together in the correct order to form a complete unit, structure, or other element.

Assessment : A determination of value, usually in dollar terms, of an asset, situation or condition that requires some action. Most often used in connection with some form of damages or valuation for insurance, taxation, etc.

Assets : Anything owned that has a monetary value, e.g. property, both real and personal, including notes, accounts and accrued earnings or revenues receivable and cash or its equivalent. Assets may be subdivided into current, fixed, etc.

Assignment : The transfer of some power such as Authority, Responsibility, Accountability, etc.

assignment indexing : A method of indexing in which a human indexer selects one or more subject headings or descriptors from a list of controlled vocabulary to represent the subject(s) of a work. The indexing terms selected to represent the content need not appear in the title or text of the document indexed. Synonymous with *assigned indexing*. Compare with derivative indexing.

Associated Revenue : That part of a project cost that is of a revenue nature and therefore charged as incurred to the profit and loss account.

association : The group of persons who have joined a formal organization devoted to pursuing a common interest or purpose, usually by applying for membership and paying an annual membership fee. Professional associations, such as the American Library Association, are dedicated to promoting the interests of a specific profession and its practitioners. The most comprehensive directory of such organizations is the *Encyclopedia of Associations* published by Gale Group, available in the reference section of most libraries in the United States. Click here to connect to an online directory of scholarly societies in North America, maintained by the University of Waterloo Library. Abbreviated *ass.*, *assn.*, and *assoc.* *See also*: library association and trade association.

association copy : A copy of a book that has a special association with the author, with a person closely connected to the author or its content, with a well-known individual other than the author, or with a particular library or collection, as indicated by an autograph, bookplate, dedication, inscription, marginalia, special binding, or other physical characteristic, or by reliable documentation.

Association of Research Libraries (ARL) : Founded in 1932, ARL is an organization of large research libraries dedicated to influencing major decisions affecting the future of research libraries and their ability to serve effectively the needs of students, faculty, and the research community, by articulating concerns, forming coalitions, suggesting policy, and supporting innovations and improvements in operations. An affiliate of the American Library Association, ARL provides access to proprietary databases, training and consultation in management and program development, directories, and statistics on its membership. The Association also publishes *ARL*, a bimonthly report on its activities. Click here to connect to the ARL homepage.

Association of Vision Science Librarians (AVSL) : An international association of information professionals employed at educational institutions, eye clinics and hospitals, and private companies whose library collections and services include the literature of vision, AVSL is a special interest group of both the Association of Schools and Colleges of Optometry and the Medical Library Association. The organization publishes standards and guideliness for vision science libraries, a union list of vision-related serials, and a core list for audiovisual collections. Click here to connect to the AVSL homepage.

associational value : The significance or utility of documents or other materials based on their relationship to a specific person, family, organization, place, or event. The connection can be one of creation, ownership, use, or subject content. Often key to the intrinsic value of archival materials, associational value can be difficult to quantify. Click here to see an image of Thomas Jefferson's portable writing desk, which he used to write the Declaration of Independence at Philadelphia (Library of Congress).

As-Soon-As-Possible ("ASAP") : An activity for which the application sets the early dates to be as soon as possible. This is the default activity type in most project management systems.

Assumption : There may be external circumstances or events that must occur for the project to be successful. If you believe such an event is likely to happen, then it would be an assumption. (Contrast with the definition of a risk.) If an event is within the control of the project team, such as having testing complete by a certain date, then it is not an assumption. If an event has a 100% chance of occurring, then it is not an assumption since there is no "likelihood" or risk involved. (It is just a fact). Examples of assumptions might be that "Budgets and resources will be available when needed..." or "The new software release will be available for use by the time the Construct Phase begins".

Assumptions List : A key part of the risk register which lists the assumptions, both explicit and implicit, on which a RAMP analysis is based. It is updated as and when previous assumptions need to be modified or new assumptions have to be made.

Assurance : To examine with the intent to verify.

at the bindery : This is the designation given to an item in the CATALOG that has been sent out of the library to be bound or repaired.

Attitude : The way a person views a situation or condition and then behaves accordingly. An important consideration in Team Building.

Attribute : An attribute defined by a class represents a named property of the class or its objects. An attribute has a type that defines the type of its instances.

attributed : A creative work ascribed to a known person or corporate body, usually on the basis of reliable supporting evidence. Degree of certainty concerning authorship depends on the strength of the existing evidence. For example, some scholars believe the plays and sonnets of

William Shakespeare to be the work of another Elizabethan writer, but the available evidence is insufficient to resolve the issue. When evidence of authorship is inconclusive, a work is said to be of unknown authorship.

Attrition : The loss of a resource due to causes beyond the jurisdiction of the project manager such as the death or resignation of an employee, or spoilage, damage, or obsolescence of material.

audience : The people who actually read a literary work or attend an artistic performance or exhibition, not necessarily the same as the target audience for whom the work is intended by the author or creator, or by the publisher or producer.

audio download : A data file containing recorded sound available over the Internet for transmission to a network user's computer, free of charge or for a fee (usually payable by credit card). Dot.com booksellers like Amazon.com offer audio downloads of popular new books. Audible.com is an example of a company specializing in downloadable audiorecordings. *See also*: peer-to-peer.

audiovisual (AV) : A work in a medium that combines sound and visual images, for example, a motion picture or videorecording with a sound track, or a slide presentation synchronized with audiotape. Directory information for products and services provided by the audiovisual industry is available in *AV Market Place (AVMP)*, published annually by R.R. Bowker. Also spelled *audio-visual* and abbreviated *a-v*. *See also*: media.

audio-visual material : These are sound or video recordings rather than textual objects. In James C. Jernigan Library, most audio-visual material is held at the Circulation Desk. You will still need the item's Call Number when you approach the desk.

Australian Library and Information Association (ALIA): The professional association for the Australian library and information services sector, ALIA seeks to empower the library profession in the development, promotion, and delivery of quality services to all Australians, through leadership, advocacy, and mutual support. Membership is open to individuals and organizations. ALIA sponsors a biennial national conference, presents national and regional awards, and publishes *Australian Library Journal (ALJ)*. Click here to connect to the ALIA homepage.

Authentication : The process of identifying an individual by a computer, usually based on a username and password. Cornell uses SideCar and CUWebLogin to authenticate members of the Cornell community.

author : Generally, this refers to the writer of a book or an ARTICLE. However, author more generally means the "creator" of material, for example the composer of music. When searching in the CATALOG, directors, actors or performers are also considered authors.

author abstract : A brief summary, called an abstract, written by the person responsible for creating the work summarized, as opposed to one written by someone other than the author, usually a professional abstractor or indexer.

author entry : The entry in a catalog, index, or bibliography under the authorized heading for the first-named author of a work, whether it be a person or corporate body. In most library catalogs, the author entry is the main entry.

author index : An alphabetically arranged index in which the headings are the names of the individuals and corporate bodies responsible for creating the works indexed. Author entries may be combined with the subject index or title index, rather than listed separately. Compare with name index.

author interview : A conversation in which a writer is questioned about his/her life and work by an *interviewer* who intends to publish the results verbatim in a book or periodical or incorporate them into a radio or television broadcast, in their entirety or excerpted. Also refers to the article or program based on such an interview. Click here to see an example, courtesy of PBS.

author's binding : A copy of an edition bound to the author's specifications for purposes of presentation, usually to a friend, associate, or public figure, normally in a more attractive style, using better materials, and exhibiting superior workmanship. According to Matt Roberts and Don Etherington (*Bookbinding and the Conservation of Books: A Dictionary of Descriptive Terminology*), gilt vellum author's bindings were common in the 16th century and paneled morocco in the 17th and 18th centuries.

author's editor : An editor familiar with the publishing industry, employed by a university or research institution to assist faculty and researchers in preparing their work for publication and to help them negotiate the intricacies of the publishing process, as distinct from an editor employed by a publishing company who helps to prepare a manuscript for printing once it has been accepted for publication.

Authoritarian : A form of Leadership in which the Leader, directs activities from a position of power and without consideration of the views of those being lead.

Authoritative : Having experience or other established grounds for the giving of information or directions.

authoritative : A source that is official. Also, a work known to be reliable because its authority or authenticity is widely recognized by experts in the field.

authority : The knowledge and experience that qualifies a person to write or speak as an expert on a given subject. In the academic community, authority is indicated by credentials, previously published works on the subject, institutional affiliation, awards, imprint, reviews, patterns of citation, etc.

authority control : The procedures by which consistency of form is maintained in the headings (names, uniform titles, series titles, and subjects) used in a library catalog or file of bibliographic records through the application of an authoritative list (called an authority file) to new items as they are added to the collection. Authority control is available from commercial service providers.

authority file : A list of the authoritative forms of the headings used in a library catalog or file of bibliographic records, maintained to ensure that headings are applied consistently as new items are added to the collection. Separate authority files are usually maintained for names, uniform titles, series titles, and subjects. All the references made to and from a given heading are also included in the file. *See also*: authority control.

Authority for Expenditure ("AFE") : A formal document requesting the expenditure of capital funds on a defined business objective. Authorized by senior management or participants, depending on the funding level.

authority record : A printed or machine-readable record of the decision made concerning the authoritative form of a name (personal or corporate), uniform title, series title, or subject used as a heading in a library catalog or file of bibliographic records, listed in an authority file governing the application of headings to new items as they are added to the library collection. An authority record may also contain *See from* and *See also from* records, as well as notes concerning the application of the authorized form. Click here to connect to *Library of Congress Authorities*, a searchable database of authority headings.

authorization : In computing, a username, password, PIN, or other access code issued to a person who is permitted to access a specific electronic resource, application program, network, or other computer system that must be entered correctly by the user in order to log on. Authorization codes are usually subject to periodic renewal. A single authentication may have multiple authorizations.

Authorize : To give final approval. A person who can authorize something is vested with authority to give final endorsement which requires no further approval

Authorized Unpriced Work : The effort for which contract cost adjustments has not been agreed to, but for which authorization to proceed has been granted.

Authorized Work : An effort that has been approved by higher authority and may or may not be definitive.

autograph book : A book with blank pages intended for the collection of signatures of friends and/or famous people, with or without accompanying inscriptions. The value of an autograph book in the collectors' market depends on the rarity of the signatures it contains. Click here to see an example.

Automated Data Processing ("ADP") : The application of electronic equipment, especially computers, to manage. manipulate, display, and store data.

Automatic Decision Event : Decision event where the decision depends only on the outcome of the preceding activities and that can be programmed or made automatic.

Automatic Generation : Spontaneous creation. Typically applies to the generation of data by software programs, following the input of the requisite data and processing instructions.

Automatic Private IP Addressing : A feature in Windows Server 2003 and Windows XP that automatically configures a unique IPv4 address from the range 169.254.0.1 through 169.254.255.254 and a subnet mask of 255.255.0.0. APIPA is used when the Internet Protocol (TCP/IP) component is configured for automatic addressing, no DHCP server is available, and the Automatic Private IP Address alternate configuration option is chosen.

Automatic Test Equipment : Equipment built to perform a test or sequence of tests. ATE ranges from simple devices to verify mechanical or electrical continuity to sophisticated computerized systems with automatic sequencing, data processing, and readout. Automatic Test Equipment may be stand alone test units or may be built into the operational equipment. If built in, it is referred to as BITE (Built In Test Equipment).

Auxiliary Ground Equipment : System support equipment that provides power or environment normally provided by internal systems.

Availability : Capable of being used. Usually refers to resources and/or funding

available : This is the designation given to an item in the CATALOG when it is in the library available for CHECK OUT.

Average Outgoing Quality ("AOQ") : The average quality of outgoing product including all accepted lots, plus all rejected lots after the rejected lots have been effectively 100 percent inspected and all defectives replaced by non-defectives.

Average Outgoing Quality Limit ("AOQL") : The maximum of the average outgoing qualities for all possible incoming qualities for a given sampling plan.

Average Sample Size Curve : The curves that show the average sample sizes which may be expected to occur under the various sampling plans for a given process quality

Avoidance : Keeping away from. Typically used as a risk reduction strategy by adopting a Workaround.

Award : The assignment of work under Contract.

Award Fee : A contract fee provision used to motivate a contractor to respond to issues that are assigned and measured periodically and subjectively. The contract specifies award fee periods, usually six to nine months long. The award fee criteria are negotiated prior to the start of the award fee period, providing the buyer flexibility to change the incentive emphasis as the project evolves. The determination is made unilaterally by the buyer and is not subject to the legal disputes clause provisions.

Award Letter : A letter sent in response to an offer that accepts that offer.

azimuth : The direction of a celestial object expressed as a angle measured clockwise from true north or magnetic north around the plane of the observer's local horizon. An object due east has an azimuth of 90°, an object due south 180°, and due west 270°. An object due north has an azimuth of 0°. The azimuth of an object on the celestial sphere and its altitude above the horizon are the coordinates used to indicate direction in the *horizontal coordinate system* (also called the *alt-az coordinate system*). Click here or here to see azimuth illustrated.

back file : All the issues of a periodical that precede the current issue, usually bound in annual volumes or converted to microfilm or microfiche to conserve space. In the catalog record, the extent of the back file is indicated in the holdings statement. *See also*: holdings.

back fold : The fold along which a signature is gathered to form the binding edge of a book, left uncut in sewn bindings but trimmed in perfect binding to allow the adhesive to bond more securely. Synonymous with *spine fold*.

back matter : The pages following the text at the end of a book on which the appendices, notes, bibliographies, list of contributors, indices, imprint, and any advertising normally appear. In scholarly works, the back matter may be considerable. Back matter is paginated in arabic numerals continuously with the text. Blank leaves may be included at the end to make up a full section. Synonymous with *end matter*, *postliminary matter*, *reference matter*, and *subsidiaries*. Compare with front matter. *See also*: parts of a book.

back order (BO) : An order for library materials that could not be filled when originally placed because at least one of the items requested was not in stock or was as yet unpublished. Back orders are held open for future delivery, usually for a designated period of time, after which they are canceled. Synonymous in the UK with *dues*. *See also*: reorder and short shipment.

back page : The last page of an issue of a periodical (verso of the last leaf), facing the inside of the back cover. In some publications (*example*: *Booklist*), the back page is reserved for a regular column or editorial. *See also*: front page.

back to back : In library cataloging, a term used in the physical description area of the bibliographic record to describe: (1) two maps that are versions of the same work in two different languages, printed on alternate sides of a single sheet; or (2) two parts of a bilingual atlas published tête-bêche in a single volume.

Backcharge : The cost of corrective action taken by the purchaser, chargeable to the supplier under the terms of the contract.

backdate : To make a document or transaction effective from a date earlier than its actual date, for example, a book order given a prior date with the publisher's permission, to allow the purchaser to qualify for an expired discount.

background : In pictorial art, the parts of a scene that lie in the distance, behind figures and objects in the foreground. In illuminated manuscripts, the background in a miniature can be undecorated, diapered, or foliate, with or without gilding, as in the preceding examples from a Gospel book and a *Bible historiale* (Getty Museum, MS

65 & 1). In the late Middle Ages, miniatures were often painted against a naturalistic background, as in this miniature from *Des Cas des Nobles* by the Boucicaut Master (Getty, MS 63).

backlist : All the publications on a publisher's active list that are no longer new, having been published prior to the current season. Kept in stock to meet future demand, backlist titles are often the most profitable part of a publisher's list. Also spelled *back-list*. Compare with frontlist. *See also*: in print, out of print, and out of stock.

backlog : An accumulation of work that remains to be done, often the cause of delays and bottlenecks in workflow. A *cataloging backlog* may result when staffing is insufficient to meet the demands of acquisitions; for example, when a substantial gift is received within a short period of time. Synonymous in this sense with arrears.

Backward Pass : Calculation of the latest finish times by working from finish to start for the uncompleted portion of a network of activities.

Bad Debts : Actual or estimated losses arising from uncollectable accounts receivable due from customers and other claims, and any directly associated costs (e.g., collection costs and legal costs).

Balance : The amount remaining after summing a set of cost data. Alternatively, to trade off one item against another.

Balanced Matrix : An organizational matrix where functions and projects have the same priority.

Balanced Scorecard Approach ("BSA") : A business methodology designed to assess the performance of an enterprise in more than just financial terms, developed by Kaplan and Norton of Harvard Business School, 1996. When applied to evaluating the relative merits of proposed projects, BSA assists in evaluating the contribution of project objectives to the enterprise based on four "balanced" perspectives of: financial, internal process, customer, and learning or growth.

balloon : In cartoons, comic books, and graphic novels, a space encircled by a line drawn from the mouth of one of the characters, containing dialogue or the character's unspoken thoughts. Click here to see examples from the comic strip "Pogo" by Walt Kelly.

bands : Raised ridges running at intervals across the spine of a hand-bound volume, caused by the bulk of the underlying sewing supports (click here to see examples, courtesy of the Harcourt Bindery). Binders sometimes cut shallow grooves in the binding edge of the sections in which sunk bands were recessed to avoid ridges in the spine. In later bindings, false bands were sometimes added for decorative effect.

Bank : A planned accumulation of work in progress to permit reasonable fluctuations in performance during times of coordination or associated operation.

Banking : Setting aside, or put in reserve. For example, holiday time may be worked instead and the corresponding hours "banked", to be drawn upon at some future time.

banned book : A book, the publication and/or sale of which has been prohibited or suppressed by ecclesiastical or secular authority because its content is considered objectionable or dangerous, usually for political and/or social reasons (*examples*: The Grapes of Wrath and Leaves of Grass). Banned Books Week has been celebrated annually in the United States since 1981. Lists of banned books are available in the reference section of most large libraries. Click here to learn about the first book banned in the New England colonies (Springfield City Library). For more examples, see *Banned Books Online*. Compare with expurgated. *See also*: censorship, challenge, *Index Librorum Prohibitorum*, and intellectual freedom.

Bar Chart : A view of project data that uses horizontal bars on a time scale to depict activity information. Frequently called a Gantt chart.

barcode : Small label of closely spaced bars that can be read by a computer. Barcodes on books and on your Tufts University ID cards are used to CHECK OUT books from the library. You will also use your barcode number when checking your borrowing information in MY ACCOUNT.

Barcode Number : The 14-digit number appearing beneath the barcode found inside the front or back cover of a book.

Barcode numbers for Cornell library books begin with the numbers "3 1924" and are used to charge, discharge, and renew books on the online computer system.

bargain book : A book offered by a bookseller for a very low sticker price (usually $1.00-5.00), as distinct from one for which the list price is discounted, usually by a fixed percentage (see these examples, courtesy of Biblio.com). Bargain book tables, often located near the cash register, are a marketing device commonly used by bookstore chains.

Bargaining : Persuasion, alteration of assumptions and positions, give-and-take, that may apply to price, schedule, technical requirements, type of contract, or other terms of a proposed contract.

Bargaining Power : The power of each party in the bargaining process is relative. It comes in many forms and is never totally one-sided, because both parties have bargaining strengths and weaknesses. It must be perceived by at least one party to have an effect on negotiations. In fact, the power does not have to be real as long it is perceived.

bark book : A book consisting of leaves made of bark cloth, usually folded accordion-style between wooden cover plates, a format used historically in Asia and the Pacific. Click here and here to see late 19th examples from Sumatra, courtesy of the Royal Library of Denmark.

bark cloth : A flexible material used as a writing surface in the Himalayas, South Pacific, and Americas, consisting of pieces of tree bark beaten smooth, then joined with a vegetable adhesive to form large sheets. In the South Pacific, the inner bark of the paper mulberry or breadfruit tree is used. Click here to see a manuscript written on bark cloth by the Batak people of Indonesia, folded accordion-style between wooden boards (Cornell University Library). Also spelled *barkcloth*.

Barriers : Obstacles in the way of progress, mutual understanding, negotiated settlements, etc.

Base : Bottom support, or initial reference, or starting point.

baseball card : A paper trading card featuring a portrait of a baseball player or other person or topic associated with the game, often issued in sets (click here to see examples, courtesy of the Library of Congress). In the period following the American Civil War, carte-de-visite and cabinet card photographs featuring famous players were collected as mementos. From the 1860s to the 1890s, printed cards became a popular form of advertising. In the 1880s, tobacco companies began using mass-produced baseball cards to stiffen cigarette packs and boost sales. After a lull during the 1920s, chewing gum companies began issuing the cards in the 1930s. Today they are highly collectible. Common sizes are 1.5 x 2.5 inches, 2.5 x 3.5 inches, and 5 x 8 inches. In *AACR2*, baseball cards are cataloged as graphic materials. Click here to learn more about the early history of baseball cards.

Baseline : The value or condition against which all future measurements will be compared.

Baseline at Completion ("BAC") : Total completed cost of work as originally planned.

Baseline Concept : Management's project management plan for a project fixed prior to commencement.

Baseline Cost : The amount of money an Activity was intended to cost when the Baseline Plan was established.

Baseline Dates : Original planned start and finished dates for an activity. Used to compare with current planned dates to determine any delays. Also used to calculate budgeted cost of work scheduled in earned value analysis.

Baseline Management : The planning, organizing and control of baseline documentation. See, for example, Configuration Management.

Baseline Plan : The original plan (for a project, a work package, or an activity), plus or minus approved changes. Usually used with a modifier, e.g., cost baseline, schedule baseline, performance measurement baseline, etc.

Baseline Review : A customer review conducted to determine with a limited sampling that a contractor is continuing to use the previously accepted performance system and is properly implementing a baseline on the contract or option under review.

basic collection : The U.S. government publications that are sent to *every* depository library under the Federal Depository Library Program (FDLP), to which the library is expected to provide easy public access. First developed in 1977, the list of titles includes basic documents considered vital sources of information in support of the public's right to know about the activities of the federal government. Proposed revisions in the basic collection are submitted by the Library Programs Service (LPS) to the Depository Library Council (DLC) for approval. Click here to see a list of the current basic collection and here to learn more about it.

Bear Access : A suite of network service applications designed to provide services specific to the needs of the Cornell community, such as CoursEnroll, Faculty Advisor, and the online timecard system (COLTS II), as well as general Internet services such as electronic mail and browsers for navigating the World Wide Web. The CU Library Catalog and Library Gateway are available through Bear Access.

beast epic : A series of stories popular during the Middle Ages in which the characters are animals with human qualities, usually written in the form of an allegory satirizing the Catholic Church, the royal court, or some other powerful person, group, or institution (*example*: Pierre de Saint-Cloud's 12th-century Roman de Renart). A more recent example is George Orwell's Animal Farm (1945), written in the same tradition. Compare with bestiary.

benedictional : From the Latin *benedictus*, meaning "blessed." A liturgical book containing a collection of blessings recited for the benefit of congregants after the consecration and before the giving of communion in the Catholic Mass. In early Church history, when blessings were said only by the bishop, a lavishly illuminated benedictional might be made for a specific bishop. In the later Middle Ages, when any priest holding a Mass could give blessings, benedictionals became more common. Click here to page through the 10th-century *Benedictional of St. Æthelwold* (British Library, MS Add. 49598) and here to view an 11th-century Ottonian benedictional (Getty Museum, MS Ludwig VII 1).

beveled boards : A technique used in hand-binding in which the upper surface of the edges of heavy boards is cut at a sloping angle, instead of the usual 90 degrees, to give the cover a more elegant appearance or in conscious imitation of an earlier style. Click here to see a 19th-century example in brown leather (Rare Books & Texana Collections, Univ. of North Texas Libraries). Also spelled *bevelled boards. See also*: beveled edge.

bibliocaper : A term coined by George Eberhart in *The Whole Library Handbook 3* (ALA, 2000) to refer to an odd or wacky event, harebrained prank, or bizarre petty crime involving libraries, librarians, library patrons, or books.

bibliographic format : The standardized sequence and manner of presentation of the data elements constituting the full description of an item in a specific cataloging or indexing system. The machine-readable MARC record format has become the standard for library catalogs in many countries of the world.

bibliographic resource : In functional terms, an expression or manifestation of a work, or a specific item, that is the basis for bibliographic description in library cataloging (*AACR2*). Such a resource may be tangible (*example*: a printed publication) or intangible (an electronic text).

bibliography : (1) A list of items gathered together while researching a paper that will appear at the end of the paper as a list of works cited. These materials are usually arranged alphabetically by AUTHOR'S last name. (2) A publication, frequently a REFERENCE book, which lists sources on a particular subject or person.

Bibliography : A bibliography is a list of citations that appear at the end of a paper, article, chapter or book. There are also books entirely made up of bibliographies. These are usually compilations of citations on a particular subject or by a particular author.

bibliography : This is a list of citations at the end of a paper, article or book. Sometimes these are referred to as "Works Cited" lists or "Reference Lists." These lists of citations allow the readers of the work to find the items in the list. There are whole books which are lists of bibliographic citations. These are often lists of citations covering a specific subject.

bibliometrics : The use of mathematical and statistical methods to study and identify patterns in the usage of materials and services within a library or to analyze the historical development of a specific body of literature, especially its authorship, publication, and use. Prior to the mid-20th century, the quantitative study of bibliographic data and usage was known as *statistical bibliography*. *See also*: citation analysis and informetrics.

bifolium : In modern bookbinding, a pair of conjoint leaves, as opposed to a single leaf, one on each side of the fold down the center of a sheet. In medieval book production, a sheet of writing material (papyrus, parchment, or vellum) was folded in half to produce two leaves or four pages. A number of *bifolia*, nested one inside the other, usually in groups of four (eight leaves or 16 pages), formed a quire. A manuscript was assembled as a sequence of quires or gatherings, each sewn through the centerfold onto cords (sewing supports) running perpendicular to the spine. Click here to see an example from a 13th-century manuscript of the *Decretals of Gratian*, courtesy of the Metropolitan Museum of Art. Synonymous with *bifolio*. Compare with singleton.

binder's board : A stiff, sturdy board made from pulped fiber derived from rope, wood, or recycled paper, used since the early 18th century to give rigidity to the covers of books published in hardcover, and preferred in hand-binding. Modern high-quality binder's board is single-ply, made by pressing pulp between heavy rollers to achieve the desired thickness and smoothness. Click here to see binder's board used to make a heavy duty box fo preservation (Univ. of Illinois at Urbana-Champaign). Synonymous in the UK with *millboard*. Compare with pasteboard.

bindery record : The systematic account maintained by a library of materials sent to the bindery and the specific treatment given them. Most bindery records include title of publication, call number (if applicable), style and color of binding, format and placement of spine lettering, description of binding unit, and any special instructions. In some automated serials control systems, bindery information is included in the check-in record. Synonymous with *binding record*.

binding error : A mistake made in binding a publication. Common errors include the incorrect folding of signatures; leaves or an entire section omitted, gathered in incorrect sequence, or bound in upside down; or application of the wrong cover to the body of the book. In most circumstances, the publisher will replace such copies at no charge. *See also*: aberrant copy.

biographical note : A brief sketch of the life of the author (composer, performer, etc.) of a work, printed at the end of a book, on the dust jacket, on the container, or elsewhere in or on the bibliographic item. Historical works sometimes contain a section of *biographical notes* in the back matter covering important persons whose names appear in the text. In library cataloging, the presence of a biographical note is indicated in the note area of the bibliographic description, with the name of the author of the note included if given on the item.

bird book : A type of natural history book containing pictures of wild bird species, with or without accompanying text (see this 18th-century engraved example, courtesy of the Koninklijke Bibliotheek). One of the most famous is John James Audubon's *Birds of America*, published in the mid-19th century. The category also includes field guides designed for bird identification.

blankbook : A book consisting of clean or ruled leaves for writing or making entries, with printing limited to page headings and/or divisions (see this example). Examples include diaries, albums, scrapbooks, guestbooks, sketchbooks, account books, minute books, log books, exercise books, etc. Because the information recorded in official blankbooks may be of permanent value, good-quality paper and durable bindings are generally used. A blankbook should open flat for ease of use. Also spelled *blank book*.

blue book : In the United States, the popular name for a manual published by a state government listing the names of elected and appointed officials and providing information about government structure, agencies, voting districts, elections, etc., usually bound in blue covers. Compare with red book.

board book : A durable book of small size designed for very young children, consisting of a few unnumbered pages made of pasteboard covered in glossy paper printed with colorful illustrations and little if any text (see these examples). Board books are often alphabet books or counting books.

Bodleian Library : The library of the University of Oxford in England. The original medieval library was severely damaged in 1542, then refounded in 1598 by Sir Thomas Bodley, a former diplomat. Its combination of buildings, constructed between 1490 and 1970, and its vast holdings make it unique among the world's great libraries. Its collections are particularly strong in English literature, history, and typography. The Bodleian has been a copyright depository library since 1662. Click here to connect to the "Bodley" homepage which provides a more detailed history of the library (see "Visitor Information"). *See also*: British Library, The

book announcement : A brief statement by the publisher announcing the availability of a new book or backlisted title, published as an advertisement in a book trade journal or review publication or in an advertising section included in another book published under the same imprint. A book announcement usually includes the title of the work, name(s) of author(s) or editor(s), ISBN, projected date of publication, list price, and prepublication price, if offered. It may also include a blurb or brief excerpts from favorable reviews and a picture of the front cover.

book drive : A campaign, usually of predetermined length, conducted by a library, school, or other organization to solicit donations of books for the purpose of expanding the existing collection or to generate funds to benefit the institution by means of a book sale. Sometimes the gifts are earmarked for a particular use, for example, distribution to disadvantaged children or shut-ins, or for a specific program, such as the Library War Service during World War I.

book lice : A species (*Liposcelis divinatorius*) of minute (one-sixteenth-inch) soft-bodied, wingless insects of worldwide distribution that damages old books by feeding on the glue and paste in bindings. Usually gray, white, or translucent in color, book lice also consume mold, cereal products, and the bodies of dead insects, which makes them a menace to botanical and zoological specimens. Keeping relative humidity low helps to control them in libraries and exhibit spaces. Book lice are prey to book scorpions. They can be exterminated by freezing the infested item. Click here to view an image of book lice. Synonymous with *book mites*. *See also*: bookworm.

book paper : A grade of paper suitable for printing books, pamphlets, periodicals, catalogs, etc., as opposed to various other grades (newsprint, tissue paper, wallpaper, wrapping paper, etc.). Book papers vary in content, color, finish, opacity, weight, and permanence. For books that are to be retained indefinitely in the collection, librarians prefer permanent papers, acid-free and of high rag content.

book report : A factual description of a book, usually submitted in fulfillment of a school assignment, including a brief bibliographic description (title, name of author, publisher, date of publication, etc.) and in the case of fiction, an account of the setting, time period, main characters, and plot, and for nonfiction, the subject of the work and a summary of the author's treatment of it. The instructor may also ask the student to give a response to the work. Click here to read the Lakewood Public Library's student guide to completing a book report.

book return : A place to bring books borrowed from the library. There is an exterior book return slot on your left as you are entering Tisch Library and another one inside Tisch Library to the left of the CIRCULATION desk.

Book Return : A place to return books borrowed from the library. The book return is a box located outside the library, near the door of the library, or near the circulation desk.

book return : This is where you will bring the books you have borrowed back to the library. There is a drop box outside of the library for returning your books. Inside the library there is a drop box at the Circulation Desk, or you can give your returned books to the Circulation employee who is staffing the desk.

book scorpion : A species of small (one-eighth-to one-quarter-inch) stingless arachnid (*Chelifer cancroides*), also known as the *false scorpion*, that diets on tiny insects such as book lice that damage books by feeding on paper and bindings.

book signing : An event scheduled at a retail bookstore or library at which the author and/or illustrator of a new book is available to autograph copies of his or her work(s), sometimes scheduled in conjunction with a book talk or a reading from the text. *See also*: autographed copy.

book stamp : A wood, metal, or rubber stamp used to make an inked impression on the cover, edge, endpaper, or title page of a book, usually as a mark of ownership (click here to see an examples on ex-library copies).

booklet : A book of small size or containing little text. Also used synonymously with pamphlet.

bookstore model : A philosophy of public librarianship based on the success of large bookstore chains, that focuses on the library patron as customer and seeks to attract users by creating an ambiance that is user-friendly. Libraries operating on the bookstore model typically strive to identify and meet the unique needs of the community served, often through outreach and a marketing plan. More books are displayed face out on bookstore-style shelving, and interiors are designed to please the eye, with comfortable seating, professionally designed signage, attractive book displays, and a coffee shop or cybercafe for people who like to "hang out" at the library. Portions of the collection may be arranged according to reading interest (health, business and finance, genre fiction, etc.). Sometimes used synonymously with *customer-driven library*.

boolean operator : Boolean Operators help you to refine your searches in electronic databases and when using the

WWW. These Operators are AND, OR, and NOT (in some databases the NOT is replaced with AND NOT; in some WWW search engines the AND is the + sign, and the NOT is the-sign.)

Boolean Operator or Boolean Logic : Boolean operators, otherwise known as logical operators, are used to construct complex searches in a database. They help make a search more accurate. There are 3 logical operators : AND, OR and NOT.

bootstrap : A program that causes the first piece of software installed on a computer (usually the operating system) to load when the power is switched on, enabling the CPU to begin executing instructions. The word *bootstrap* originally referred to a leather strap or tab attached to the back of a boot to help the wearer pull it on—hence the expression "to pull oneself up by one's bootstraps." In computing, it has spawned boot, cold boot, reboot, etc.

Borrow Direct : A rapid book request and delivery system. It enables Cornell faculty, staff, and students to search the combined library catalogs of Brown, Columbia, Cornell, Dartmouth, University of Pennsylvania, Princeton, and Yale a collection of over 40 million volumes and directly request expedited delivery of circulating items.

borrowing : Being able to take books and other materials from the library. It is the same as CHECK OUT.

borrowing privileges : The rights to which a library borrower is entitled, usually established by registering to receive a library card. Such privileges normally include the right to check out books and other materials from the circulating collection for a designated period of time, interlibrary loan, use of special collections, etc. They may be suspended if fines remain unpaid. In most public libraries, all registered users enjoy the same privileges, but in academic libraries, certain privileges, such as length of loan period, may depend on borrower status. In special libraries, borrowing privileges may be determined by a person's rank in the parent organization.

bound periodical : Several issues, often a year's worth, of JOURNALS or MAGAZINES that are fastened together (bound) between hard covers.

boxed : A set of books or other documents stored in a close-fitting box-shaped container, usually to keep the volumes together and provide protection but sometimes for decorative effect. *See also*: slipcase.

Bradford's Law : The bibliometric principle that a disproportionate share of the significant research results on a given subject are published in a relatively small number of the scholarly journals in the field, a pattern of exponentially diminishing returns first noted by Samuel C. Bradford in 1934, who proposed the formula $1:n:n^2$ to describe the phenomenon, based on his examination of a bibliography of geophysics. He found that a few core journals provide 1/3 of the articles on a given subject, a moderate number of less-than-core journals provide a further 1/3 of the articles on the subject, and a large number peripheral journals provide the remaining 1/3 of the articles. The pattern exists in the literature of the natural sciences but not in the humanities and social sciences. Identification of the core journals in a scientific specialization can therefore facilitate not only the research process, but also serials collection development. Click here to learn more about Bradford's Law, courtesy of *Wikipedia*. Synonymous with *Bradford's Distribution*, *Law of Scatter*, and *Law of Scattering*.

branch library : An auxiliary service outlet in a library system, housed in a facility separate from the central library, which has at least a basic collection of materials, a regular staff, and established hours, with a budget and policies determined by the central library. A branch library is usually managed by a *branch librarian* who may have responsibility for more than one branch. The Association of College and Research Libraries (ACRL) publishes *Guidelines for Branch Libraries in College and University Libraries* (June 1990). In a public library system, new branches may be sited on the basis of a comprehensive plan for the entire city, county, region, or library district served by the system. Compare with affiliated library. *See also*: bookmobile and books-by-mail.

British Film Institute (BFI) : Established by Royal Charter as a registered charity in 1933, BFI is devoted to promoting understanding and appreciation of Britain's film and television heritage and culture. In 1934, BFI received its first annual grant from the Cinematograph Fund (administered by the Privy Council) and assumed editorial responsibility for the magazine *Sight & Sound*. In 1935, the Institute set up the National Film Library, now named the National Film and Television Archive (NFTA), the largest moving image archive in the world. In 1951, BFI built and managed the Telekinema, a special theater that showed 3-D and other experimental films for the Festival of Britain and was eventually converted into the National Film Theater owned and operated by the Institute, which today screens over 1,000 motion pictures annually. BFI also owns and operates an IMAX Cinema in London and sponsors the London Film Festival, which runs for two weeks every autumn, showcasing the best in contemporary cinema from around the world at venues across London. The Institute also maintains a national library on film and television. Charged with promoting media literacy, BFI produces a range of resources for teachers and hosts conferences, seminars, and workshops for learners of all ages. Click here to connect to the BFI homepage. *See also*: American Film Institute.

British Library, The : Located mainly in London, the British Library is the national library of the United Kingdom (UK), created in 1973 by an act of Parliament that merged the British Museum Library, the National Central Library, and the National Lending Library for Science and Technology (Patent Office Library). In later years, the *British National Bibliography*, the National Sound Archive, and the India Office Library and Records were added to the institution. In 1997, its constituent parts were brought together in a new building at St. Pancras, with the exception of the Newspaper Library which remains at Colindale. Covering all known languages and periods of history, its collections are a resource for scholars worldwide. The British Library is also the legal depository for UK publications. Click here to learn more about the history of the British Library, and here to connect to its homepage. *See also*: Bodleian Library.

broadcast flag : A sequence of status bits embedded in the data stream of a digital television (DTV) program that can be turned "on" or "off" by broadcasters to prevent copyright infringement, restricting unauthorized redistribution of digital content. In the United States, the Federal Communications Commission (FCC) ruled in November, 2003 that all new television receivers using the ATSC (Advanced Television Systems Committee) standard were to include this new functionality by July 1, 2005. In March, 2004, the American Library Association and other advocacy groups filed suit against the FCC, contending that the regulation would deny libraries and consumers the right of fair use under U.S. copyright law and restrict interoperability between playback devices. In a setback for Hollywood, the U.S. Court of Appeals for the District of Columbia ruled on May 6, 2005 that the FCC exceeded its authority in prohibiting the manufacture of computer and video hardware without "content protection" technology. Click here to learn more about the issue, courtesy of *Wikipedia*.

brocade paper : A type of decorated paper in which an embossed pattern is pressed into colored or uncolored paper in real or imitation gold or silver foil, using thick copper plates or cylinders bearing the design in positive or negative relief. Click here and here to see samples made in Nuremberg and Augsburg in the 18th century, courtesy of the Koninklijke Bibliotheek, Netherlands.

Browser : Software program used to view web pages. Browsers like Internet Explorer, Netscape, and Firefox allow you to click on a link to another document, and get information from a different computer where that resource is stored.

browser : This is a software program that allows you to view pages on the WWW. These programs make it possible to click on links to other documents which are stored on other computers.

built number : In Dewey Decimal Classification, a class number constructed according to add instructions stated or implied in the schedules or tables. Number building is employed

used in libraries in India and in research libraries throughout the world. To learn more about colon classification, try *Wikipedia*.

Colon Hexadecimal Notation : The notation used to express IPv6 addresses. The 128-bit IPv6 address is divided into eight 16-bit blocks. Each block is expressed as a hexadecimal number, and adjacent blocks are separated by colons. Within each block, leading zeros are suppressed. An example of an IPv6 unicast address in colon hexadecimal notation is 2001:DB8:2A1D:48C:2AA:3CFF:FE21:81F9.

color balance : In the graphic arts, the range of colors in an image, especially as regards deviation from the accurate reproduction of tones in the original subject (e.g., the skin tones of a face), inaccurate color balance giving a general cast, subtle or pronounced, to the image. Color balance can be manipulated by the artist to express mood or to create the desired impression. In video production and transmission, color balance is tested and calibrated by means of color bars. Also refers to the ability of photographic materials to reproduce colors accurately, which may diminish as the material ages, posing problems for preservation.

column picture : A miniature in a medieval manuscript that fills the entire width of a column of text but not necessarily it full height, as in this example in an early 15th-century French manuscript (British Library, Lansdowne 1178).

comes-with title : In acquisitions, a title that is not a supplement, received by a library at no additional charge as a result of purchasing another title, for example, a newsletter or directory supplied by an academic society or professional association with a paid subscription to a journal.

comic book : A booklet, usually printed in color on paper made from wood pulp, containing one or more stories told pictorially in a continuous strip of panels drawn in cartoon style, with dialogue or monologue enclosed in balloons or given in captions. An extended form of the comic strip published in daily newspapers, comic books are often issued in series and classified by genre (adventure, fantasy, romance, science fiction, etc.). They are acquired by libraries for special collections on popular culture and are of considerable interest to private collectors. For early examples, see the British Comics Collection at the British Library and *Comic Books in the '50s* (SUNY Buffalo). Similarity between contemporary comics and medieval manuscript illustration is the subject of the online exhibition *Comics before Comics*, courtesy of the Bibliothèque Nationale de France. *See also*: Big Little Book, comic strip, and graphic novel.

commemorative print : A print bearing an image of a significant event, such as the signing of an important document, the founding of an institution, or a decisive military battle, shown in narrative or allegorical style, often bearing text indicating commemorative intent ("in honor of..." or "in memory of..."). Click here to see a commemorative print of the campus of Princeton University as it appeared in 1996.

commercial journal : A scholarly journal or trade journal published by a for-profit company, as opposed to a journal published by a university press or nonprofit organization, such as a scholarly society or professional association. Click here to see a list of examples. Relentless price increases have become an important issue for libraries that subscribe to commercially published journals.

commercial publisher : A publisher in the business of producing and selling books and/or other publications for profit, as opposed to a university press or the publishing arm of a scholarly society, professional association, or other nonprofit organization operating on a cost-recovery basis. The term includes trade publishers and popular presses. In commercial publishing, the decision to publish is influenced by sales potential, sometimes at the expense of originality and quality.

commercial television : Television broadcast stations for which profit is the prime concern. In the selection of programming, commercial stations rely heavily on ratings because their advertisers are motivated by the desire to reach the widest possible viewing audience. Compare with public television.

Commission on Preservation and Access (CPA) : A non-profit organization incorporated in 1988 for the purpose of fostering development and supporting systematic and purposeful collaboration in order to ensure the preservation of the public and documentary universe in all formats and to provide equitable access to that information.

Common Gateway Interface (CGI) : A program interface installed on a Web server that allows Web pages to be linked to databases and other programs in such a way that input can be entered via the Web page and sent to a database management system for searching. Results are sent back by the DBMS and presented to the user in HTML format.

community service volunteer (CSV) : A person convicted of a misdemeanor assigned volunteer work in his or her community as a form of restitution. Community service volunteers are typically recommended by a probation officer based on criteria established by the library, with most libraries reserving the right of refusal. Because one of the goals of such work is to teach responsibility, attendance is closely monitored, but duties that involve handling money or accessing nonpublic computer systems are generally not assigned. Some libraries accept adult offenders but not teenagers. In most cases, the program coordinator and supervising librarian are the only employees in the library who know the volunteer is completing community service. The library benefits from unpaid labor, but CSVs often require closer supervision than paid employees. Synonymous with *probation volunteer*.

companion book : A book published in conjunction with a motion picture or television program or series, usually a work of nonfiction intended to complement documentary or instructional content, for example, Lewis and Clark: An Illustrated History by Dayton Duncan, based on the PBS television mini-series *Lewis and Clark: The Journey of the Corps of Discovery* by Ken Burns. In library cataloging, the note *Companion volume to:* is included in the bibliographic description, followed by the title of the work on which the book is based. Compare with tie-in. *See also*: companion.

competitive intelligence (CI) : In business, the collection, analysis, and assessment of information about a company's markets and competition, for use in strategic decision-making. CI involves monitoring the environment external to the company for information pertinent to the decision-making process, which is then analyzed into accurate, usable strategic knowledge about the firm's markets and competitors, including position, performance, capabilities, and intentions. For example, a CI professional might wish to learn about a competitor's research and development initiatives or the best way to bid against another company to win a contract. Ethical CI is conducted openly, but the target company is generally kept in the dark. Fuld & Company, a specialist in CI, has developed the *Internet Intelligence Index* to help CI professionals gather information from a variety of public sources. CI practitioners are organized in the Society of Competitive Intelligence Professionals (SCIP). CI is one aspect of business intelligence.

composite daguerreotype : A daguerreotype consisting of more than one image, usually made in a studio from a series of individual daguerreotypes (see this composite portrait of the Princeton University Class of 1852, courtesy of the Princeton University Archives).

composite photograph : A photograph in which the image is produced by (1) multiple exposure of negatives, (2) sandwiching two or more negatives, or (3) some other method of combining negatives (click here to see an example, courtesy of the Library of Congress).

comprehensive : All-inclusive or all-encompassing. An index, bibliographic database, or other work of reference compiled with the stated goal of covering all possible aspects of a subject or all the published literature on a subject or in a given discipline or field. In bibliography, an attempt to list of *all* the works that meet the criteria for inclusion established by the bibliographer as to author, subject, publication type, currency, etc. The opposite of selective.

compulsory arbitration : The process in which representatives of organized labor and management, having reached an impasse in contract negotiations, submit their differences to a legally designated *arbitrator* or *arbitration board* authorized to hear arguments from both sides on unresolved issues and reach a final binding decision. Both sides are required to accept the outcome. *See also*: collective bargaining agreement.

computer literacy : The skills required to retrieve information efficiently and communicate effectively using computer hardware and software, based on a conceptual understanding of computer technology and how it can be used to accomplish specific tasks, including an awareness of its inherent limitations, as well as its advantages. Because hardware and software are progressively upgraded, an ongoing effort is required of the user to remain computer literate. Compare with information literacy.

computer output microform (COM) : Computer output produced directly on microfiche or microfilm without ever having been printed on paper. A device called a *COM recorder* converts digital data into a form that can be read by the human eye before recording it on film. *See also*: computer output microform catalog.

computer output microform catalog : A library catalog produced directly on microfiche or microfilm from a file of machine-readable bibliographic records, using a special recording device called a *COM recorder*. *Comcatalog*s are more compact than card catalogs, but a microform reader-printer machine is required to display and print individual catalog records. Prior to the development of online catalogs, this format was preferred for state, regional, and consortial union catalogs.

Conservation : The treatment of library or archival materials, works of art, or museum objects to stabilize them chemically or strengthen them physically, sustaining their survival as long as possible in their original form. Conservation implies the restoration of an item to a state close to the original by means of physical treatment. See also preservation.

conservation board : An archival quality board, used in bookbinding, book boxes, picture framing, and archival storage, containing no harmful properties, such as acid or lignin, that might migrate to materials that come in contact with it.

conservation box : A type of book box designed to protect books of an age or condition requiring additional preservation. Made of acid-free materials, they can be hand-made or commercially manufactured and are designed to allow the volume to be easily removed and reinserted. Click here to see the process of manufacture, courtesy of the Etherington Conservation Center and George Mason University.

contemporary binding : A binding made in the same time period as the text block, but not necessarily at the same time the text was printed or hand-copied. Older books are often rebound in the style of a later period and the original binding discarded when badly worn.

contraction : A shortened form of a word or phrase used for brevity in place of the whole, formed by the omission of one or more letters or sounds, usually replaced by a hyphen (**e-mail** for *electronic mail*) or an apostrophe (**isn't** for *is not*). Compare with abbreviation and elision.

co-publishing : The simultaneous publication of an edition by two or more publishers, usually in different countries, to achieve economies of scale when the home market is not sufficient to guarantee a reasonable profit. Typically, a work is printed in the country of the originating publisher and then supplied to a publisher in another country with a title page bearing the imprint of the second publisher (or both). Subsequent printings may occur independently or cooperatively. In journal publishing, the result may be separate editions for each country or a bilingual edition marketed in both countries. Compare with export edition.

Copyright : Copyright is a form of protection provided by the laws of the United States (title 17, U.S. Code) to the authors of "original works of authorship," including literary, dramatic, musical, artistic, and certain other intellectual works. For more information about copyright, see the United States Copyright Office web site-which includes definitions, frequently asked questions, and basic information about copyright.

copyright depository : A library designated by law or custom to receive and preserve a specified number of free deposit copies of works published under national copyright law. In the United States, the copyright depository is the U.S. Copyright Office at the Library of Congress. In Great Britain it is the Bodleian Library. In Canada, copyright law is administered by the Canadian Intellectual Property Office (CIPO). Synonymous with *copyright library*.

correctional library : A type of special library maintained inside the walls of a prison or other correctional institution for the use of inmates and staff, usually managed by a *prison librarian* (*example*: Federal Bureau of Prisons Library). The collection usually includes general interest titles for recreational reading, educational and vocational materials, and legal resources. Synonymous with *prison library*.

Correspondence : Letters, postcards, memoranda, notes, printed e-mail, and any other form of addressed, written communications sent and received.

cost projection : In acquisitions, a forecast made by a vendor, based on information on current economic trends and from publishers and other sources, concerning the future inflation rate for various categories of materials (books, periodicals, etc.). Libraries use such informed estimates in collection management to allocate budgets, particularly for serials collections.

cottage binding : A style of leather binding, popular in England during the 17th and 18th centuries, in which the center panel is surrounded by decoration tooled to resemble the gables of a building, with the design of the binding bearing no relationship to the content of the work. According to *The Bookman's Glossary* (R.R. Bowker, 1983), this ornamental style, developed by Samuel Mearne, binder to King Charles II, was particularly popular on Bibles and prayer books. Click here to see a 17th-century gold-tooled example in black goatskin (Princeton University Library) and here to see the style used on a book of common prayer of the same period (Glasgow

University Library, Special Collections, Ds-f.3). To see other examples, try a search on the keyword "cottage" in the British Library's *Database of Bookbindings*. Synonymous with *cottage style*.

Council of Literary Magazines and Presses (CLMP) : Founded in 1967 as the Coordinating Council of Literary Magazines (CCLM), CLMP serves the independent publishers of exceptional fiction, poetry, and prose, who accomplish the backstage work of American literature by discovering new writers, supporting mid-career writers, publishing the creative voices of communities under-represented in mainstream commercial culture, and preserving literature for future readers by keeping books in print. Supported in part by the National Endowment for the Humanities (NEH), CLMP publishes the newsletter *CLMP Newswire*. Click here to connect to the CLMP homepage.

Council on Library and Information Resources (CLIR) : Originally named the Council on Library Resources, CLIR is an independent foundation that supports initiatives in preservation awareness, digital libraries, information economics, resources for scholarship, and international developments in library and information science. CLIR publishes the bimonthly newsletter *CLIR Issues*. Click here to connect to the CLIR homepage. *See also*: Access to Learning Award.

Council on Library Resources (CLR) : A private operating foundation based in Washington, DC, which aims to assist libraries, especially academic and research libraries, to take advantage of emerging technologies to improve operational efficiencies and services for library users.

counting book : A picture book designed to teach preschool children to count (usually from 1 to 10 or 12) by providing illustrations in which the number of objects displayed on each page or double spread corresponds to the numeral printed with them. Click here to see a narrative example. Compare with alphabet book. *See also*: horn book.

Course Reserves : In academic libraries, course reserves are library items given a shorter loan period (one-hour, three-hours, overnight, 3-day, etc.) for a limited period of time (usually one term or semester) at the request of the instructor, to ensure that all the students enrolled in a course have an opportunity to use them. These materials are usually kept together in a particular area of the library, such as a graduate reading room or behind the circulation desk. Each library has its own reserve system; however, many reserve items may also be accessed through the CU Library Catalog as Electronic Course Reserves (or e-Reserves). See the Electronic Reserves help page for more information.

course reserves : These are items kept at the Circulation Desk and placed on Reserve by your professors. These items have shorter checkout times than material in the Main Collection. These checkout times have been determined by your professor and may range from one hour to a day or two. You may look up Course Reserves on the computer by the Circulation Desk or in the Electronic Resource Center by Course Number or Professor's Name. You will need the item's Call Number when you go to the Circulation Desk to request the item.

courtesy book : A literary genre popular during the Renaissance, devoted to the detailed description of the code of personal conduct, training, and view of life expected of a gentleman, soldier, and courtier by the society in which he lived (*example*: Castiglioni's *The Courtier*).

cover letter : A letter of introduction, usually no longer than one page, sent with a resume or *curriculum vitae* when applying for employment. A good cover letter usually indicates that the applicant meets all the qualifications listed in the job posting, and expresses an interest in being considered for the position. In a more general sense, a brief letter of explanation sent with a document.

CRL : The Center for Research Libraries (CRL) is an international not-for-profit consortium of colleges, universities, and libraries that provides access to a variety of scholarly research resources, including newspapers, serials, archival materials in microform, microform sets, and foreign government publications in many subject areas. The CRL catalog is available from the Library Gateway. CRL resources are available to Cornell researchers through interlibrary loan.

cross classification : In Dewey Decimal Classification (DDC), the assignment of two different class numbers to works on the same subject, an accident most likely to happen when the works deal with two or more characteristics (facets) of the subject in the same class. Notes on preference order are intended to prevent this type of classification error.

Cross-Reference : Directions that lead you from one subject or name to another in a catalog or index.

CU Library Catalog : An online catalog that contains records for materials in the Cornell University Library collection including the holdings of all 17 libraries on the Ithaca campus, in addition to those of the Geneva Experiment Station and the CISER Data Archive. The catalog contains records for books, computer files (including CD-ROM's and networked resources), government documents, journal titles, manuscripts and archives, maps, microforms, musical scores, serials, sound recordings, and visual materials.

Cubic Foot : An archival term used to describe the quantity of a collection. A bankers box, or records centre carton, holds one cubic foot.

CUL : The Cornell University Library (CUL) is one of the largest academic research libraries in the United States. Composed of 20 libraries, CUL holds over seven million printed volumes, subscribes to more than 65,000 journals, and is networked to over 40,000 electronic databases. Please see About the Library and Libraries/Departments on the Library Gateway for information on collections, organization, policies, and services.

current awareness service : A service or publication designed to alert scholars, researchers, readers, customers, or employees to recently published literature in their field(s) of specialization, usually available in special libraries serving companies, organizations, and institutions in which access to current information is essential. Such services can be tailored to fit the interest profile of a specific individual or group. Some online catalogs and bibliographic databases include a "preferred searches" option that allows the library user to archive search statements and re-execute them as needed. Synonymous with *selective dissemination of information*. *See also*: current contents.

CUWebLogin : CUWebLogin allows you to access restricted library resources in the Library Catalog and Find Articles/ Find Databases/Find e-Journas without needing SideCar. It does this by allowing you to log in to a web form, and then passing your authentication information back to the web server in a cookie. For more information about how CUWebLogin works, see the help page for CUWebLogin.

dandy roll : The cylinder that exerts pressure in mechanized papermaking, smoothing the surface and creating designs such as the watermark, countermark, and the lines characteristic of laid and wove paper (see this example).

dasymetric map : A thematic map similar to a choropleth map in the use of areal symbols (tint, shading, hatching, etc.) to represent quantitative data, but instead of mapping the data to areas that correspond to administrative or enumeration units, ancillary variables are employed to change the boundaries of the areas to better represent the areal distribution of classes of data. Click here to see an example showing the distribution of population density in Greece in 1973, courtesy of the Perry-Castañeda Library (to enlarge click on lower right corner of image).

Data Documentation Initiative (DDI) : A project of the social science community to develop a standardized XML markup and representation for codebooks, the primary metadata describing social science data sets. Click here to learn more about the DDI.

database : Databases are electronic collections of computer records, often records that contain either citations or full text of journal articles. Jernigan Library has more than 100 electronic databases, many of them offering full text of periodical articles and other types of print resources. Many of these are also accessible electronically from outside the library.

date due slip : A card or slip of paper inserted in an item charged from a library collection or a small printed form attached to the inside of the front or back cover or to one of the free endpapers, on which is stamped the date the item is due back in the library (see this example). The paper on which they are printed should be acid-free. Date due slips are sometimes removed by borrowers in an attempt to avoid overdue fines, but the advent of automated circulation systems has nixed this strategy. Synonymous with *charge slip*.

Deaccession : The process of removing material from the care and custody of an archives, either because the material has been reappraised and found to be unsuitable for the archives, or because the legal owner has requested its return, or because it has been agreed to transfer it to another repository. Deaccessioning is a serious matter which requires careful consideration and documentation because of legal ramifications and possible donor reaction.

Dead Sea Scrolls : Ancient papyrus and parchment manuscripts stored inside large pottery jars, discovered in caves in the Judean Desert in 1947 by Bedouin shepherds. Radiocarbon dating has established that the scrolls, and the Essene community at wadi Quram with which they are believed to be associated, date from 250 B.C. to A.D. 65. Written in Aramaic, the scrolls comprise about 800 documents of which most are in fragmentary condition. They include the oldest extant text of the Old Testament. The tedious work of piecing them together has taken decades. The scrolls are in the possession of the Israel Antiquities Authority in Jerusalem, where they are being prepared for publication by Oxford University Press in what will eventually be a thirty-five volume work entitled *Discoveries in the Judaean Desert* (see Dead Sea Scrolls Foundation). The Library of Congress provides the online exhibit *Scrolls from the Dead Sea*. Examples can also be seen in the Schøyen Collection (Oslo and London) and *Treasures from the World's Great Libraries*, courtesy of the Israel Antiquities Authority and the National Library of Australia.

Decision Document : The official document sent to the dean of a library and information studies program and to the institution?s chief executive officer conveying the accreditation action taken by the Committee on Accreditation (COA) of the American Library Association (ALA) as the result of a two-year comprehensive review to verify that the program conforms to the ALA's *Standards for Accreditation of Master's Programs in Library and Information Studies* (1992). If accreditation is withdrawn or denied, the program or institution may appeal the decision. *See also*: special report.

decomposition vent : An opening in a storage chamber made to allow the escape of gases (usually toxic or flammable) produced in the deterioration of the stored material. For example, the National Fire Protection Association (NFPA) has established a standard requirement for decomposition vents in chambers used to store chemically unstable cellulose nitrate film.

dedicated line : A direct pathway to the Internet or some other computer network via a separate telecommunications channel not shared with multiple users as in dial-up access but available around the clock to a specific user or group of users for a designated purpose. When accessed through a common carrier, the channel is called a *leased line*.

dedication copy : A copy of a book or other work inscribed by the author, editor, or illustrator to the person or persons to whom the work is dedicated. In the antiquarian book trade, a dedication copy may be of substantially greater value than a copy with no inscription and is considered one of the most collectible presentation copies of an edition. Click here to see the hand-colored copy of *Le Jardin de Plaisance & Fleur de Rhetorique*, an anthology of poems edited by Anthoine Vérard, dedicated to the French King in about 1500 (Royal Library of Denmark).

Default Gateway : A configuration parameter for the Internet Protocol (TCP/IP) component that is the IPv4 address of a neighbouring IPv4 router. Configuring a default gateway creates a default route in the IPv4 routing table.

Default Route : A route that summarizes all possible destinations and is used for forwarding when the routing table does not contain any other more specific routes for the destination. For example, if a router or sending host cannot find a subnet route, a summarized route, or a host route for the destination, IP selects the default route. The default route is used to simplify the configuration of hosts and routers. For IPv4 routing tables, the default route is the route with the network destination of 0.0.0.0 and netmask of 0.0.0.0. For IPv6 routing tables, the default route has the address prefix::/0.

definitive edition : An edition of the complete text of an author's work or works, usually edited and published after the individual's death in a form considered final and authoritative, often including the critical apparatus documenting variations in the work and explaining the editor's choice of version. Also refers to the text of an anonymous work considered by scholars or other experts, upon close examination, to be closest to the original version. Compare with authorized edition. *See also*: critical edition and variant edition.

dentelle binding : A style of 18th-century leather binding in which the covers are decorated on the outer and/or inner surface with broad, full borders gold-tooled in a finely detailed pattern resembling lacework. Click here to view a blankbook gold-tooled in dentelle style (Koninklijke Bibliotheek) and here to see dentelle decoration of the turn-ins on a deluxe binding (University of Pittsburgh Libraries). To see more examples, try a keyword search on the term in the British Library's *Database of Bookbindings*.

departmental library : A type of academic library that serves the information and research needs of the faculty members of a department within an institution of higher learning, usually a large university. Departmental libraries are also used by students enrolled in courses in the discipline(s) taught by the department, especially graduate students. If acquisitions are funded through the department, selection is usually the responsibility of the teaching faculty in collaboration with the departmental librarian.

Deposit Agreement and Instrument of Transmittal : A legal document that designates The University of Texas at Arlington Libraries as official depository for the records of a labour union, which are to be donated at scheduled intervals. The agreement permits the union to retain ownership of its records or to transfer ownership to the university. The agreement may be amended or terminated at any time by mutual consent. Both the union representative and a university representative must sign and date the agreement.

Depository Library Council (DLC) : Formally established in 1972, the Depository Library Council is appointed by the Public Printer to advise on matters pertaining to the Federal Depository Library Program (FDLP) as provided in *Title 44 U.S.C.* The mission of the DLC is to assist the U.S. Government Printing Office (GPO) in identifying and evaluating alternatives for improving public access to government information through the FDLP and for optimizing available resources. Its 15 members are selected to provide a diverse range of opinion and expertise, and to represent a cross section of the various types of DLP libraries, with at least half of the members employed in depository libraries in positions that provide experience in a documents department. Click here to learn more about the DLC.

depository library number : The unique identification number assigned by the U.S. Government Printing Office (GPO) to each depository library in the Federal Depository Library Program (FDLP), consisting of four digits (*example*: **0063**) or four digits plus an alphabetic character (**0063B**), used to record the library's selections and to distribute materials. The number can also be used to view an online list of the item numbers selected for receipt by the library (see the *Item Lister*). The depository library number is included at the beginning of each entry in the online directory of depository libraries available via *GPO Acccess* (click here to connect). Synonymous with *depository number*.

Description : The process of establishing intellectual control over holdings through the preparation of finding aids.

descriptive cataloging : The part of the library cataloging process concerned with identifying and describing the physical and bibliographic characteristics of the item, and with determining the name(s) and title(s) to be used as access points in the catalog, but not with the assignment of subject and form headings. In the United States, Great Britain, and Canada, descriptive cataloging is governed by *Anglo-American Cataloguing Rules* (**AACR2**). *See also*: authority control and subject analysis.

designer binding : A bookbinding bearing decoration done by an artist skilled in graphic design, usually in a style contemporary with the period in which it was made. This type of binding began to appear in trade editions in the second half of the 19th century and remained popular into the early 20th century. Click here to see examples of 19th-century gold-stamped publisher's bindings done in designer-style (Rare Books and Manuscripts Library, Columbia University). For an example of 20th-century book design, see this binding by Paul Bonet (National Art Library, Victoria and Albert Museum). Click here and here and here to see other contemporary examples.

desktop publishing (DTP) : The use of microcomputer hardware and software for page layout, graphic design, and printing to produce professional-quality camera-ready copy for commercial printing at a fraction of the cost of using the services of a commercial publisher. Used extensively to produce in-house brochures, fliers, newsletters, posters, etc., DTP requires desktop publishing software and a high-speed PC equipped with a large monitor and high-resolution laser printer to produce text and graphics in WYSIWYG format. *See also*: self-publishing.

Dewey Decimal Classification (DDC) : A hierarchical system for classifying books and other library materials by subject, first published in 1876 by the librarian and educator Melvil Dewey, who divided human knowledge into 10 main classes, each of which is divided into 10 divisions, and so on. In Dewey Decimal call numbers, arabic numerals and decimal fractions are used in the class notation (*example:* **996.9**) and an alphanumeric book number is added to subarrange works of the same classification by author and by title and edition (**996.9 B3262h**). Click here to see a list of DDC summaries. Developed and updated continuously for the past 125 years, most recently by a 10-member international Editorial Policy Committee (EPC), DDC is the most widely used classification system in the world. According to OCLC, it has been translated into 30 languages and is used by 200,000 libraries in 135 countries. The national bibliographies of 60 countries are organized according to DDC. In the United States, public and school libraries use DDC, but most academic and research libraries use Library of Congress Classification (LCC) because it is more hospitable. The abridged edition (ADC), intended for general collections of 20,000 or fewer titles, is a logical truncation of the notational and structural hierarchy of the *full edition*. OCLC has also developed *WebDewey* for classifying Web pages and other electronic resources. Click here to connect to the DDC Web site maintained by OCLC and here to read OCLC's *Introduction to Dewey Decimal Classification*. *See also*: Universal Decimal Classification.

dictionary catalog : A type of catalog, widely used in the United States before the conversion of the card catalog to machine-readable form, in which all the entries (main, added, subject) and cross-references are interfiled in a single alphabetic sequence, as opposed to a catalog divided into separate sections by type of entry (author, title, subject). Compare with classified catalog.

digital archaeology : The process of reclaiming digital information that has been damaged or become unusable due to technological obsolescence of formats and/or media. The most common causes of damage are storage under conditions of high temperature and/or relative humidity, contact with magnetic fields, natural disaster (i.e., lightning strikes), manufacturer's defects, and normal wear-and-tear. Reclamation techniques vary.

digital asset management (DAM) : Systems designed to organize and display digital content produced in a variety of media types. The content is usually locally owned and controlled, rather than licensed from a third party. Most of the DAM systems offered by the leading library automation vendors use standards other than the MARC record, such as XML, the Open Archives Initiative Protocol for Metadata Harvesting (OAI-PMH), Metadata Encoding and Transmission Standards (METS), and JPEG2000. The rapid pace of archival and special collections digitization projects has created the need for DAM systems. Synonymous with *digital object management*. Compare with electronic resources management.

digital elevation model (DEM) : A digital representation of cartographic information in the form of a raster grid of regularly spaced elevation values for ground positions derived primarily from the conversion of contours on printed topographic map series and from photogrammetry (click here to see a DEM of Lake Tahoe). Resolution depends on the distance between adjacent grid points. The U.S. Geological Survey publishes 7.5-minute DEMs derived from its 1:24,000-and 1:25,000-scale topographic quadrangle maps; 30-minute DEMs corresponding to the east half or west half of its 30-minute by 60-minute topographic quadrangle maps; and 1-degree DEMs corresponding to the 3 arc-second (or 1:250,000-scale) topographic map series. DEMs can be combined with other digital data to provide additional visual detail (see this example of a digital orthophoto overlaid on a DEM). Click here to learn more about digital elevation models, courtesy of the USGS, and here to learn more about USGS DEM products. Click here to see a practical application of digital elevation modeling in the conservation of the mountain gorilla. Synonymous with *digital terrain model*. *See also*: National Elevation Dataset.

Digital Libraries Initiative (DLI) : A multi-agency interdisciplinary research program of the National Science Foundation (NSF) that provides grants to facilitate the creation of large knowledge bases, develop the information technology to access them effectively, and improve their usability in a wide range of contexts. Click here to see a list of projects funded by DLI Phase 2.

digital library : A library in which a significant proportion of the resources are available in machine-readable format (as opposed to print or microform), accessible by means of computers. The digital content may be locally held or accessed remotely via computer networks. For a distributed example, see the Mountain West Digital Library established by the Utah Academic Library Consortium. In libraries, the process of digitization began with the catalog, moved to periodical indexes and abstracting services, then to periodicals and large reference works, and finally to book publishing. Abbreviated *d-lib*. Compare with virtual library. *See also*: Digital Library Federation and National Science Digital Library.

Digital Library Federation (DLF) : A consortium of major libraries and library-related agencies dedicated to promoting the use of electronic technologies to extend collections and services, DLF is committed to identifying standards and best practices for digital collections and network access, coordinating research and development in the use of information technology by libraries, and assisting in the initiation of projects and services that individual libraries lack the means to develop on their own. Click here to connect to the homepage of the DLF.

digital orthophoto quadrangle (DOQ) : The standard product for the initial national orthoimagery coverage of the United States, the DOQ is a digital orthophotograph at a scale of 1:12,000 centered on a quarter-quadrangle at 1-meter pixel resolution (click here to see a DOQ of Lake Tahoe). DOQs are cast on the Universal Transverse Mercator (UTM) projection from black and white or color infrared digital aerial photographs. Each DOQ includes an ASCII keyword header containing descriptive information about the image data, including photographic source type, date taken, software systems used in creating it, and production date of the digital elevation model (DEM) metadata used in the orthophoto rectification process. 3.75-minute DOQs are available from the U.S. Geological Survey. Click here to learn more about USGS DOQs. Synonymous with *digital orthographic quadrangle* and *digital orthophoto quarter-quadrangle* (DOQQ).

digital orthophotograph (DOP) : A black and white or infrared aerial photograph taken with digital equipment, instead of a conventional film camera, then rectified to eliminate displacement and other image distortions to conform to measurements taken on the ground (this example). A DOP has uniform scale and can be used like a map. DOPs can also be combined in a photomosaic to create a single image of a larger area, or with other digital products such as digital elevation models (DEMs) to provide additional detail. Click here to see digital orthophotographs used in a study of the Waller Creek floodplain in Texas. DOPs are also available from *TerraServer*. Click here to learn more about orthoimagery, courtesy of the U.S. Geological Survey. Abbreviated *digital orthophoto*. *See also*: digital orthophoto quadrangle.

digital publishing : The activities involved in the business of preparing, processing, producing, protecting, and preserving information content in digital form, whether the result is delivered in print or electronic format (e-journal, e-book, Web document, etc.). In 2005, the Pennsylvania State University Libraries formed a partnership with Penn State Press to create an Office of Digital Scholarly Publishing which will use new media technology to advance scholarly communication at Penn State and within the wider academic community. One goal of the new Office will be to make research publications available online by moving existing print journals and monographs to a digital environment. The role of libraries in digital publishing is discussed by Kate Wittenberg in the article *Librarians as Publishers: A New Role in Scholarly Communication* in the November/December 2004 issue of *Searcher*. For a full treatment of the topic, see *The Columbia Guide to Digital Publishing* edited by William Kasdorf (Columbia University Press: 2003).

digital raster graphic (DRG) : A digital image of a standard-scale topographic quadrangle originally published on paper by the U.S. Geological Survey, including all marginal data, optically scanned at high resolution (250 or more dots per inch). The image inside the neat line is georeferenced to the surface of the earth, with horizontal positional accuracy and datum matching that of the source map (click here to see a DRG of Lake Tahoe). DRGs can be used as background images on which other digital data is overlaid and as base maps in any GIS, GPS, or graphics software system capable of displaying GeoTIFF images. DRGs can also be combined with other digital products, such as digital elevation models (DEMs) and digital orthophoto quadrangles (DOQs) to provide additional visual detail. DRGs are available from *TerraServer*. Click here to learn more about USGS DRGs. Compare with digital line graph. *See also*: raster data.

digital talking book (DTB) : Unlike the traditional audiobook, which is an analog representation of a print publication, the digital talking book is a collection of electronic files arranged as a multimedia representation of information traditionally imparted in print. Special playback equipment is required. DTBs enable the target population to receive information as human or synthetic speech, refreshable Braille, or alternative visual display (e.g., large print). When created and assembled in accordance with the ANSI/NISO Z39.86 *Specifications for the Digital Talking Book*, the files make possible such features as rapid, flexible navigation; bookmarking and highlighting; keyword(s) searching; spelling of words on demand; and user control over the presentation of footnotes, page numbers, etc., enabling readers with physical and visual disabilities to access information flexibly and efficiently, and sighted users with learning or reading disabilities to receive information through multiple senses.

digital thesis : A master's thesis or Ph.D. dissertation created in electronic form ("born digital"). Most universities require a paper or microform copy for archival purposes, but for some hypermedia theses, a print version may not be an accurate representation of the original (or even possible). Preservation dilemmas posed by the rapid obsolescence of digital equipment and formats underscore the need for standards. See the Networked Digital Library of Theses and Dissertations (NDLTD) and the Australasian Digital Theses Program (ADT).

Direct Delivery : The delivery of an IP packet by an IP node to the final destination on a directly attached subnet.

display matter : Any printed matter that is not part of the text of a work, including illustrations, headings, captions, printer's ornaments, etc. To distinguish it from body matter, textual display matter is set in type of a different size and/or font.

Disposal : Removal of an item, or items, in a collection following the appraisal process.

Distance Learning Section (DLS) : The section of the Association of College and Research Libraries (ACRL) within the American Library Association (ALA) that provides leadership, support, and new ideas for librarians involved in all aspects of distance learning. Click here to connect to the DLS homepage.

Distance Vector : A routing protocol technology that propagates routing information in the form of an address prefix and its "distance" (hop count).

document camera : A tabletop device used in bibliographic instruction and other visual presentations to project text and/or images from an opaque surface or transparency onto a large screen using an LCD projector. Document cameras have superseded overhead projectors in well-equipped libraries. To see examples, try a keywords search on the term in *Google Image Search*.

document delivery service (DDS) : The provision of published or unpublished documents in hard copy, microform, or digital format, usually for a fixed fee upon request. In most libraries, document delivery service is provided by the interlibrary loan office on a cost-recovery basis. The patron is usually required to pick up printed material at the library, but electronic full-text may be forwarded via e-mail. Also refers to the physical or electronic delivery of documents from a library collection to the residence or place of business of a library user, upon request. Click here to connect to *DocDel.net*, a directory of document suppliers provided by Instant Information Systems. *See also*: *Ariel* and electronic document delivery:

document delivery services : You may request materials not owned by Tisch Library, such as photocopies of articles or books, from other libraries using document delivery services. Requests can be made using the online form on the Tisch Library webpage or directly from certain DATABASES such as Ovid, FirstSearch, and Cambridge Scientific Abstracts.

documentarian : A person who makes one or more documentary motion pictures. Notable examples include Robert Flaherty (*Louisiana Story* and *Nanook of the North*), Ken Burns (*Baseball* and *Jazz*), and Michael Moore (*Bowling for Columbine* and *Fahrenheit 9/11*). Academy Awards are given annually for the best documentary feature and short subject. Also, a photographer who specializes in a form of photojournalism devoted to producing objective, usually candid photographs of a particular subject (often a person) for publication or exhibition.

documentation center : An organization or agency that specializes in receiving, processing, preserving, abstracting, and indexing publications, usually within a scholarly discipline or field of research and study (*example*: ERIC). Documentation centers also issue bulletins on the progress of such work for distribution to interested parties and may also prepare bibliographies on special topics, make copies or translations, and engage in bibliographic research.

Donation : A voluntary deposit of records involving the transfer of legal ownership, as well as custody, to the archives.

Dotted Decimal Notation : The notation most commonly used to express IPv4 addresses. The 32-bit IPv4 address is divided into four 8-bit blocks. Each block is expressed as a decimal number, and adjacent blocks are separated by periods. An example of an IPv4 unicast address in dotted decimal notation is 131.107.199.45.

Double Colon : The practice of compressing a single contiguous series of zero blocks of an IPv6 address to "::". For example, the multicast address FF02:0:0:0:0:0:0:2 is expressed as FF02::2.

double numeration : A system of enumeration, used mainly in textbooks, law books, and technical publications, in which *two* numbers are assigned, usually separated by a period, hyphen, or other symbol, the first being the number of the chapter or other major division of the work, and the second indicating a section of the text or one of several illustrations, maps, graphs, charts, etc., numbered in the sequence in which they appear within the division, for example, *Fig. 12.10* to indicate the tenth figure in chapter 12.

drop initial : A large decorated or undecorated initial letter in a manuscript or printed work aligned horizontally with the tops of succeeding letters in the same line but extending below the line into a space left by indenting the next line (or lines). Drop initials are used mainly at the beginning of a chapter or other major division of a work. Click here to see an illuminated example in a 15th-century manuscript, here to see a decorated example in a 16th-century printed book, and here to see a 20th-century rubricated example (Cary Collection, Rochester Institute of Technology). Synonymous with *drop cap.* Compare with raised capital.

due date : Each time you check out a book, you will be told when it is due back to the library. There will also be a slip of paper in the book stamped with the due date. Undergraduates can check out books for 2 weeks, graduate students can check out books for 1 month. Both undergraduate and graduate students can renew their items online as long as the item is renewed BEFORE the due date. To renew an item, you must go to your library record, enter your name and University ID (this should be your social security number), and then select the item(s) you wish to renew. If you wait until the due date, you must bring the item to the library to renew it. Other items have different check out lengths. For instance, theses and dissertations can be checked out for 1 week and videos can be checked out for 3 days. Remember, if your items are overdue, there will be fines and Jernigan Library can put a hold on your account so that you cannot register for classes until the fines are paid.

duplicate publication : A published article that substantially duplicates another published article without acknowledgment, both articles having one or more authors in common and a substantial amount of identical text.

Duplication may be intentional, often to achieve wider dissemination of the content, especially of a specific type of article, such as a policy statement, or inadvertent through multiple submissions of a manuscript to different journals. In some bibliographic databases, such as *MEDLINE*, the publication type "Duplicate Publication" may be assigned to a citation with or without formal notification from the author(s) or journal editor, often by an indexer who notices substantial similarity.

ead : Encoded archival description. EAD is a nonproprietary encoding standard for machine-readable finding aids.

easy book : A heavily illustrated book with limited text written to appeal to the interests and reading ability of children from preschool to third grade, usually shelved in a separate section of a school library or children's room in a public library. Synonymous with *easy reader*.

economies of scale : The decrease in cost of production that occurs as the extent of an operation is enlarged, for example, reduction in the cost of preparing new items for circulation, achieved by processing them in large batches rather than a few at a time, an argument used to justify centralized ordering and processing in library systems. If marginal cost (cost of producing an additional unit) is less than average cost, an economic incentive exists to produce additional output. *Diseconomies of scale* occur when average cost increases as output increases. In large libraries, efficiency can be enhanced by taking advantage of economies of scale. Synonymous with *scale economies*.

economy binding : Any one of a variety of methods for binding library materials that are less expensive than standard binding, generally used for volumes expected to receive limited circulation. The material is bound as received, with no mending or collation, and the width of inner margins may not be checked by the binder. The preferred method of leaf attachment in economy binding is double-fan adhesive or side sewing, rather than sewing through the fold, and the volume is given little or no rounding and backing, producing a flat back. A lower grade of covering material is used and the color may be selected by the binder, or from a limited number of choices. Click here to compare images of standard versus economy periodical binding, courtesy of Roswell Bookbinding.

edge painting : A picture drawn or painted on the edges of the sections of a book with its leaves closed, a common form of decoration in the Middle Ages. On some books, painting was done on all three edges but on most only on the fore-edge. Click here to see a 19th-century example from the MacDonald Collection at Mount Saint Vincent University, Nova Scotia, and here to see an example from the Ransom Collection at the University of Texas at Austin. In England during the late 18th and early 19th centuries, the technique was refined to make the picture visible only when the leaves were slightly fanned. In *double fore-edge painting*, two different images are displayed by fanning the leaves first in one direction, then in the other. Edge painting may also be concealed beneath gilt or combined with gauffering for an especially elegant effect (see this example, courtesy of the Princeton University Library).

edible book : An object made of ingredients that can be consumed and digested as food, which has the appearance of a book or makes reference to a book title, format, or structure, for example, a "rare book" made of thin slices of roast beef bound together by a scallion. Click here to see examples from an edible book festival sponsored by Yale University. To see other examples, try a keywords search on the term in *Google Image Search*. The concept adds a new dimension to the phrase "eat your words."

edition statement : In library cataloging, the portion of the edition area of the bibliographic description in which the edition of the work is indicated by ordinal number (*7th ed.*) and/or description (*Rev. ed.*) as found on the item, using standard abbreviations found in *Appendix B* of *AACR2*. If an item lacks an edition statement but is known to include important changes from previous editions, a brief statement in the language and script of the title proper is provided by the cataloger in square brackets. In the MARC record, the edition statement is given in subfield *a* of field 250.

editorial content : The portions of a newspaper or periodical containing content controlled by the editor(s) or editorial board (articles, columns, editorials, letters to the editor, illustrations, political cartoons, etc.), as opposed to the space devoted to advertisements, notices and announcements, etc.

Educational and General Expenditures (E&G) : The sum of total institutional expenditures for instruction, research, public service, academic support, student services, institutional support, operation and maintenance of plant, scholarships and fellowships, mandatory transfers, and (in recent years) non-mandatory transfers.

Electronic Frontier Foundation (EFF) : A group of people (lawyers, technologists, volunteers, and visionaries) who share a passionate commitment to defending digital information, innovation, and technology from attempts by government and business to restrict freedom of expression. Current key issues include censorship, copyright law, digital rights management, *DMCA*, e-voting, file sharing, privacy, RFID, spam, and the *USA Patriot Act*. Click here to connect to the EFF homepage.

electronic journal : Journals that are available online. Electronic journals that the Tufts libraries subscribe to can be found using the Electronic Journals link on the Tisch Library webpage or the CATALOG. Check both for the most accurate information.

electronic publication : A work in digital form capable of being read or otherwise perceived, distributed to the general public electronically. The category includes electronic journals and e-prints, electronic magazines and newspapers, electronic books, Web sites, Weblogs, etc. Some electronic publications are online versions of print publications; others are born digital. Synonymous with *e-publication*.

electronic resources management (ERM) : Systems developed to assist librarians in the control of licensed third-party resources published electronically (databases, e-books, e-journals, etc.), including license management, renewal, legal use, access management, and collection development. In 2001, a small group of academic librarians began to create metadata specifications for managing electronic subscriptions and their associated titles. The group was later asked by the Digital Library Federation (DLF) to deliver formal specifications for vendors, as a replacement for various homegrown systems. Innovative Interfaces Inc. was the first library automation vendor to market an ERM software module based on the DLF specifications, and other vendors have followed suit. Compare with digital asset management.

e-mail reference : Jernigan Library has now added a service called E-mail Reference. This service is monitored from : Mon through Fri, 8am to 5pm, excluding holidays. Responses to questions you may submit are normally sent by email within 72 hours. If you have a question that requires significant interaction with library staff you will want to visit the library rather than ask an email question. Types of questions that can be answered via E-mail Reference include : availability and location of materials in Jernigan Library; inquiries about library services or hours; requests for brief statistical or other factual data; verification of citations; requests for brief biographical data or business/organization contact information; assistance on the use of OASIS (our online catalog) or the databases made available by Jernigan Library.

emblematic decoration : Pictorial motifs used in the manner of a badge in bookbinding and manuscripts to indicate the name or identity of the author, the owner of the volume, its country of origin or ownership, or its subject content. Click here to see an example indicating the identity of the owner, courtesy of the British Library's *Database of Bookbindings*. *See also*: armorial binding.

emendation : Correction or improvement, especially of a literary or artistic work or written document, by alteration of the text, whether done by the author or another person, such as an editor. Also, a specific instance of such an alteration. Click here to see holograph emendations in a typescript of Philip Roth's *Patrimony*, courtesy of the Library of Congress. In textual criticism, the correction (usually by judicious inference or informed conjecture) of a text found to have been corrupted in transmission, restoring it to a state presumed to be closer to the original.

emergency plan : A set of guidelines or steps prepared in advance to help the staff of a library deal with unusual occurrences that may temporarily disrupt normal operations (assaults, bomb threats, security violations, etc.) but are not usually disastrous. Compare with contingency plan and disaster plan.

Encapsulation; Polyester Encapsulation : A protective enclosure for papers and other flat materials that involves placing the item between two sheets of transparent polyester film that are then sealed around all the edges. The object is physically supported and protected from the atmosphere, although it may continue to deteriorate within the capsule. It can be removed easily from the capsule by cutting one or more of the edges of the polyester. Ideally an item should be deacidified before it is encapsulated.

EndNote : EndNote is citation management software produced by ISI. A free 30 day trial is available through the EndNote website. The software can be purchased at the Cornell Campus Store.

engraved edition : An edition of a book or other publication printed from engraved plates, rather than by the setting of movable type, a process generally reserved for limited editions due to the additional expense. Click here to see an 18th-century edition of a work by Franz Anton Mesmer (1734-1815) printed by this method (Bakken Library and Museum). From the late 16th to the early 20th century, engraving was also one of the methods used to print music scores. Engraving services are still available to composers and songwriters (see Soundsmith Music).

entry level : Employment at the lowest grade in a system of classified positions, suitable for candidates who are beginning their careers and lack experience. Promotion usually depends on a vacancy occurring at a higher grade or classification, rather than on the development of the initial position into one requiring greater skill or responsibility. Synonymous with *entrance level*.

entry word : The word under which a record in a catalog, index, or bibliography is filed and searched, usually the first word of the heading, initial articles excluded. In retrieving information from an online catalog or bibliographic database, the order of terms typed as input may determine the success or failure of a search by author, title, subject heading, or descriptor, but in a keywords search, word order should not affect results if Boolean logic is correctly used. Synonymous with *filing word*.

epistolary novel : A form of novel that reached its greatest popularity during the 18th century, in which the narrative is developed by the author in a series of letters (*example*: Clarissa by Samuel Richardson). Sometimes a novelist begins a work in epistolary style, then switches to conventional narrative (Busman's Honeymoon by Dorothy L. Sayers).

escapist literature : Fiction written as light entertainment, intended mainly to divert the mind of the reader into a world of imagination and fantasy. Popular genres include romance, science fiction, thrillers, etc.

ETC : The Electronic Text Center (ETC), located on the first floor of Olin Library, provides access to scholarly electronic text and multimedia documents from a set of dedicated workstations in the library and from the Center's Web site. For more information about the ETC and the resources available there, see the ETC web site.

Etruscan binding : A style of leather binding developed during the late 18th century by William Edwards of Halifax in which the panel on each cover, decorated by means of acid staining, is surrounded by borders of classical design (fretwork, etc.). A vase of classical shape sometimes adorns the center of each panel. Click here to view an early 19th-century example with an inner border of palmettes acid-stained terracotta and black to replicate the colors of an antique vase (Glasgow University Library, Special Collections, BD14-i.28). To see other examples, try a search on the keyword "etruscan" in the British Library's *Database of Bookbindings*.

EUI-64 Address : A 64-bit link-layer address that is used as a basis for an IPv6 interface identifier.

exhibition catalog : An art book in hard or softcover containing reproductions of the works of art displayed at an exhibition or series of exhibitions held in a museum or gallery. The illustrations are usually numbered and may be arranged in the order in which the items are exhibited, with or without prices. Accompanying text may be minimal. Exhibition catalogs are often issued by museum publishers. For examples, see the "Books" section of the Metropolitan Museum of Art's online Met Store. Synonymous with *exhibit catalog*.

ex-library copy : A copy of a book or other item once owned by a library and subsequently acquired by a used book dealer, usually identified by an ownership mark, library binding, and/or spine label. An ex-library copy may also show signs of heavy use. Condition may reduce its value to collectors. If not stamped "discard," the volume may still belong to the library. Click here to see examples of ex-library markings, courtesy of My Wings Books. Abbreviated *ex-lib* or *x-lib*.

export edition : An edition of a publication prepared by the publisher specifically for distribution or sale in another country (or countries). Compare with co-edition.

Extended Unique Identifier : A link-layer address defined by the Institute of Electrical and Electronics Engineers (IEEE).

External Review Panel : A group of educators and practitioners in the field of library and information studies (usually six) selected to visit a program under evaluation for accreditation to verify information provided in the Program Presentation document submitted as part of the two-year comprehensive review. Panelists are appointed by the Committee on Accreditation (COA) with the cooperation of the dean of the program and the Office for Accreditation of the American Library Association (ALA). When possible, panelists are selected to reflect the emphasis indicated in the program?s Plan for the Program Presentation and to meet requests for areas of special expertise.

faceted classification : A classification system developed through analysis of the fundamental characteristics of subjects by which they can be divided into subclasses. For example, in his *Colon Classification*, S.R. Ranganathan identifies five basic characteristics: personality, matter, energy, space, and time (abbreviated PMEST). In such a system, the notation representing a subject is created by combining the notations of its facets.

faceted initial : An initial letter in an illuminated manuscript or early printed book drawn to appear three-dimensional, like a gemstone cut into a number of intersecting plane surfaces, or a Roman capital carved in stone, a style inspired the antiquarian movement in Renaissance Italy (see this example, courtesy of the British Library, Burney 353). Other examples can be seen by browsing images in this 15th-century Virgil (British Library, King's 24).

faceted notation : A notation in which the facets of the classification system are indicated by symbols, for example, the colon in S.R. Ranganathan's *Colon Classification*.

facsimile atlas : A bound collection of facsimile maps or a printed reproduction of an older atlas made to duplicate as closely as possible the physical appearance of the original. Click here to see several openings in an example.

facsimile binding : A binding intended to duplicate as closely as possible the binding on a previously published edition of the same work or an earlier style of binding typical of the period in which the work was first published (click here to see a modern example). Compare with retrospective binding.

facsimile catalog : A catalog that includes in each entry a small reproduction of the picture, slide, map, or other item it represents, usually affixed to or printed on cards larger than standard size or on sheets of heavy paper filed in a loose-leaf or other type of binder.

fair copy : In publishing, the final version of the manuscript or typescript of an original work, containing few mistakes and no corrections, having been carefully prepared from the final draft by the author, or by a copy editor, for the use of the printer. Click here to see the autograph fair copy of a concerto by Mozart (Cornell University Library). Synonymous with *clean copy*.

false date : A date such as a birth or death date or publication date given incorrectly, whether intentionally or inadvertently. In library cataloging, the correct date is interpolated in square brackets following the incorrect date in the bibliographic description (*example*: 1950 [1952]).

fascicle : For convenience in publishing or printing, a book or other item is sometimes issued in numbered or unnumbered installments, each incomplete and not necessarily coincident with any formal division of the work. Usually issued in paper wrappers, fascicles may eventually be bound together in correct sequence to form a complete volume or uniform set of volumes (*example*: **Middle English Dictionary**, published by the University of Michigan Press). They differ from parts in being temporary rather than permanent. Click here to see an 18th-century Chinese edition published in this manner (Bibliothèque Nationale de France) and here to see a contemporary example published under a separate title. Abbreviated *fasc.* Synonymous with *fascicule* and *fasciculus*.

fat matter : A printer's term for copy that does not take long to set because it contains a high proportion of white space, for example, extended passages of dialogue in a work of fiction. The opposite of lean matter.

Federal Depository Library Program (FDLP) : Established by Congress as part of the Printing Act of 1895 to assure access for the American public to government information, the FDLP authorizes the U.S. Government Printing Office (GPO) and contractors to distribute without charge copies of federal government documents to designated depository libraries in the United States (and its territories) that agree to provide unrestricted access and professional assistance at no charge to the user. The legal requirements of the FDLP are found in *Chapter 19* of *Title 44, U.S. Code*. There are currently about 1,350 depository libraries, some receiving less than the full complement of available publications. The FDLP also provides free online public access to government information via *GPO Access*. The Public Printer and Superintendent of Documents are advised on policy matters concerning the FDLP by the Depository Library Council (DLC) established in 1972. Click here to connect to the FDLP homepage. *See also*: state plan.

federal library : A library owned and operated by the federal government of the United States, usually containing a collection of government documents pertaining to the field(s) it is mandated to cover. The largest are the Library of Congress, the National Library of Medicine, the National Library of Education, and the National Agricultural Library. The Federal Library and Information Center Committee (FLICC) of the Library of Congress has provided the FEDLINK guide to federal libraries since 1965. Federal librarians are organized in the Federal and Armed Forces Libraries Round Table (FAFLRT) of the American Library Association (ALA).

fence diagram : In cartography, a three-dimensional rendering of the subsurface of a geographic area consisting of three or more geologic cross sections in which the perspective is created by the intersection of the sections and their correlation lines. Click here to see an archaeological example and here to see a generalized fence diagram of the Floridan Aquifer System, courtesy of the U.S. Geological Survey. To see other examples, try a keywords search on the term "fence diagram" in *Google Image Search*.

field : When searching most databases, you will see boxes for entering search terms in various "fields." A field consists of one part of a bibliographic citation. For instance, there is an author field, an [article] title field, a journal title field, a publisher field, etc. Keep in mind that not all databases offer the same searchable fields.

figure of speech : A form of expression employed mainly in rhetoric and literary writing in which words or entire sentences are used in a way that deviates from conventional order or literal meaning to achieve an unusual or unexpected poetic or aesthetic effect, for example, the phrase "a flood of tears." Click here to learn more about figures of speech in *Wikipedia* or see Grant Williams' Figures of Speech Tables. *See also*: metaphor.

film library : A type of special library containing a collection of 8, 16, 35, or 70mm motion pictures, videorecordings, DVDs, and other materials related to cinematography and film studies, classified for ease of access and retrieval, for example, the New York Public Library for the Performing Arts. Viewing or borrowing privileges may be restricted to registered members or subscribers who are required to pay fees. Compare with film archives.

Find Articles : Find Articles identifies and locates articles, or article citations, from a select group of online periodical indexes. The Find Articles interface allows users to search multiple indexes simultaneously using simple keywords. Search results will lead to articles available online or, if online access is not available, to the Library Catalog for the location of the periodical in the library's print collections.

Find Databases : Find Databases provides direct access to all of the catalogs, periodical indexes (including full-text sources), newspaper databases, numeric files, and other online reference sources licensed by Cornell. In addition, Find Databases includes links to public websites reviewed and selected by Cornell librarians. All of the resources in Find Databases may also be accessed through the CUL online catalog.

Find e-Journals : Find e-Journals provides a convenient list of electronic journals licensed by CUL. Every title in Find e-Journals may also be accessed through the CUL online catalog.

finding aid : A published or unpublished guide, inventory, index, register, calendar, list, or other system for retrieving archival primary source materials that provides more detailed description of each item than is customary in a library catalog record (see this online example, courtesy of the Avery Architectural & Fine Arts Library at Columbia University). Finding aids also exist in nonprint formats (ASCII, HTML, etc.). In partnership with the Society of American Archivists, the Library of Congress maintains a standard called Encoded Archival Description (EAD) for encoding archival finding aids in Standard Generalized Markup Language (SGML) and/or Extensible Markup Language (XML). Click here to connect to a list of online finding aids for Library of Congress collections. Compare with finding tool.

First Amendment : Amendment I to the *United States Constitution*, ratified in 1791, which guarantees freedom of speech: "Congress shall make no law respecting an establishment of religion, or prohibiting the free exercise thereof; or abridging the freedom of speech, or of the press; or the right of the people peaceably to assemble, and to petition the government for a redress of grievances." The *Freedom to Read Statement* and the *Library Bill of Rights* of the American Library Association (ALA) are based on this constitutional protection.

fixed-length data elements : Field 008 of the MARC record, containing 40 characters used to encode information that allows records meeting certain criteria to be identified and retrieved, for example, materials in a specific format, published in a specific language or country, or intended for a particular audience.

flock paper : A type of specialty cover paper, originally intended to simulate tapestry or velvet brocade, produced by coating the sheet with size (all over or in patterns or designs), applying specially dyed flock powder (pulverized fiber), and removing any excess that does not adhere to the surface (adapted from Roberts and Etherington, *Bookbinding and the Conservation of Books: A Dictionary of Descriptive Terminology*).

focus group : A small group of people assembled by a researcher to identify through informal discussion the key issues and/or themes related to a research topic, often to facilitate development of a more quantitative methodology, such as a survey. An effort may be made to select a representative sample of the larger cohort used in subsequent research. Focus groups are sometimes used in library research and strategic planning, for example, to determine user needs and preferences in the development of a technology plan. The technique is also used extensively in business for qualitative research on consumer behavior. Online focus groups are used in the evaluation of Web-based services.

format integration : The concept that separate cataloging rules and documentation should not be maintained for each bibliographic format (books, music scores, maps, etc.). The MARC record is designed to allow a given field to be used for any format for which it is appropriate. In the United States, MARC format integration was defined in the 1980s and implemented in the 1990s.

formatting : The appearance of printed text, including font, type size, alignment, boldface, italic, underlining, etc. In word processing software, options allow the user to specify formatting. In HTML documents, the same effects are achieved through the use of fixed tags embedded in the text.

frequently challenged book : A book purchased for school and/ or public library collections whose removal is often demanded by parents or other patrons based on the appropriateness of its content, usually for children and/ or young adults. The American Library Association (ALA) publishes the *100 Most Frequently Challenged Books* list, with information on challenges by initiator, institution, type, and year. *See also*: banned book and parenting collection.

frozen catalog : A library catalog to which no new bibliographic records are added and from which no existing records are removed, even when revisions or corrections are made or existing records are converted to machine-readable format. Compare with closed catalog and open catalog.

full score : A music score in which each of the parts is written on a separate stave, usually for the use of the conductor. For orchestral and choral works, this usually requires a large page size. From top to bottom, the standard arrangement of instrumental parts in a full score is: woodwinds, brass, percussion, and strings, with any solo part in a concerto appearing above the violins. Voice parts, arranged in descending order of vocal register, are placed above the string section, with any solo parts given above the chorus. Only the largest music libraries collect this type of score. Click here to see the full score of *The Mighty Casey*, an opera by American composer William Schuman (Library of Congress) and here to see the conducting score of Stravinsky's *Le Sacre du Printemps* marked for performance by Leopold Stokowski (University of Pennsylvania Library).

full text : Many of the library's databases link directly from online search results to the article in its entirety, or to the "full text" of the item.

Full text database : A full text database is a resource that provides access to the complete text of an item. In a full text periodical resource, both the bibliographic descriptions and the articles themselves will be available. An example of this type of resource is ProQuest Direct.

full-text : An electronic resource that provides the entire text of a single work (*example*: **Britannica Online**) or of articles published in one or more journals, magazines, and/or newspapers. For example, a bibliographic database that provides the complete text of a significant proportion of the works indexed, in addition to the bibliographic citation and (in many cases) an abstract of the content (*example*: *JSTOR*). Also spelled *full text* and *fulltext*.

full-text search : A search of a bibliographic database in which the entire text of each record or document is searched and the entry retrieved if the terms included in the search statement are present. Most Web search engines are designed to perform full-text searches. This can pose a problem for the user if a search term has more than one meaning, resulting in the retrieval of irrelevant information (false drops). For example, in a medical database, the query "treatment of AIDS" might retrieve entries for sources containing the phrase "treatment aids in geriatrics" (with "of" a stopword). Compare with free-text search.

full-time equivalent (FTE) : A measure of the total number of students, undergraduate and graduate, enrolled for the number of credit hours considered by an institution of higher learning to be a full schedule, sometimes used by vendors to determine subscription rates charged on a sliding scale for access to electronic resources such as bibliographic databases. In the United States, there is no national standard for computing FTE—each institution has devised its own formula. A typical example: FTE = total number of undergraduate credit hours divided by 15, plus total number of graduate credit hours divided by 12.

furlough : A temporary leave of absence granted without pay to an employee. Some libraries and library systems use mandatory furloughs to cut costs in a budget crisis, electing to close for one or more weeks, usually during periods of low usage (end of summer, week before Christmas, etc.), instead of laying off workers. This option spreads the impact of cuts over all employees and administrative units within the organization.

galley proof : An impression taken from type composed in long columns, arranged in trays called galleys, before it has been made up into pages, to allow the author and proofreader to inspect the text and make any corrections before the work goes to press. Although galley proofs usually do *not* include illustrations and indexes, reviews may be written from them. Synonymous with *galleys* and *slip proof*.

gate count : The number of times a mechanical counting device, located at the entrance to or exit from a library, is automatically activated whenever a person enters or leaves during a designated period of time (day, week, month, year), an important measure of library use. In most facilities, the counter is located near, attached to, or part of the security gate. Totals are recorded at regular intervals, usually by the staff at the circulation desk. Gate counts provide statistical information on traffic patterns, helpful in establishing library hours and anticipating staffing needs. Synonymous with *door count*.

gauffered edges : A small wavy or crimped repeating pattern impressed as decoration on the gilt edges of a book by the use of heated finishing tools called *gauffering irons*, popular on ornamental bindings of the late 15th to 17th centuries. The designs were sometimes built up through repeated impressions. Click here to see an elaborate Renaissance example (Saxon State Library), and here to see two 19th-century examples (Otto G. Richter Library, University of Miami, Florida). When the technique is combined with edge painting, the results can be very elegant (see this example, courtesy of the Princeton University Library). Also spelled *goffered edges*. Synonymous with *chased edges*.

gelatin silver print : The result of a photographic process in which a negative is printed on a sheet of paper or other support coated with an emulsion of gelatin (an animal protein) containing light-sensitive silver salts. After brief exposure to the negative, the paper is immersed in a chemical solution that allows the latent image to develop. Invented in 1873 by Peter Mawdsley, gelatin silver papers were commercially available by 1885. Within a decade, prints made on gelatin papers superseded the earlier albumen print because they were more stable, did not yellow, and were easier to produce. Glossy, matte, or textured, gelatin prints are the standard medium in modern black and white photography. Click here to see a selection of early gelatin silver prints from the Victoria & Albert Museum and here to see examples from the Getty Museum.

gem photograph : A very small tintype, usually a portrait, about 1/2 x 1 inch in size for mounting in jewelry or in a carte-de-visite size cardboard holder designed to be inserted into a Victorian carte-de-visite photograph album, popular from the mid-1860s until about 1880 (see this example).

general material designation (GMD) : An optional term added in square brackets to the bibliographic description of a nonbook item following the title proper to indicate type of material (*example*: **[videorecording]**). Separate lists of general material designations are provided in *AACR2* for British and North American libraries. In some categories, the British list is more general (*object* includes diorama, game, microscope slide, model, and realia). The Library of Congress does *not* include the GMD in catalog records for manuscripts, maps, music, and textual works. Compare with material type. *See also*: specific material designation.

geologic column : A composite diagram showing, in vertical sequence, the geologic strata underlying a given location or area of the earth's surface, usually color-coded when printed as an index on a geologic map, with the names of the various rock formations indicated along one side of the column. Click here to see examples on a series of geologic maps of Great Britain, courtesy of the School of Ocean and Earth Science, Southampton University, and here to see examples detailing a geologic cross section. Geologic columns often appear in conjunction with a geologic time scale (see this example). Also refers to the sequence of strata shown in such a diagram. Synonymous with *geologic section* and *stratigraphic column*.

ghost writer : A person who writes or prepares a work for, and in the name of, another person who may be famous but is usually not a writer by profession (see this example). Autobiographies and memoirs are often written in this way. Although a ghost writer normally receives compensation for services rendered, sometimes even a share of royalties, the writer's name may or may not be listed as joint author on the title page. Also spelled *ghostwriter*.

gift book program : A formal library program allowing users to purchase items for the library collection in memory of a deceased person or in honor of a special occasion for a loved one (birthday, anniversary, etc.), with selections usually made by the library. Some programs offer a memorial bookplate and may give the honoree the privilege of "first read" (see this example at a public library). Click here to see an example at an academic library.

gift collection : The donation to a library of a significant volume of materials, usually about a specific subject or person, in a particular genre, of a certain format, etc., assembled by one or more persons based on personal interests. Such gifts may be unsolicited or solicited by the library. When the collection contains rare and valuable items, the donor(s) may be honored by the library at a special reception or in other ways. The materials may be housed separately, given special honorary bookplates, or distinguished by some other method. If the collection is archival, the donor may specify restrictions on use. Recent examples include the donation in 2003 by Edwin and Terry Murray of over 55,000 comic books and thousands of fanzines to the Duke University Rare Book, Manuscript, and Special Collections Library, giving it one of the largest archival comics collections in the United States, and the donation in 2002 of a portion the Hatch/Billops Collection to an African-American studies archive at Emory University.

global positioning system (GPS) : A worldwide navigational system based on the triangulation of radio signals transmitted by a network of 24 satellites in orbit around the earth, allowing the coordinates of any point on or near the surface of the planet to be determined with a high degree of accuracy at any time and in any weather. GPS receivers have been miniaturized to just a few integrated circuits, making them economical to incorporate into a variety of products. To learn more about GPS, try Peter H. Dana's *Global Positioning System Overview* or *How GPS Receivers Work* in HowStuffWorks. For the latest developments in GPS technology, see *GPS World* or the *Yahoo!* list of GPS Web sites.

Global Unicast Address : An IPv6 unicast address that is globally routable and reachable on the IPv6 portion of the Internet. IPv6 global addresses are equivalent to public IPv4 addresses.

GNP Deflator : An updated version of the general price index used to adjust the U.S. gross national product (GNP) for inflation.

government library : In the United States, a library maintained by a unit of government at the local, state, or federal level, containing collections primarily for the use of its staff. Some government libraries have a wider mandate that includes accessibility to the general public (*example*: Smithsonian Institution Libraries). Government librarians are organized in the Government Documents Round Table (GODORT) of the American Library Association (ALA). *See also*: federal library, military library, national library, and state library.

government publication : Under *Title 44, Section 1901* of the *United States Code*, a government publication is defined as "information matter" published as a separate document at government expense or as required by law. *Section 1902* states that government publications, except those "required for official use only or for strictly administrative or operational purposes which have no public interest or educational value and publications classified for reasons of national security," are to be made publicly available to depository libraries by the Superintendent of Documents. The term is also used in a broader sense to include documents published by local, state, territorial, and foreign governments. *See also*: *Monthly Catalog of United States Government Publications.*

government publications : This refers to an area on level 1 in Tisch Library that contains materials produced by the federal government on a wide variety of topics. Government publications are also available from the Tisch Library webpage under Government Information.

GPO bookstore : As of September 1, 2003, the U.S. Government Printing Office (GPO) closed all its regional bookstores, except the main outlet in Washington, D.C. The closures were the result of an overall decline in sales due to increasing access to government information via the Internet and the shift from walk-in traffic at bookstores to purchases from the U.S. Government Bookstore.

graduate library : The academic library at a university that maintains separate collections (and usually facilities) for undergraduates and graduate students, containing the major research collections, staffed and equipped to meet the information needs of graduate students and faculty but also open to undergraduates (*example*: Suzzallo and Allen Libraries, University of Washington).

Grolier binding : A style of ornamental bookbinding named after bindings commissioned by the 16th-century French bibliophile Jean Grolier, Vicomte d'Aguisy (1479-1565) for books in his personal collection, the decoration typically consisting of open interlace strapwork, plain or polychromatic, in a geometrical pattern (circles, squares, lozenges), often with a tooled central motif, plain gilt edges, and vellum paste-down endleaves. Click here to view an example in brown calf (University of London Library) and here to see a more ornate example (Royal Library of Denmark). Click here to see a late-19th-century retrospective example (Princeton University Library). To see other examples, try a keyword search on the term "grolier" in the British Library's *Database of Bookbindings.*

guard book : A book that includes short compensation stubs, called guards, sewn into the sections, equal in thickness to material to be inserted between the leaves subsequent to binding. Their purpose is to keep the volume from bulging open. A guard book may consist entirely of blank leaves interleaved with stubs. Also spelled *guardbook.*

Guide : A descriptive list of a repository's holdings.

guidebook : A handbook that provides useful current information for travelers to a city, state, region, country, or other geographic area or for visitors to a museum, park, historical site, etc. Click here and here to see online examples.

hagiography : A form of biography, popular during the Middle Ages and Renaissance, in which the life described is that of a saint. Also refers to a book containing such accounts, often a collective biography covering the lives of two or more saints. The lives of early saints were included in the Martyrology, which became one of the liturgical readings in the Divine Office. As new saints were canonized, accounts of their lives (*vitae*) were written in Latin by *hagiographers* and translated into the vernacular for the laity. Click here to page through *Vita Beatae Hedwigis*, a 14th-century narrative of the life and works of Saint Hedwig of Silesia (Getty Museum, MS Ludwig XI 7). Click here to learn more about hagiography, courtesy of *The ORB: On-line Reference Book for Medieval Studies.*

hand-binding : The art and craft of binding books by hand without the aid of mechanization. Medieval manuscripts and early printed books were hand-bound in wooden boards covered in leather. Today, trade editions are case bound, and hand-binding is limited to fine books (click here to see the process illustrated). For a very extensive online exhibition, see *Hand Bookbindings: Plain and Simple to Grand and Glorious* (Princeton University Library). The Harcourt Bindery is one of the largest binderies in the United States devoted exclusively to fine bookbinding by hand. Synonymous with *craft binding.*

handbook : A single-volume reference book of compact size that provides concise factual information on a specific subject, organized systematically for quick and easy access. Statistical information is often published in handbook form (*example*: **Statistical Handbook on the American Family**). Some handbooks are published serially (**CRC Handbook of Chemistry and Physics**). Synonymous with vade mecum. *See also*: companion and manual.

hand-colored : A print, illustration, map, or photograph to which tint is added manually, rather than applied during printing or by some other mechanical process, a practice now limited to deluxe collector's editions. Click here to see hand-colored woodcuts in the 15th-century *Nuremberg Chronicles* (Royal Library of Denmark) and here to see them in another copy of the same work (Bryn Mawr College Library). Click here to see a 19th-century hand-tinted lithograph map of the Gold Regions of California and here to see hand-colored copper-etched plates in *Curtis' Botanical Magazine* which began publication in 1787(Glasgow University Library). Also spelled *hand-coloured.*

handling : The physical manipulation of library materials with the hands or by automated equipment, usually in technical processing, circulation, or transportation from one location to another (see this example). Because careless handling can cause damage, proper techniques are particularly important in the preservation of items that are rare and/or valuable and restrictions are often applied. Click here for an online tutorial on the hazards of improper handling (University of Illinois Library). The Heritage Collections Council of Australia also provides useful information on handling various media.

handmade paper : Paper made without the aid of mechanization, usually from pulp made from various vegetable fibers and/or cotton or linen rags. Handmade papers often bear a watermark identifying the papermaker. Click here to view a medieval illuminated manuscript written on handmade paper prior to the invention of printing (Glasgow University Library, Hunterian Add f91). For contemporary examples, see Creative Papers Online. *See also*: deckle edge.

hanging caption : A heading in a book, printed adjacent to the text to which it refers, as a vertical column in the margin rather than horizontally across the page. Click here to see an example, courtesy of the Lehigh University Library.

headpiece : A decoration printed in the blank space at the beginning of a chapter or other division of a book, usually a printer's ornament or a small illustration done by a professional illustrator. Michelle Brown notes in *Understanding Illuminated Manuscripts* (Getty Museum/ British Library, 1994) that decorative panels began appearing at the beginning of texts in late Antiquity, a practice that continued in medieval manuscript and Renaissance book production (click here and here to see examples in Byzantine illuminated manuscripts). Zoomorphic and anthropomorphic motifs can be seen in this headpiece in a 15th-century Greek manuscript (British Library, Burney 75). Click here to see a headpiece in the first edition of the New Testament in Greek, translated into Latin by Erasmus and published in Basel in 1516 (Georgetown University Library). Also spelled *head-piece*. Synonymous with *headband* and *head ornament*. Compare with tailpiece. *See also*: sinkage.

hierarchical classification : A classification system in which the classes are subdivided on the principle of logical subordination, from the most general subjects to the most specific. Hierarchical classification can be broad or close. Click here to explore hierarchy in Dewey Decimal Classification (DDC). Synonymous with *analytic classification*. *See also*: enumerative classification, synthetic classification, and tree structure.

Higher Education General Information Survey (HEGIS) : The predecessor of the IPEDS surveys of post-secondary education institutions by the National Centre for Education Statistics, U.S. Department of Education.

high-risk collection : An archival or library collection for which the likelihood of vandalism or theft is higher than normal due to its exceptional value (rare books) or unusual content (special collections). Tighter security precautions are taken, especially when such items are placed on exhibit.

historiated border : An ornamental band around a miniature and/or portion of text on the page of an illuminated manuscript or early printed book, decorated with figures of animals and/or humans in a scene that illustrates the accompanying text or tells an unrelated story. Click here to see an illuminated example in a 16th-century German psalter (*Leaves of Gold*) and here to view a hand-illuminated border in a breviary printed in Venice in 1478 (Glasgow University Library, Special Collections, Hunterian Bf.1.18). Click here to see a printed border in an early edition (University of Pittsburgh Libraries). *See also*: historiated initial.

historical society : A nonprofit organization devoted to preserving the historical record of a state or municipality (*example*: Oregon), place (Martha's Vineyard), institution (U.S. Supreme Court), people (Huguenots), activity (seafaring), achievement (Titanic), or event (World War II). Well-established historical societies often support a public museum, maintain an archive or library for the use of members, and may publish books and other materials related to their sphere of interest. Click here to connect to a directory of the affiliates of the American Historical Association (AHA).

Hold : When a book or other item is currently on loan, the library permits another borrower to place a "hold" on it by contacting the circulation desk. The patron who has the item checked out will not be permitted to renew it, and the person placing the "hold" will be entitled to check it out after it has been returned. The CU Library online catalog includes a feature that allows the user to place an item on hold without staff assistance. This service is available through the REQUESTS link at the top of any online catalog record.

Holdings : The total stock of materials, print and nonprint, owned by a library, usually listed in the catalog. Synonymous with library collection.

holdings statement : A note added to the catalog record for an item in a library collection indicating, in an open or closed entry, all the copies, volumes, issues, or parts held by the library or library system, usually with information concerning the location of the item. For serials, separate notes may be provided for print and microform holdings. ANSI/NISO standard Z39.71-1999 *Holdings Statements for Bibliographic Items* specifies rules for the construction and display of holdings statements for all non-unitary publications. Compare with numeric and/or alphabetic, chronological, or other designation. *See also*: completeness.

holograph manuscript : The text of an original work written entirely in the hand of the author. Click here to view holograph manuscripts of Sigmund Freud in the collections of the Library of Congress.

hospital library : A medical library maintained within the walls of a hospital, containing a collection of print and online resources on medicine and allied health to serve the information and research needs of doctors, nurses, patients, and staff, usually managed by a medical librarian. Hospital librarians are organized in the Hospital Libraries Section of the Medical Library Association.

Host : A node that is typically the source and a destination of IP traffic. Hosts silently discard received packets that are not addressed to an IP address of the host.

Host Route : A route to a specific IP address. Host routes allow packets to be routed on a per-IP address basis. For IPv4 host routes, the route prefix is a specific IPv4 address with a 32-bit prefix length. For IPv6 host routes, the route prefix is a specific IPv6 address with a 128-bit prefix length.

HTML : HTML is a programming language used to create Web pages. The acronym stands for Hypertext Markup Language.

Huntington Library : Located in San Marino, California, the Huntington Library is one of the world's leading libraries of Americana and English literature, surpassed only by the British Library and the Bodleian. Its collections include over 5 million manuscripts, rare books, reference works, and other materials on Anglo-American history, literature and the arts, the history of science, and maritime history. The library includes a conservation center, exhibition hall, art collection, and botanical gardens.

Click here to connect to the homepage of the Huntington Library.

Hypertext : Transparent linkage of textual documents to other related documents on the World Wide Web.

Hypertext Transfer Protocol (HTTP) : The communications protocol used in Web browser software to establish the connection between a client computer and a remote Web server, making it possible for data files in HTML format to be transmitted over the Internet from the server to the client machine on which the browser is installed. Most Web browsers are designed to default to **http://** whenever a user enters a Web address (URL) without the protocol.

ICMP : See Internet Control Message Protocol.

iconic document : A publication or other document in which the content is presented in predominantly graphic or pictorial form. Examples include atlases, children's picture books, exhibition catalogs, visual dictionaries, posters, postcards, etc.

IEEE : Institute of Electrical and Electronics Engineers.

IEEE 802 Address : A 48-bit link-layer address defined by the IEEE. Ethernet and Token Ring network adapters use IEEE 802 addresses.

IGMP : See Internet Group Management Protocol.

Illegal Address : A duplicate address that conflicts with a public IPv4 address that the ICANN has already assigned to another organization.

Image Permanence Institute (IPI) : Founded in 1985 through the combined efforts of the Rochester Institute of Technology and the Society for Imaging Science and Technology, IPI is a university-based nonprofit laboratory devoted to scientific research in the preservation of visual and other forms of recorded information. IPI studies the effects of light, temperature, humidity, pollutants, and other factors on imaging materials (film, videotape, optical disks, etc.). The Institute developed the Photographic Activity Test (PAT), a worldwide standard (ISO 14523) for archival quality in photographic enclosures. Click here to connect to the IPI homepage.

in print : A book currently available from the publisher, either as a frontlist or backlist title, as opposed to a title no longer available. Books currently in print in the United States are listed annually in *Books in Print, Children's Books in Print*, and *El-Hi Textbooks & Serials in Print*. The opposite of out of print.

in Transit : If an item has been returned to the library, but has not been re-shelved in its call number location, the catalog will indicate the items status as In Transit. If patrons need In Transit items immediately, they may inquire at the circulation desk.

inactive records : Records no longer required by an agency or individual in the daily conduct of business or affairs, which may be placed in intermediate storage, transferred to archival custody, destroyed, or disposed of in some other way without affecting normal operations. The opposite of active records. Synonymous with *nonactive records. See also*: intermediate records.

independent librarian : A provider of library services who works outside traditional library settings, for example, an information broker who works from a home office. Independent librarians are organized in the Independent Librarian's Exchange (ILEX), a section of the Association of Specialized and Cooperative Library Agencies (ASCLA) of the American Library Association (ALA). Also used synonymously with solo librarian. Recently, the term has been used in reference to Cubans who, in response to Fidel Castro's 1998 announcement that there are no prohibited books in Cuba (only books that no one had the money to buy), began lending banned materials from their homes. The following year, human rights activists in the United States formed the group Friends of Cuban Libraries to oppose the intimidation and arrest of "independent librarians" in Cuba, including confiscation of their book collections, and began lobbying the ALA in support of the position that intellectual freedom was at issue. After hearing arguments on both sides of the controversy at its January 2001 meeting, the International Relations Committee (IRC) of the ALA issued a report recommending that no action be taken, based on information that the Cubans suffering persecution were not librarians but political dissidents supported by anti-Castro groups.

Independent Librarian's Exchange (ILEX) : The section of the Association of Specialized and Cooperative Library Agencies (ASCLA) within the American Library Association (ALA) that seeks to expand the definition of librarianship by supporting ALA members who work outside traditional library settings and by providing programs, information exchange, and networking opportunities for them. Click here to connect to the ILEX homepage. *See also*: solo librarian.

Independent Media Arts Preservation (IMAP) : Established in 1999 with the assistance of New York State Council on the Arts (NYSCA) and Electronic Arts Intermix (EAI), IMAP is a nonprofit service, education, and advocacy organization committed to the preservation of non-commercial electronic media. IMAP provides archivists, artists, conservators, curators, librarians, media makers, producers, distributors, scholars, and other professionals with accessible solutions to facilitate the documentation and preservation of media collections (audio, video, film, etc.). IMAP?s Cataloging Template and online tutorial is a standards-based tool for cataloging media collections, created specifically for individuals without professional training in archival management and information science, but is also useful to archivists and librarians affiliated with institutions. Click here to connect to the IMAP homepage.

index : An index is a tool used to locate information such as JOURNAL and newspaper articles (and sometimes books or book chapters). Some indexes are general, covering many topic areas, others cover only one topic but in great depth. Indexes can be in online or paper format. Generally a person searches the index using subject words, AUTHOR'S name or words from the title. The index may retrieve a list of CITATIONS (the information necessary to find the item such as dates and page numbers) or it may retrieve the actual text of the resource.

Indirect Delivery : The delivery of an IP packet by an IP node to an intermediate router.

Information and Communication Technology (ICT) Literacy Assessment : A scenario-based test under development by the Educational Testing Service (ETS) to measure a student's cognitive and technical ability to find and evaluate information on the Internet. Because computer skills are a fundamental predictor of how well a student is prepared to handle college-level studies, one of the primary goals of the ICT test is to identify at-risk students before they enter college. Institutions of higher education may also use the test to improve retention by weeding out applicants who are unprepared. Click here to learn more from ETS.

information literacy (IL) : Skill in finding the information one needs, including an understanding of how libraries are organized, familiarity with the resources they provide (including information formats and automated search tools), and knowledge of commonly used research techniques. The concept also includes the skills required to critically evaluate information content and employ it effectively, as well as an understanding of the technological infrastructure on which information transmission is based, including its social, political, and cultural context and impact. Click here to connect to the Web site on information literacy maintained by the Association of College and Research Libraries (ACRL) or try *Information Literacy on the WWW*, a site maintained by the Florida International University Libraries. Synonymous with *information skills*. Compare with computer literacy and media literacy. *See also*: bibliographic instruction and Institute for Information Literacy.

initial letter : A large capital letter at the beginning of the first word of a paragraph, chapter, or other division of a text. In medieval manuscripts and early printed books, initial letters were often decorated or illuminated, for example, the "B" at the beginning of the text of a psalter (the first letter of *Beatus*, the first word of the first Psalm). Click here to see a large historiated example in a 13th-century Gallican psalter (*Leaves of Gold*) and here to see a delicately gilded 14th-century example (Koninklijke Bibliotheek). Size of letter and amount of decoration indicate the relative significance of the division within the text, with gradations measured in number of lines (height). Initials of varying size can be seen on a page of the *Murthly Hours* (National Library of Scotland). In manuscripts and incunabula, large initial letters were inserted by a rubricator or illuminator in spaces left blank when the sheets were hand-copied or printed. Other examples can be seen by paging through the *Burnet Psalter* (University of Aberdeen).

Institute of Certified Records Managers (ICRM) : An independent nonprofit organization established in 1975 to meet the need for standards by which the experience and capabilities of persons involved in records and information management can be measured, accredited, and recognized according to criteria recognized by their peers. ICRM develops and administers a program of professional certification of records managers that includes examinations and a certification maintenance program. Click here to connect to the ICRM homepage.

Institute of Museum and Library Services (IMLS) : An independent federal grant-making agency created under the Museum and Library Services Act of 1996 to foster leadership, innovation, and lifelong learning by supporting museums, archives, and libraries of all types and by encouraging partnerships among them. IMLS administers four grant-in-aid programs for libraries, including LSTA grants to state library agencies. IMLS publishes the monthly e-mail newsletter *Primary Source*. A report on the library programs of the IMLS is published in *The Bowker Annual Library and Book Trade Almanac*. Click here to connect to the IMLS homepage. *See also*: National Awards for Museum and Library Service.

Integrated Tool for Selection and Ordering (ITSO) : Software developed at the Cornell University Library (CUL) to consolidate into a single interface the new title information provided weekly by multiple book vendor Web systems for electronic selection and acquisitions. Developed in response to the move by the Library of Congress Alert

Service from paper to electronic notification, ITSO also serves as a source of precatalog records. Incoming records are matched at initial load against the OPAC using LCCN and ISBN to detect duplicates. Once the record is available in ITSO, the selector can click to perform an automatic author, title, or subject search in the OPAC. To learn more about ITSO, see "Many Vendors, One Face: Acquisitions' Next Wave," an interview with the developers by Rick Lugg and Ruth Fischer in the Summer 2005 issue of the *Netconnect* supplement to *Library Journal*.

Intellectual property : Intellectual property refers to creations of the mind : inventions, literary and artistic works, and symbols, names, images, and designs used in commerce. Intellectual property is divided into two categories : Industrial property, which includes inventions (patents), trademarks, industrial designs, and geographic indications of source; and Copyright, which includes literary and artistic works such as novels, poems and plays, films, musical works, drawings, paintings, photographs and sculptures, and architectural designs. More information is available from the World Intellectual Property Organization.

Interface : The representation of a physical or logical attachment of a node to a subnet. An example of a physical interface is a network adapter. An example of a logical interface is a tunnel interface that is used to send IPv6 packets across an IPv4 network.

Interlibrary Loan : Interlibrary loan is a form of resource sharing among libraries nation-and world-wide. When a book or other item needed by a Cornell user is checked out, unavailable for some other reason, or not owned by the library, a patron may request that it be borrowed from another library by submitting an interlibrary loan request form.

interLibrary loan : Sometimes referred to as ILL, InterLibrary Loan is a way libraries share resources for their users. When a title you want is not available at your library, you can fill out an InterLibrary Loan request online. Books, Dissertations, Government Reports, Proceedings,

Journal Articles and other materials may be borrowed. Keep in mind that items you receive through ILL, such as journal articles, may be photocopies of originals. Please allow two weeks for your request to arrive. The InterLibrary Loan office is located on the first floor of Jernigan Library.

International Association of School Librarianship (IASL) : Founded in 1971, IASL provides an international forum for the promotion of effective school library media programs as instruments in the educational process, and guidance and advice in the development of school library programs and the school library profession. Its membership includes school librarians and teachers, consultants, educational administrators, and others responsible for library and information services in schools, as well as professors and instructors at universities and colleges offering programs for school librarians, and students enrolled in such programs. IASL sponsors an annual conference and publishes the semiannual journal *School Libraries Worldwide* and the *IASL Newsletter* three times per year. Click here to connect to the IASL homepage.

International Association of Social Science Information Service and Technology (IASSIST) : An international organization of professionals working with information technology and data services to support research and teaching in the social sciences, IASSIST seeks to (1) to foster and promote excellence in data service delivery, (2) advance infrastructure in the social sciences, and (3) provide opportunities for collegial exchange of sound professional practices. Its 200 members work in a variety of settings, including data archives, statistical agencies, research centers, libraries, academic departments, government departments, and nonprofit organizations. Click here to connect to the IASSIST homepage.

International Association of Sound and Audiovisual Archives (IASA) : Founded in Amsterdam in 1969 as a forum for international cooperation between archives that preserve recorded sound and audiovisual documents, IASA supports information exchange and fosters international cooperation between audiovisual archives in all fields, especially in the areas of acquisition and exchange, documentation and metadata, resource discovery and access, copyright and ethics, conservation and preservation, and research and publication. IASA sponsors an annual conference and publishes the semiannual *IASA Journal*. Click here to connect to the IASA homepage.

International Association of Technological University Libraries (IATUL) : Founded in Germany in 1955, IATUL provides an international forum for the exchange of ideas pertinent to librarianship in technological universities and the discussion of opportunities for collaboration in the solution of common problems. Its member libraries are represented by their directors and senior managers. IATUL publishes the quarterly newsletter *IATUL News*. Click here to connect to the IATUL homepage.

International Federation of Library Associations and Institutions (IFLA) : An independent international nongovernmental association of library associations, libraries and related institutions, sponsors, and individuals, IFLA was founded in 1927 by 15 countries as the International Library and Bibliographical Committee to promote global cooperation, communication, and research in library science and librarianship. With association and institutional members in over 130 countries, IFLA has a democratic structure in which a general assembly of members (the Council) is the highest governing organ. The organization maintains a Secretariat headed by a Secretary-General in The Hague and sponsors an annual conference, the World Library and Information Congress, in a different member country each year. Click here to connect to the IFLA homepage.

International League of Antiquarian Booksellers (ILAB) : An organization encompassing 20 national associations representing antiquarian booksellers in 30 countries, ILAB was founded in Amsterdam in 1947 to uphold and improve professional standards in the antiquarian book trade, promote honorable conduct in business, and contribute to a broader appreciation of the art and history of the book. Click here to connect to the ILAB homepage.

International Literary Market Place (ILMP) : A directory of the international book publishing industry issued annually by R.R. Bowker, *ILMP* provides information on publishers, literary agents, book manufacturing, book clubs and dealers, major libraries and library associations, and literary associations, periodicals, and awards for over 180 countries. The directory also includes an industry yellow pages. The most recent edition of *ILMP* is usually shelved in the reference section of large academic and public libraries. *See also*: *Literary Market Place*.

International Serials Data System (ISDS) : An intergovernmental network established under the auspices of UNESCO to develop and maintain an international registry of serial publications containing the information necessary for identification and bibliographic control, including the International Standard Serial Number (ISSN) and key title. The ISSN center for the United States is the National Serials Data Program (NSDP) administered by the Library of Congress. Click here to connect to the Web site maintained by the ISSN International Centre in Paris, France.

internet : The Internet is the infrastructure including a worldwide network of computers which allows a local computer to access information from other computers around the world. People often use the terms Internet and WWW interchangeably; however, the World Wide Web is only one part of the Internet.

Internet Control Message Protocol (ICMP) : A protocol in the IPv4 Internet layer that reports errors and provides troubleshooting facilities.

Internet Control Message Protocol for IPv6 (ICMPv6) : A protocol in the IPv6 Internet layer that reports errors, provides troubleshooting facilities, and hosts ND and MLD messages.

Internet Group Management Protocol (IGMP) : A protocol in the IPv4 Internet layer that manages multicast group membership on a subnet.

Internet Protocol (IP) : For IPv4, a routable protocol in the IPv4 Internet layer that addresses, routes, fragments, and reassembles IPv4 packets. Also used to denote both IPv4 and IPv6 sets of protocols.

IP : Features or attributes that apply to both IPv4 and IPv6. For example, an IP address is either an IPv4 address or an IPv6 address.

IPv4 : The Internet layer in widespread use on the Internet and on private intranets. Another term for IP.

IPv6 : The Internet layer protocols of the TCP/IP protocol suite as defined in RFC 2460. IPv6 is gaining acceptance today.

ISBN : This acronym stands for "International Standard Book Number." ISBN's are unique to each edition of a title and consist of ten digits, thus identifying the exact title. Book stores and libraries often use ISBN's to order and track titles. Some countries do not use ISBN's.

ISSN : This acronym stands for "International Standard Serial Number." Each ISSN is a unique eight digit code that identifies a specific serial title. (Serials are items published on a continuing, regular basis.)

jeweled binding : A binding in which the boards are covered in designs done in gold or silver inset with ivory and/or precious or semiprecious stones, usually with a similarly decorated clasp to keep the leaves pressed firmly together. During the Middle Ages, this style was used for liturgical and devotional books commissioned by the Catholic Church and by members of the nobility from the 6th century on. The lavish use of costly materials was considered an act of religious piety rather than ostentation, and the colors of the gems often had symbolic significance. Extremely valuable, the rare survivals are sold by the world's most prestigious auction houses. Click here to view the jeweled binding on the *Lindisfarne Gospels* and here to see the repoussé gold and jeweled front cover of the *Lindau Gospels*. Click here to see an 11th-century Iberian example (Metropolitan Museum of Art). Jeweled binding underwent a revival in the late 19th and early 20th centuries. Click here to see a 19th-century example (Ransom Center, University of Texas at Austin) and here to see a 20th-century example on a copy of the *Rubaiyat of Omar Khayyam* (Princeton University Library). Compare with treasure binding.

job rotation : The systematic movement of employees from one job to another within an organization or between organizations, usually to a new position for a fixed period of time and then back to the former position. Uncommon in libraries, the practice has been tried with veteran librarians in both public and academic libraries. Participants report that the voluntary experience can provide a broader perspective on the profession, clarify job content and process, lead to improvements in procedures and collections, enhance capacity to cope with change, provide networking opportunities, and renew commitment. Rotation can be particularly rewarding for employees at risk of stagnation because their careers have reached a plateau. Disadvantages include temporary loss of productivity and increased stress for co-workers. Planning can mitigate negative effects. Compare with job sharing.

joint author : In *AACR2*, a person who collaborates with one or more others to produce a work in which all who contribute perform the same function. The contributions of the individual collaborators may not be indicated and are usually not separable. In cataloging, main entry is made under the name of the author listed first on the chief source of information (the primary author), with added entries for the other authors, unless primary responsibility clearly rests with one author. Bibliographic style manuals differ in the maximum number of joint authors included in a citation. Synonymous with *coauthor*. Compare with composite work. *See also*: et al. and shared responsibility.

Joint Committee on Printing (JCP) : The congressional committee responsible under *Title 44 U.S.C.* for overseeing the functions of the U.S. Government Printing Office (GPO) and general printing procedures of the federal government. The Committee includes members of the Senate and House of Representatives from both political parties. Click here to connect to the JCP homepage.

joint publication : Publication (by prior agreement) of the same work by two different publishers in separate editions, often in hardcover by a university press and in paperback by a trade publisher. Compare with co-edition. *See also*: simultaneous publication.

journal : A journal is a periodical (or serial) which publishes peer-reviewed articles written by scholars in a specific field. Journals are quite different from popular magazines, which contain articles which, while they have gone through the editorial process, have not gone through a peer-review process. Journal articles tend to look different than magazine articles : they are longer, often with statistical data in the form of charts, graphs or tables, usually have extensive footnotes and/or bibliographies and often contain little or no advertising.

journal of commentary : A periodical that specializes in the publication of news analysis and discussion of political, social, and cultural issues, usually from an editorial position somewhere on the political spectrum, for example, the *National Review* on the Right and *The Progressive* on the Left. Journals of commentary are usually issued monthly and sold at newsstands, in bookstores, and by subscription. Compare with journal and magazine.

keynote address : A formal speech delivered at the beginning or on the first day of a library conference, often by a prominent person in or from outside the profession, usually on a topic related to the overall theme of the conference. The keynote address is intended to stimulate thought and set the tone for subsequent discussion.

keyword searching : In our online catalog (OASIS) and in most electronic databases available through Jernigan Library, users have the option to search for materials by keyword. These are descriptive words that relate to the specific topic forwhich you need material. The online catalog or database which you are using will retrieve all records which contain the words you enter in any field, (i.e. title field, subject heading field, etc.) Sometimes keyword searches yield too many results. When this is the case, you may have the option to use Boolean Operators to limit your search results.

labeling : The controversial practice of affixing a warning mark or label to library materials considered unsuitable for young children or that contain language or images that some readers or viewers might find offensive or distressing. The practice is followed by some public television stations in the United States when programs containing adult language or graphic images of sex and/or violence are broadcast at times when children are likely to be watching. *See also*: content rating.

Lambda Literary Awards : A series of literary awards given annually by the Lambda Literary Foundation in recognition of the best in lesbian, gay, bisexual and transgender (LGBT) literature. A panel of judges selected to represent the diversity of the LGBT literary community determines the finalists in over 20 categories, including lesbian fiction, gay men's fiction, lesbian poetry, gay men's poetry, lesbian mystery, gay men's mystery, drama, fiction anthology, nonfiction anthology, memoir/autobiography, biography, children/young adult, erotica, humor, romance, science fiction/fantasy, transgender/genderqueer, and so on. Also known as *Lammys*. Click here to connect to the official homepage of the Lambda Literary Awards to see lists of past winners.

LAN segment : A portion of a subnet that consists of a single medium that is bounded by bridges or Layer 2 switches.

last copy : A book or other item in a library collection, of which no copy is owned by any other library, often an older title lost or weeded by all libraries save one. The uniqueness of last copies makes them a preservation priority. In January 2005, the *WorldCat* bibliographic database maintained by OCLC contained 24 million records for items held by a single OCLC member library. For more on this subject, see the article "Last Copies: What's at Risk?" by Lynn Connaway, Edward O'Neill, and Chandra Prabha in the July 2006 issue of *College & Research Libraries*.

law library : A type of special library with a collection consisting primarily of materials for legal research and study, including case law, federal and state statutes, international legal agreements, treatises, reference works, legal periodicals, and electronic search tools (see this example). A law library maintained by a court, law school, or legal firm is normally managed by a *law librarian* who may hold a J.D. degree in addition to the M.L.S. or M.L.I.S. *See also*: American Association of Law Libraries.

leaf book : A book written about another book, with a leaf from the subject volume included (adapted from Jane Greenfield's *ABC of Bookbinding*, Oak Knoll/Lyons Press, 1998).

learning management system (LMS) : An integrated set of online applications providing access to course assignments and materials, tests and test results, e-discussion and chat space, and other features in support of education, particularly in colleges and universities. Learning management systems offer some functions that overlap with library systems, such as the provision of electronic reserves, and their content may overlap with that delivered through library portals.

learning resources center (LRC) : Synonymous in the United States with school library.

lending library : A library or other institution that sends materials on request to another library, usually via interlibrary loan. Compare with borrowing library. *See also*: net lender.

librarian : A professionally trained person responsible for the care of a library and its contents, including the selection, processing, and organization of materials and the delivery of information, instruction, and loan services to meet the needs of its users (to see examples, try a keyword search on the term in *Google Image Search*). In the online environment, the role of the librarian is to manage and mediate access to information that may exist only in electronic form. In the United States, the title is reserved for persons who have been awarded the M.L.S. or M.L.I.S. degree, or certified as professionals by a state agency. Also refers to the person responsible for the overall administration of a library or library system, synonymous in this sense with library director. Classified by functional specialization (acquisitions librarian, cataloger, instruction librarian, reference librarian, serials librarian, systems librarian, etc.), librarians in the United States are organized in the American Library Association (ALA) and its affiliates and the Special Libraries Association (SLA). Compare with support staff. *See also*: Librarian of Congress, renaissance librarian, scholar-librarian, and solo librarian.

Librarian of Congress : An office created in 1802, two years after the Library of Congress was established, for which no qualifications were specified. The position is filled by presidential appointment for no fixed term. In 1897, the Senate acquired the power to approve the president's nomination, and the Librarian of Congress was given the authority to appoint the staff of the Library of Congress and to establish its rules and regulations. In the 20th century, a precedent was established for appointing the Librarian of Congress for life. Click here for biographical information about the Americans who have served as Librarian of Congress since the office was created.

librariana : A catch-all term for the body of information, works, and memorabilia that has accumulated on the subject of libraries, librarians, and related topics, particularly items of historical interest. Click here to browse a collection of librariana, courtesy of The Library History Buff. *See also*: Molesworth Institute.

librarianship : The profession devoted to applying theory and technology to the creation, selection, organization, management, preservation, dissemination, and utilization of collections of information in all formats. In the United States, often used synonymously with library science. A person formally trained or certified to perform such services is a librarian. Librarianship is a very old profession. The founder and organizer of the great classical library at Alexandria (c. 300 B.C.) was Demetrius of Phaleron. The ancient Egyptians and Babylonians probably had librarians to organize and preserve their extensive collections of papyrus scrolls and clay tablets. *See also*: comparative librarianship.

Libraries Serving Special Populations Section (LSSPS): The section of the Association of Specialized and Cooperative

Library Agencies (ASCLA) within the American Library Association (ALA) whose members are committed to improving the quality of library service for people with special needs, including users who (1) are elderly; (2) have vision, hearing, mobility, or developmental impairments; and/or (3) are in correctional institutions, health care facilities, and other types of institutions. LSSPS is also committed to improving library service for families and professionals working with people who have special needs. Click here to connect to the LSSPS homepage.

library : From the Latin *liber*, meaning "book." In Greek and the Romance languages, the corresponding term is *bibliotheca*. A collection or group of collections of books and/or other print or nonprint materials organized and maintained for use (reading, consultation, study, research, etc.). Institutional libraries, organized to facilitate access by a specific clientele, are staffed by librarians and other personnel trained to provide services to meet user needs. By extension, the room, building, or facility that houses such a collection, usually but not necessarily built for that purpose. Directory information on libraries is available alphabetically by country in *World Guide to Libraries*, a serial published by K.G. Saur. Two comprehensive worldwide online directories of library homepages are *LibDex* and *Libweb*. See also the UNESCO Libraries Portal. Abbreviated *lib. See also*: academic library, government library, monastic library, new library, proto-library, public library, special library, and subscription library.

library administration : The control and supervision of a library or library system, including planning, budgeting, policymaking, personnel management, public relations, and program assessment, with responsibility for results. Also refers collectively to the persons responsible for managing a library, usually a board of trustees or dean, library director, and his or her immediate staff. *See also*: Library Administration and Management Association.

Library Administration and Management Association (LAMA) : A division of the American Library Association

(ALA) founded in 1957, LAMA has a membership consisting of library directors and persons with an interest in improving the quality of administration and management in libraries of all types. LAMA publishes the quarterly journal *Library Administration & Management (LA&M)*. Click here to connect to the LAMA homepage.

library advisory committee : A standing committee at an academic institution, composed of members of the teaching faculty, library professionals, and students who have an interest in library services, charged with advising the library administration on policies and decisions affecting teaching and learning, such as library hours and the allocation of funds to academic departments for new acquisitions, and with acting as library advocates in institution-wide decision-making (see this example). Not all colleges and universities have such a committee. Synonymous with *faculty library advisory committee*.

library advocate : A person who appreciates libraries and their role in society to the extent of speaking and acting publicly in their support, especially when funding and the freedom to read are at stake. The American Library Association takes an active role in training library advocates by maintaining an Issues and Advocacy section at its Web site. The Advocacy Institute offers workshops on advocacy skills and strategies at the annual and midwinter ALA conferences. *See also*: Friends of the Library, library trustee, and National Library Legislative Day.

Library and Archives Canada/Bibliothèque et Archives Canada : The combined national library and national archives of Canada, established in 2002 by the merger of the National Library of Canada (NLC/NIC) and the National Archives of Canada. Located in Ottawa, the new institution is charged with acquiring, preserving, and facilitating access to the documentary heritage of Canada in all its forms for present and future generations of Canadians. Its collections are focused primarily on Canadiana (works written by, about, or of interest to Canadians, published in Canada or abroad). Click here to connect to the Library and Archives Canada homepage. *See also*: *Canadiana*.

Library and Information Science Abstracts (LISA) : An abstracting and indexing service devoted to the literature of library science and information science, published quarterly from 1950 to 1968 under the title *Library Science Abstracts*, and bimonthly from 1969 to 1982 and monthly since 1982 under the current title, by the Library Association of Great Britain. Available online from R.R. Bowker, *LISA* provides abstracts of articles from over 500 periodicals published in 68 countries, as well as papers from major English-language conference proceedings, updated biweekly. ISSN: 0024-2179. *See also*: *Library Literature & Information Science*.

Library and Information Technology Association (LITA) : A division of the American Library Association (ALA) since in 1966, LITA has a membership of librarians and other information professionals concerned with all aspects of the acquisition, organization, storage, retrieval, and dissemination of information in electronic formats, including digital libraries, metadata, authorization and authentication, electronic journals and electronic publishing, telecommunications, networks, computer security and intellectual property rights, technical standards, online catalogs and bibliographic databases, optical information systems, desktop applications, software engineering, etc. LITA publishes the quarterly journal *Information Technology and Libraries (ITAL)* and the *LITA Newsletter*. Click here to connect to the LITA homepage.

Library Annex : The Library Annex is a storage facility for lesser-used materials from the collections of CUL. Materials held in the Annex can be delivered to any of the libraries on campus or used in the Annex reading room. Annex requests can be made through the online catalog, through the link Annex Requests available under the Circulation Services section of the Library Gateway, or at any circulation desk on campus.

library anxiety : Confusion, fear, and frustration felt by a library user, especially someone lacking experience, when faced with the need to find information in a library. Among college and university students, library anxiety may be one cause of academic procrastination. The first formal study of this phenomenon was conducted by Constance Mellon in the mid-1980s using qualitative methods. In 1992, Sharon Bostick developed the Library Anxiety Scale (LAS) to quantitatively measure: (1) barriers with library staff, (2) affective barriers, (3) comfort with the library, (4) knowledge of the library, and (5) mechanical barriers. In 2001, Doris Van Kampen developed the Multidimensional Library Anxiety Scale (MLAS) to reflect changes in information theory and search methods. The new questionnaire instrument was successfully pilot-tested on doctoral students in 2002. For more information, see Van Kampen's article in the January 2004 issue of *College & Research Libraries.*

library architect : An architectural firm that specializes in the design of structures for housing libraries. Because most library buildings are intended to be permanent and their physical appearance makes a statement about the institution or community they serve, the selection of an architect is an important decision in planning new construction or renovation. A directory of architects with experience in the design of libraries is included in the annual *Buyer's Guide* supplement to *Library Journal*, published each December. Since 1963, the American Institute of Architects and the Library Administration and Management Association (LAMA) of the American Library Association (ALA) have jointly sponsored biennial awards for distinguished accomplishment in library architecture by an American architect without regard to location or library type. The award-winning structures are shown in the April issue of *American Libraries*, which features new and renovated library facilities in the United States.

Library Association (LA) : Founded in 1877, LA is the leading library association in the United Kingdom, with a membership of 25,000 librarians and other information professionals, approximately 5.5 percent of whom are employed overseas. Divided into 12 geographic branches and over 20 special interest groups with headquarters in London, LA publishes the monthly journal *Library Association Record*. Its publishing arm, Library Association Publishing Limited (LAPL), issues approximately 30 new titles each year and maintains a backlist of over 200 titles. In April 2002, LA merged with the Institute of Information Scientists (IIS) to form the Chartered Institute of Library and Information Professionals (CILIP). Click here to connect to the CILIP homepage.

library association : A membership organization consisting of a group of librarians, library directors, and other persons involved with libraries who meet periodically to discuss matters of professional interest. Library associations represent the interests of their members, sponsor conferences, elect officers, select committees to address specific issues, publish newsletters and professional journals, and charge dues to support the organization's activities. The largest library association in the United States is the American Library Association (ALA). Its counterparts in Canada and Great Britain are the (CLA) and the Chartered Institute of Library and Information Professionals (CILIP). The major library and information industry associations of the United States and Canada are listed in *The Bowker Annual Library and Book Trade Almanac*, which also provides information about international library associations and a list of regional and national library associations around the world. The ALA provides an online list of Library Associations Around the World. Library associations are organized in the International Federation of Library Associations and Institutions (IFLA). *See also*: American Society for Information Science and Technology and Special Libraries Association.

library automation : The design and implementation of ever more sophisticated computer systems to accomplish tasks originally done by hand in libraries. Beginning in the 1960s with the development of the machine-readable catalog record (MARC), the process of automation has expanded to include the core functions of acquisitions, cataloging and authority control, serials control, circulation and inventory, and interlibrary loan and document delivery. The library automation field is currently dominated by a handful of systems vendors (Auto-Graphics, Brodart, EOS International, Ex Libris, Follett, Innovative Interfaces, Polaris Library Systems, SirsiDynix, TLC, and VTLS). Recent trends in library automation include the growing importance of "add-ons" mostly related to the delivery of digital content (link resolvers, portal and metasearch interfaces, and e-resource management modules often provided by third-party vendors), better integration with the Web environment (rewriting fat PC clients as browser applications, using XML and style sheets for display, and developing XML import and export capabilities) and for academic libraries, closer integration of library systems with learning management systems.

library award : Special recognition given to an individual, group, or library in honor of outstanding achievement and/or distinguished service to the profession. Major awards given annually often include a monetary prize funded by an individual or corporate donor or by a library association. Recipients of library awards and scholarships are listed in the *The Bowker Annual Library and Book Trade Almanac*. A less extensive list is provided in the *American Library Directory*. Click here to see a list of awards and scholarships in the ALA Awards Program.

Library Awareness Program : An attempt by the FBI to recruit librarians in the United States as "cold warriors" during the 1970s and 1980s by suggesting that they restrict public access to unclassified scientific research, particularly information available from the National Technical Information Service (NTIS). Librarians were asked to report on individuals requesting certain categories of scientific information, especially foreign nationals from countries in the Soviet Union. The FBI had the support of the National Commission on Libraries and Information Science (NCLIS) in this effort, which undermined the confidentiality of library lending records and open access to library resources. In *Free Expression and Censorship* *in America: An Encyclopedia* (Greenwood, 1997), Herbert Foerstel writes that the FBI conducted a 16-month investigation of librarians who openly opposed the Library Awareness Program, even accusing them of being dupes of the Soviet Union. The program was also opposed by the American Association of University Professors (AAUP), the American Federation of Teachers (AFT), and other organizations. In response to public indignation, many state legislatures passed statutes making it illegal for any librarian to reveal library records or patron requests without a court order. For more information, see *Surveillance in the Stacks: The FBI's Library Awareness Program* by Herbert Foerstel (Greenwood Press, 1991). *See also*: *USA Patriot Act*.

library binder : A commercial binder that specializes in serving the needs of libraries. Many libraries regularly send their periodical back files to a library binder to be bound into annual volumes. Special binding may also be needed for heavily used items and trade paperbacks. Library binders are organized in the Library Binding Institute. *See also*: library binding.

library binding : An especially strong, durable binding used for periodical back files and for rebinding worn volumes and new paperbound publications for which circulation is expected to remain high over a comparatively long period, usually more expensive than the standard publisher's binding (click here and here to see examples). Includes prelibrary binding. The ANSI standard for library binding, established by the American Library Association (ALA) and the Library Binding Institute (LBI), requires that a book have a spine glued with polyvinyl acetate adhesive, strong endpapers, reinforced hinges, and boards covered in buckram coated or impregnated with nonmigratory resin. Click here to read the full-text of *ANSI/NISO Z39.78-2000 Library Binding*, courtesy of Conservation OnLine (CoOL). Compare with library edition. *See also*: Library Binding Institute and oversewing.

Library Binding Institute (LBI) : A trade association of commercial library binders doing business in the United

States, Canada, and the United Kingdom, LBI was established in 1935 to create and maintain standards for library rebinding and prebinding, improve binding methods, and facilitate cooperation between library binders and between binders and their customers. Membership is also open to suppliers of library binders and organizations with an interest in the preservation of books and periodicals. LBI developed the ANSI standard for library binding in cooperation with the American Library Association (ALA). The Institute publishes the magazine *The New Library Scene* and technical papers on binding and related topics. Click here connect to the LBI homepage.

library bond : An interest-bearing or discounted security issued by a library district, or by the government entity of which a library or library system is a part, usually to finance the construction and/or renovation of facilities or some other major capital project. A bond places the library district under a general obligation to pay the bondholder (investor) a specified amount of interest, usually at regular intervals, and to repay the principal amount of the loan within a designated period of time. The bond is backed by a majority of voters in the district, who consent to be taxed at a slightly higher rate to raise sufficient revenue to pay the interest and principal on the loan. Bond measures pass more easily in times of prosperity than in economic recession.

library book : A book that is the property of a library, usually bearing an ownership mark and labeling. Library books allowed to circulate are usually barcoded, with a date due slip attached inside the cover. Some are given a more sturdy binding than the trade edition, or a plastic sleeve to protect the dust jacket and cover. A book no longer owned by a library is usually stamped "discarded" or "withdrawn." Some libraries sell their discards in an annual or continuing book sale, usually as reading copies. *See also*: ex-library copy.

library card : A small paper or plastic card issued by a library in the name of a registered borrower, to be presented at the circulation desk when checking out materials from its collections. Identification is usually required of new applicants. In most libraries in the United States, library cards are barcoded for electronic circulation (see this example). Periodic renewal may be required to verify contact information (current street address and telephone number). Synonymous with *borrower card. See also*: library card campaign and patron ID.

library card campaign : An organized publicity effort conducted by a public library or library system over a finite period of time aimed at encouraging the adult and juvenile residents of the district or area served to become registered borrowers and active library users. Successful library card campaigns have been conducted in many communities in the United States, sometimes in conjunction with National Library Week. Collateral benefits often include increased visibility and enhancement of the library's image in the community. For more information, see *Running a Successful Library Card Campaign: A How-to-Do-It Manual* by Patrick Jones (Neal-Schuman, 2002).

library closure : The closing of a library or branch in a library system, temporarily or permanently, usually due to budgetary constraints or demographic changes in the area served. Library closings are announced in the news section of *American Libraries*, the monthly magazine of the American Library Association (ALA).

library collection : The total accumulation of books and other materials owned by a library, cataloged and arranged for ease of access, often consisting of several smaller collections (reference, circulating books, serials, government documents, rare books, special collections, etc.). The process of building a library collection over an extended period of time is called collection development. Synonymous with holdings. Compare with collection. *See also*: digital collection, high-risk collection, hybrid collection, opening day collection, rental collection, subject collection, and test collection.

library conference : A formal gathering of librarians, library directors, and others associated with libraries for the purpose of meeting colleagues, discussing issues and events, and learning about new products, services, technologies, and recent developments in the library science and information science profession. Most library associations sponsor regular conferences at which officers are elected, committees and task forces organized, policies formulated, awards announced, etc. *Conferees* are generally charged a registration fee based on the sections of the conference they plan to attend. *See also*: preconference and proceedings. The American Library Association sponsors a national conference during the summer and a midwinter meeting in different cities each year. The state chapters of the ALA. and some of its major divisions, sponsor their own conferences, as does the Special Libraries Association (SLA) and ASIST. The permanent round tables of the ALA convene concurrently with the national conferences. Library conferences are listed online in the *Librarian's Datebook* and in Douglas Hasty's *Library Conference Planner*

library cooperation : Methods by which libraries and library systems work together for the mutual benefit of their users, including centralized processing, cooperative cataloging, international exchange of bibliographic information, union catalogs, resource sharing, etc.

library director : The person who has overall responsibility for supervising the operations of a library or library system, including planning, budgeting, policymaking, personnel management, and program assessment. In public libraries, the library director is usually subject to the oversight of a board of trustees; in academic libraries, by a dean of academic affairs or provost. *See also*: library administration and Library Administration and Management Association.

library discount : A discount off the list price of a book or other publication, given by most publishers and jobbers on purchases made by an institutional library. Most publishers offer a flat rate, usually 5-10 percent. Jobbers may link the discount rate to size of order or volume of purchasing. As a general rule, specialized titles are given a shorter discount than trade books or not discounted at all because of their limited sales potential.

library district : An officially delineated geographic area in which the residents decide by popular vote whether to provide tax support for a public library or library system, or one of the geographical areas into which a state is divided for the purpose of administering libraries in accordance with a comprehensive statewide tax plan. *See also*: service area.

library edition : An edition, often of a children's book, published in a binding stronger and more durable than the usual publisher's binding, for marketing specifically to libraries, usually more expensive than the trade edition of the same title. *See also*: library binding and prelibrary binding.

library education : Educational programs designed to prepare students for the postbaccalaureate degree of M.L.S. or M.L.I.S., taught by the faculty of a university department known as a library school (or school of librarianship). Modern library education began in 1887 when Melvil Dewey founded the first school for training professional librarians at Columbia University. *See also*: Association for Library and Information Science Education and information studies.

library equipment : Mechanical and electronic devices purchased by a library for staff use or to facilitate patron use of its services and collections, including photocopy machines, microform reader-printers, video and CD players, projection equipment, computers and computer peripherals, security devices, office equipment, etc.

library extension : Programs and activities that enable a library or library system to deliver traditional services outside the physical walls of its facilities, including bookmobiles, books-by-mail, and direct delivery of library materials to patrons. Compare with outreach.

library facility : The physical structure housing a library, or part of a library, as distinct from the collections and equipment it contains, and the personnel who operate and maintain it. A library facility can be stand-alone or a multi-purpose structure of which the library is one of two or more components. Some libraries in the United States occupy landmark buildings, for example, the New York Public Library at 5th Avenue and 42nd Street in

Manhattan. *See also*: auxiliary facility, Carnegie library, expansion, new construction, and renovation. In the plural (*facilities*), the term is often used for the physical conveniences of a library building that are designed to facilitate the use of services and resources, such as a reading room, listening and/or viewing room, instruction lab, children's room, meeting room, conference room, cybercafe, gift shop, etc.

library faculty : The professionally trained librarians employed at an academic institution that grants faculty status to librarians. One of the advantages of faculty status is the right to participate in governance. At some institutions, library faculty are members of the same collective bargaining unit as the teaching faculty. Whether they are eligible for tenure and promotion to the same ranks as the teaching faculty depends on the contract governing employment. *See also*: academic status.

library hand : A highly legible, uniform style of handwriting traditionally used by librarians for making entries in manuscript catalogs before the typewriter came into widespread use. With the conversion of card catalogs into files of machine-readable records, catalog cards have fallen into disuse, and handwritten catalog entries are rarely seen.

library historian : A researcher who writes about the history of libraries and librarianship, from ancient to modern times (*example*: Michael H. Harris, author of *History of Libraries in the Western World*, Scarecrow, 1995). Librarians with an interest in library history are organized in the Library History Round Table (LHRT) of the American Library Association (ALA).

library history : The study of the historical development of libraries and librarianship, beginning with the Sumerian archives of clay tablets (third millennium B.C.) and including the papyrus manuscript collections of ancient Egypt, the private collections of ancient Greece, the public libraries of ancient Rome, the cathedral and monastic libraries of medieval Europe, the university and humanist libraries of the Renaissance, and finally modern libraries. Click here to learn more about the history of libraries, or see *History of Libraries in the Western World* by library historian Michael H. Harris (Scarecrow, 1995). Library history is also studied in non-Western cultures. *See also*: Alexandrian Library, Carnegie library, Library History Round Table, and proto-library.

Library History Round Table (LHRT) : A round table of the American Library Association (ALA) dedicated to facilitating communication among scholars and students of library history, supporting research in library history, and addressing current issues of concern to library historians, such as conservation and preservation. LHRT publishes the semiannual *LHRT Newsletter*. The International Federation of Library Associations and Institutions (IFLA) also has a Library History Section. Click here to connect to the LHRT homepage.

library hours : The times during a day, week, and year when a library is open to its users, usually posted near the front entrance and available by phone and via the library's Web site, including any days the library is closed, usually holidays (most libraries have a book drop to allow borrowers to return materials when the facility is closed). A library's hours are determined by the needs of its users and budgetary constraints. Also refers to the times during which a specific service is available from a library, which may be shorter (or longer) than the hours the facility is open.

library humor : Jokes, cartoons, anecdotes, unusual reference questions, witticisms, satire, occupational folklore, etc., having to do with libraries and librarianship (see this example). Library-related cartoons are usually included in each issue of the professional magazine *American Libraries*, published by the American Library Association (ALA). Click here to connect to a the IFLANET library humor site. *See also*: Molesworth Institute.

Library Instruction Round Table (LIRT) : A round table of the American Library Association (ALA) dedicated to promoting formal and informal library instruction in all types of libraries as a means of helping library users acquire the information literacy skills essential for lifelong learning. Click here to connect to the LIRT homepage.

library legislation : Laws passed by a federal or state legislative body pertaining to or affecting the interests of libraries and related institutions (*example*: *Digital Millennium Copyright Act* of 1998). Through their professional associations, librarians and library advocates seek to influence legislative decision-making in ways that will benefit libraries and their users. Federal legislation affecting libraries is summarized in *The Bowker Annual Library and Book Trade Almanac*. Each May, the American Library Association co-sponsors National Library Legislative Day with the District of Columbia Library Association. Click here to explore the ALA's Web site on issues and advocacy. Synonymous with *library law*.

library literature : The body of published information pertaining to libraries, library and information science, and librarianship, including books, journal articles, conference proceedings, reports, guidelines and standards, etc. The literature of the profession is indexed in *Library Literature & Information Science (LLIS)*, published by H.W. Wilson, and in *Library and Information Science Abstracts (LISA)*. New publications are reviewed in the "Professional Media" section of *Library Journal*. *The Bowker Annual Library and Book Trade Almanac* includes a selective bibliography ("The Librarian's Bookshelf") of professional literature published in the last three years, arranged by specialization, with a list of library periodicals at the end.

library mail : A significantly lower postal rate charged to libraries and related nonprofit institutions by the U.S. Postal Service for books and other educational materials sent by mail. The law was amended in 1976 to allow publishers and distributors to use the rate when shipping books and other materials to libraries. The lower rate has allowed public libraries to offer books-by-mail programs to homebound patrons and has helped keep down the cost of interlibrary loan service. Click here to learn more about library mail. Synonymous with *library rate*. Compare with media mail.

library management system (LMS) : In automated systems, an integrated set of applications designed to perform the business and technical functions of a library, including acquisitions, cataloging, circulation, and the provision of public access. In alphabetical order, the leading vendors of library management software are: Auto-Graphics, EOS International, Ex Libris, Follett, Innovative Interfaces, Polaris Library Systems, SirsiDynix, TLC, and VTLS. Synonymous with *integrated library system (ILS).*

library market : The portion of the market for books and other publications generated by sales to libraries, library systems, and related organizations such as museums, archives, and research institutions. The library market is segmented by type of library (public, academic, school, special, etc.). Publishers and jobbers market their products to libraries by exhibiting at library conferences, advertising in library trade journals and review publications, offering special library discounts and prepublication prices, and direct mail advertising (trade catalogs and brochures).

library materials : All the items purchased by a library or library system to satisfy the information needs of its users, including books, newspapers and periodicals, reference materials, music scores, maps, microforms, and nonprint media, as distinct from equipment and supplies. Some libraries include subscriptions to electronic resources in the materials budget; others fund them separately. Except for gifts and special endowments, the acquisition of library materials is normally funded through the operating budget. The rapid escalation of journal subscription prices over the past decade has forced many academic libraries to cancel periodical subscriptions to maintain balance between expenditures for books and serials.

library media specialist (LMS) : A librarian trained to deliver library services to students in a school library media center on a walk-in basis or at the request of the classroom teacher. In addition to managing daily operations, the library media specialist supports the curriculum through collection development, teaches research and library skills appropriate to grade level, assists students with reading selections appropriate to reading level, helps classroom teachers integrate library services and multimedia materials into instructional programs, establishes standards of behavior for the library, and assists students in developing information-seeking skills and habits needed for lifelong learning. Certification is required in many states. Synonymous with *school librarian.*

library newsletter : A publication of no more than a few pages issued by a library to its clientele on a regular or irregular basis to inform them of the availability of services and resources, describe new and ongoing initiatives, and announce upcoming events, exhibitions, etc. For an example of an online library newsletter, see the *Haverford College Library Newsletter*. *ALiNUS*, maintained at Southern New Hampshire University, is an Internet gateway to over 600 online academic library newsletters published by institutions of higher education in the United States.

Library of Congress (LC) : Established by Congress in 1800 to function as a research library for the legislative branch of the federal government, the Library of Congress eventually became the unofficial national library of the United States. Located in Washington, D.C., LC houses a collection of over 120 million items and administers the U.S. copyright system, serving as the nation's copyright depository. LC is also the primary source of original cataloging in the United States. The machine-readable cataloging (MARC) and cataloging-in-publication (CIP) programs originated at the Library of Congress. Click here to see a photograph of the exterior of the Library of Congress and here to see the interior of the main reading room. Click here to learn more about the history of the Library of Congress, and here to connect to the LC homepage. Compare with National Archives and Records Administration. *See also*: Congressional Research Service and Librarian of Congress.

Library of Congress Classification (LCC) : A system of classifying books and other library materials developed and maintained over the last 200 years by the Library of Congress in Washington, D.C. In LCC, human knowledge is divided into 20 broad categories indicated by single letters of the roman alphabet, with major subdivisions indicated by a second letter, and narrower subdivisions by decimal numbers and further alphabetic notation.

Library of Congress Classification : A classification system developed by the Library of Congress (LC) that is used to organize the collections of many academic and research libraries, including Cornell. This alpha-numeric system arranges materials by subject. Each subject or class is represented by a series of letters and numbers, which are used to create an LC call number. To see the main classes in the LC system, go to Library of Congress Classification. For a more detailed outline of the LC system, go to Library of Congress Classification Outline.

library of congress classification cystem : This system of classifying library materials was developed by the Library of Congress, as the name implies. It is the system used by most academic and research libraries. Materials are assigned unique alpha-numeric identifiers which organize the material by subject. These alpha-numeric identifiers are called Call Numbers and each begin with a letter or letters, followed by a series of letters and numbers, and sometimes include the publication date of a particular book.

Library of Congress Control Number (LCCN) : When the Library of Congress began printing catalog cards in 1898 and distributing them in 1901, a unique Library of Congress Card Number was assigned to each item for identification and control. With the development of machine-readable cataloging in the late 1960s, LCCN became the Library of Congress Control Number. It is used in bibliographic records and also in authority and classification records. The LCCN is assigned to a publication after the deposit copy is received by the U.S. Copyright Office or in advance of the publication date if a publisher requests cataloging-in-publication. *See also*: accession number.

Library of Congress subject heading (LCSH) : A descriptive word or phrase selected by a subject specialist at the Library of Congress from the list of *Library of Congress*

Subject Headings and assigned to a book or other item when first published to indicate its subject. Multiple subject headings are assigned when necessary or desirable. The complete list of LC subject headings is published annually in a multivolume set colloquially known as "the big red books," usually available in the reference section of most large public and academic libraries and in the cataloging department of smaller libraries. Click here to learn more about *LCSH*, courtesy of the University of Oregon Libraries. Compare with Sears subject heading. *See also*: controlled vocabulary.

Library of Congress Subject Headings (LCSH) : The multi-volume set *Library of Congress Subject Headings* is an alphabetic guide to and list of the official subject headings used for searching in the CU Library Catalog. These sets can be found in most libraries on campus in the reference area or at locations near the public workstations.

library of congress subject headings : Use these terms to search the CATALOG by subject. These terms were devised by the Library of Congress and are used by to divide knowledge into related subject areas. These terms are published in large red volumes, often called LCSH, and are located near the reference desk.

Library of the Year : An annual award honoring the library that most profoundly demonstrates outstanding community service, based on nominations received from the library community. Selected by members of the editorial board of *Library Journal*, representatives from Thomson Gale's Executive Committee, and librarians from around the United States, the winning library receives $10,000 in cash, a feature story in *LJ*, and a gala reception at the American Library Association's annual conference. Click here to see a list of past award winners.

library organization : The systematic demarcation of functional activities within a library or library system and the establishment of formal relationships between functional units to maximize operational efficiency, for example, the decision by many libraries to administer systems separately from both public services and technical services.

For some libraries, organizational structure is indicated in a chart of official positions arranged to show lines of supervisory authority. Generally, the larger the library, the more hierarchical the organizational structure. Sociological research has shown that formal and informal organizational structure do not necessarily coincide. *See also*: Library Organization and Management Section.

Library Organization and Management Section (LOMS) : The section of the Library Administration and Management Association (LAMA) within the American Library Association (ALA) responsible for investigating issues concerning efficient operations in all types of libraries and for disseminating information on management issues to its members, the LAMA membership, and all librarians. Areas of current focus include comparative library organization, financial management, planning and evaluation of library services, and risk management. Click here to connect to the LOMS homepage.

library pet : An animal that lives in the care of a library, often a domestic cat (see this example). Exotic pets are more common in school libraries than in other types of libraries. Some public libraries have adopted a *pet ban* to accommodate patrons with pet allergies. The behavior of a library pet is not always docile—library cats have been known to attack assistance dogs used by the visually impaired.

library portal : Software that allows a computer user to customize online access to collections of information resources by creating a list of Internet connections, much like a personalized directory of street addresses and telephone/fax numbers (*example*: **MyLibrary**). Library portals are designed to reduce information overload by allowing patrons to select only the resources they wish to display on their personal interface.

Library Programs Service (LPS) : The arm of the U.S. Government Printing Office (GPO) responsible for administering the Federal Depository Library Program (FDLP), LPS consists of a Library Division, responsible for performing library-related functions (acquisitions, classification, format conversion, cataloging, inspections, etc.), and a Depository Distribution Division, responsible for the receipt, shipment preparation, and physical distribution of government publications, and for processing claims for LPS-shipped paper and electronic publications. Out of a total GPO work force of over 3,200, LPS has slightly more than 100 employees. Click here to learn more about the LPS, or read its annual reports.

library publication : A work produced and distributed by a library, for example, a brochure intended for users, describing the library facility, its resources, and the services provided by its staff. Most library publications are ephemeral, but large academic and research libraries publish more permanent works. A recent example: Alixe Bovey's Monsters and Grotesques in Medieval Manuscripts published in 2002 by the British Library.

library rating : The practice of evaluating libraries on the basis of formal criteria and ranking them according to the results. A prime example is *Hennen's American Public Library Ratings* (*HAPLR*). Created and maintained by library administrator Thomas J. Hennen, Jr., *HAPLR* ranks U.S. public libraries on 15 weighted input and output measures based on statistical data from the U.S. Federal-State Cooperative Service. Published annually, *HAPLR* also lists the top 10 public libraries in the United States by size of community.

library referendum : An election by the registered voters of a library district or other governmental jurisdiction on a ballot measure concerning local libraries. Most library referenda fall into two categories: *operating referenda* in support of the ongoing operating expenses of the local library or library system and *building referenda* to provide one-time funding for new construction and major renovations. A *tiered referendum* provides voters with options for levels of support. *Library Journal* reports annually on the success and failure of library referenda, usually in the March 15th issue.

library representative : A publisher's sales representative responsible for calling on libraries, usually within an established territory, to solicit orders for titles on the publisher's list. Contacts are made, usually by telephone or in person, with librarians responsible for collection development and acquisitions. Also refers to a vendor's representative, responsible for soliciting subscriptions to online bibliographic databases and full-text resources, usually trained to give demonstrations to library selection committees. Abbreviated *library rep.*

library research : Systematic study and investigation of some aspect of library and information science in which conclusions are based on the statistical analysis of data collected in accordance with a pre-established research design and methodology. Results are usually published in a professional LIS journal or presented at a library conference and subsequently published in its proceedings. Library research helps expand the theoretical base of library and information science and also provides data necessary for effective administrative decision-making and problem solving. Research on libraries and librarianship published in the previous year is reported in an essay in *The Bowker Annual Library and Book Trade Almanac*. For more information, see Beth Ashmore's Web site for *The Researching Librarian*. *See also*: Library Research Round Table, library survey, and Office for Research and Statistics.

Library Research Round Table (LRRT) : Founded in 1968 as a permanent round table of the American Library Association, LRRT is dedicated to fostering library research by providing program opportunities for researchers to describe and disseminate their work and by informing and educating ALA members about research techniques and the importance of research as a foundation for effective administrative decision-making and problem solving. LRRT also gives annual awards for distinguished published research and excellence in doctoral research. Click here to connect to the LRRT homepage. *See also*: Office for Research and Statistics.

library school : A professional school or department qualified to grant the postbaccalaureate degree of M.L.S. or M.L.I.S., supported and administered by an institution of higher learning to prepare graduate students for employment in professional positions in libraries and as information service providers. The first modern library school was established by Melvil Dewey at Columbia University in 1887. Library schools may be accredited or approved (or both). Length of program varies. Synonymous with *school of librarianship*. The term is becoming archaic as more and more institutions use "library and information studies" or simply "information studies" to describe the expansion of their LIS schools to include allied fields (informatics, information management, etc.). Accredited library and information studies programs in the United States and Canada are listed in *American Library Directory* and *The Bowker Annual Library and Book Trade Almanac*. Click here to connect to T.D. Wilson's online *World List of Departments and Schools of Information Studies, Information Management, Information Systems, etc.*

library science : The professional knowledge and skill with which recorded information is selected, acquired, organized, stored, maintained, retrieved, and disseminated to meet the needs of a specific clientele, usually taught at a professional library school qualified to grant the postbaccalaureate degree of M.L.S. or M.L.I.S. The term is used synonymously in the United States with librarianship. Compare with information science.

library security officer (LSO) : The person appointed by the director of a library or library system who is authorized by the library and its parent institution to act on their behalf in working with the institution's administration and staff, legal counsel, security force, and outside agencies to develop and implement an effective *security plan*, based on a thorough understanding of security needs, particularly those of special collections. Such a plan should include a survey of the library's collections, review of the layout of the physical facility, staff training, and standard operating procedures for dealing with theft and other common security problems.

library staff : The entire group of paid employees responsible for the operation and management of a library or library system, including its director, librarians, paraprofessionals, technical assistants, clerical personnel, and pages or student assistants. In academic libraries at institutions that grant librarians faculty status, a distinction is usually made between faculty members and nonfaculty staff. In other types of libraries, a distinction may be made between professionally trained librarians and support staff. Volunteers are not considered part of the staff because they are unpaid. *See also*: Staff Organizations Round Table.

library statistics : Numerical data assembled, classified, and tabulated to present useful facts and information about the operation of a library or library system or about the activities of libraries at the local, state, provincial, or national level, usually presented in the form of a periodic report. The ANSI/NISO Z39.7 standard identifies data categories for basic library statistics applicable to four types of libraries (academic, public, school, and special) and additional data categories that may be collected by one or more types of libraries but not all. Click here to connect to the Web site maintained by the National Center for Educational Statistics (NCES) as part of the Library Statistics Program. The Association of Research Libraries (ARL) publishes statistics on academic libraries as part of its Statistics & Measurement Program. *Statistics About Libraries* are also available via the Office of Research and Statistics (ORS) of the American Library Association (ALA). For other sources of library statistics, see *LibraryHQ.com*. *See also*: circulation statistics and Integrated Postsecondary Education Data System.

library supplies : Expendable materials used in the operations of a library, including office supplies, cleaning and maintenance supplies, paper and toner for printers and photocopy machines, and items needed for technical processing (book covers, magnetic strips, book cards, labels, date due slips, bookends, mending tape, etc.). The category does not include equipment or bibliographic items acquired for collections. In the United States, the leading library suppliers are Brodart, Demco, Gaylord, and Highsmith.

Library Support Staff Interests Round Table (LSSIRT): A permanent round table of the American Library Association (ALA), LSSIRT provides a forum for addressing issues of concern to library support staff, such as training and continuing education, career development, job responsibilities, and compensation. Click here to connect to the LSSIRT homepage. *See also*: paraprofessional.

library survey : A written or oral question-and-answer instrument designed to elicit feedback from library users about the quality of services and resources and the existence of unmet needs. Library surveys are administered by staff, or by an outside agency, to determine how well the library's services, programs, and collections meet user needs and any objectives established by the library administration and/or governing institution. They are also used to generate data for library research. Also refers to the report produced as the result of such a study. Also refers to an instrument used to query libraries about the current state of services and resources, for example, the federal surveys of academic, public, school, and state libraries administered periodically by the National Center for Educational Statistics (NCES) as part of its Library Statistics Program.

library system : A group of libraries administered in common, for example, a central library and its branches or auxiliary outlets. Also, a group of independently administered libraries joined by formal or informal agreement to achieve a common purpose. Under such an arrangement, each library is considered an affiliate. Compare with consortium.

library tour : A guided walk through a library facility, usually conducted by a librarian or library assistant, to orient new users to the location of services and resources. Some libraries have installed online library tours on their Web sites, which include clickable floor plans linked to photographs and descriptive text. Not to be confused with bibliographic instruction.

library trustee : A member of an appointed or elected board responsible for overseeing the growth and development of a library or library system, including long-range planning and policymaking, public relations, and fundraising. Trustees are usually library advocates but may sometimes be political appointees. *See also*: Association for Library Trustees and Advocates.

library use : The extent to which the resources and services of a library are utilized by its clientele (students and faculty in the case of academic libraries; the general public for public libraries). Common measures include overall or per capita circulation, turnover of collection(s), gate count, program attendance, Internet use within the building, interlibrary loan and reference transactions, etc. Accurate statistics on library use are essential in documenting effectiveness and justifying funding. A study commissioned in 2006 by the American Library Association (ALA) of a random sample of 1,003 people revealed that two-thirds of adult Americans (about 135 million) visited their public libraries in the previous year. Nearly two-thirds of Americans have library cards. According to the survey, use of library services by Americans has grown in every category since the previous survey in 2002—from borrowing books and consulting librarians to checking out CDs, videos, and computer software and attending cultural programs. The most frequent library users are women, younger adults (age 25-44), college-educated adults, and parents of younger children. Click here to learn more about the survey results.

library use only : A circulation status code written on or affixed to a physical item in a library collection and entered in the item record in the catalog, indicating that it is available for use within the walls of the library but may not be checked out and removed from the premises except by special arrangement. The use of reference books, periodical indexes, and in some cases bound and/or unbound periodicals is generally restricted to the library. Use of items in special collections, such as rare books and manuscripts, may even be restricted to a designated room or area of the library (and other conditions of use). Compare with noncirculating. *See also*: in-house use.

Library War Service : A program sponsored by the American Library Association (ALA) during World War I, which provided library services to soldiers and sailors in camps and hospitals in the United States and distributed reading materials to U.S. military personnel stationed overseas. Headquartered at the Library of Congress, the program included a books-by-mail program that was granted free franking privileges by General Pershing. To help support the program, the ALA sponsored a War Service Library Week, conducted book drives, and solicited periodicals from publishers and subscribers. The Library War Service became the basis for today's armed forces libraries. Click here to see a copy of the official ALA War Service Library bookplate.

Lignin : A component of the cell walls of plants that occurs naturally, along with cellulose. It is largely responsible for the strength and rigidity of plants, but its presence in paper and board is believed to contribute to chemical degradation. It can be, to a large extent, removed during manufacture. No standards exist for the term "lignin free," and additional research is needed to determine the precise role of lignin in the durability and permanence of paper.

Linear Feet : 1. A measurement for descriptive and control purposes of shelf space occupied by archives, records, or manuscripts. For vertical files (records filed on edge), the total length of drawers, shelves, or other equipment occupied is calculated; in the case of material filed horizontally (flat or piled up), the total vertical thickness is used. Linear feet, except for card indexes, may be equated with cubic feet on a one-to-one basis for descriptions of textual records. 2. A measurement for descriptive and control purposes of length of film, tape, or microfilm. (Usually expressed as feet.)

Link State : A routing protocol technology that exchanges routing information consisting of a router's attached subnet prefixes and their assigned costs. Link state information is advertised upon startup and when changes in the network topology are detected.

Link-local Address : A local-use address with the prefix of FE80::/64 and whose scope is the local link. Nodes use link-local addresses to communicate with neighbouring nodes on the same link. Link-local addresses are equivalent to Automatic Private IP Addressing (APIPA) IPv4 addresses.

Loan Period : The amount of time a patron may borrow a book or other item from the library. The time varies depending on the type of material borrowed and the status of the borrower.

loan period : The length of time library materials may be borrowed. The time period varies depending on the borrower's STATUS.

Local Address : An IPv6 address identified by the prefix FC00::/7. The scope of a Local address is an organization. Local addresses are reachable from other sites in an organization, but not from the IPv6 Internet.

Longest Matching Route : The algorithm used to select the routes in the routing table that most closely match the destination address of the packet being sent or forwarded.

Loopback Address : For IPv4, the address 127.0.0.1. For IPv6, the address 0:0:0:0:0:0:0:1 (or::1). Nodes use the loopback address to send packets to themselves.

made-up copy : A copy of a book assembled from parts taken from one or more defective copies of the same edition, or a copy in which imperfections are corrected by adding or substituting parts taken from other copies of the same edition. In the antiquarian book trade, the practice is not considered unethical as long as the manner in which the volume is composed is revealed rather than concealed.

magazine : (see also Journal) Magazines are periodicals/serials, meaning they are published on a continuing, regular basis. They contain articles written by various authors, often journalists. Magazines are quite different from journals. Often they contain advertising; articles are usually shorter than in journals, and they do not usually contain bibliographies and footnotes.

management information system (MIS) : A computer-based information system developed and maintained by a commercial enterprise to integrate data from all its departments (product development, production and inventory, marketing and sales, personnel administration, etc.) to support managerial and supervisory decision-making with real time analysis. MIS systems are designed to track progress toward achievement of a company's goals and objectives and to aid in identifying problems or obstacles that must be resolved or removed by upper-level management. In the plural, the term refers to the study and teaching of such systems. Courses on MIS are offered as a major by some business schools in the United States.

Manuscript : A handwritten, typed, or electronically reproduced document or communication.

manuscript book : A book written entirely by hand, particularly one produced prior to the invention of printing from movable type, usually copied by medieval monks or scribes on leaves of parchment or vellum, bound in leather-covered wooden boards. Medieval manuscript books were often rubricated, illuminated, and/or embellished with miniatures. For examples, see the online exhibitions *Leaves of Gold*, courtesy of the Philadelphia Museum of Art, and *Celebrating the Liturgy's Books*, courtesy of the libraries of New York City.

Manuscripts : Documents or written compositions, such as letters or diaries, which have not been printed. Often, an author's written (or typed) original "copy" as distinguished from a printed or published version of the same material. Cornell's primary collections of manuscripts are located in the Rare Books & Manuscripts Collections in Kroch Library.

manuscripts : These are documents which have not been printed by a publisher, often personal papers such as letters or diaries. TAMUK's manuscripts are housed in the South Texas Archives and Special Collections, a division of James C. Jernigan Library.

map library : A library or unit within a library, which has collections consisting primarily of cartographic materials of current or historic interest, including maps and charts, globes, relief models, remote sensing images, spatial data, atlases, gazetteers, and books about cartography and cartographers, for example, the Perry-Castañeda Library Map Collection at the University of Texas, Austin. The

Geography and Map Reading Room at the Library of Congress also provides digital images of items in its collections. The John R. Borchert Map Library at the University of Minnesota provides an online directory of *Map Libraries on the World Wide Web*. Map librarians are organized in the Map and Geography Round Table (MAGERT) of the American Library Association (ALA), in the Geography and Map Section of the Special Libraries Association (SLA), and in the Association of Canadian Map Libraries and Archives (ACMLA). *See also*: Cartographic Users Advisory Council.

MARC : Derived from "machine-readable cataloguing," U.S. MARC is a standard for representation and communication of bibliographical and related information in machine-readable form.

Marc Formats : The Library of Congress developed the MARC formats in the late 1960s for communication of bibliographic information in machine-readable form. These MARC (for Machine-Readable cataloging) formats identify bibliographic data for computer recognition and manipulation. In the mid-1970s as variations were developed, the formats used by the Library of Congress became known as "LC-MARC formats." Since the early 1980s, however, LC-MARC formats have come to be referred to as "USMARC formats" because they are standards for MARC records in the United States.

mass-market paperback : A new work or reprint of a title previously published in hardcover or trade paperback, produced and distributed in paperback for sale at newsstands and in supermarkets, drugstores, chain stores, etc., rather than trade bookstores. Copies are usually of standard rack size (4 x 7 inches), printed on poor-quality paper, bound with hot-melt adhesive in covers designed for sales appeal, and priced to sell to the widest possible audience. The format is used extensively for popular fiction and genre fiction. Libraries prefer them for books-by-mail programs to keep mailing costs down. In some public libraries, mass-market paperbacks received as gifts are circulated on the honor system. *See also*: pulp fiction.

Materials and Binding : Materials are expenditures for items purchased in a given time period, usually a fiscal year, to be added to a library's collections, including books (monographs), periodicals and other serials, microforms, audiovisual materials, and other library materials; also sometimes includes expenditures for electronic searching and other modes of access to information that is not added to library collections in traditional ways. Binding is expenditures for contract binding, usually by commercial binders.

Mauchline binding : A decorative technique that originated in the 1830s in the Scottish town of Mauchline in which a transfer print of a wood engraving, often a color design (tartan or floral motif), was applied to a lacquered wooden object, such as the boards of a bookbinding. In the 1860s, photographs and stencils began to be used in the design process. Mauchline ware reached a peak of popularity in the 1880s, disappearing in the 1920s. Click here to see an example in a bright tartan and here to see an example that combines photographic with stenciled images.

Media : Films, tapes, and other audio-visual materials that require the use of special listening or viewing equipment.

media center : The Media Center is located on level 3 of Tisch Library. It contains viewing rooms and thousands of videos and DVDs that may be viewed in the center or checked out. All Media Center materials are listed in the CATALOG.

media literacy : The ability to access, analyze, evaluate, and create messages in a variety of forms (print, audio, film/video, Internet, etc.) based on an informed, critical understanding of the nature of mass media, the techniques used by producers of media, and the impact of those techniques on the individual and society. An interdisciplinary field, media literacy has evolved as a necessary response to the complex, pervasive, ever-changing electronic communication environment of the 21st century. Click here to connect to the homepage of the Center for Media Literacy. Compare with information literacy.

medical book : A book published in print, on CD-ROM, or online for the use of medical practitioners, researchers, and/or students (*example*: **Physician's Desk Reference**) or for laypersons with an interest in health care (**Harvard Medical School Family Health Guide**). The category includes textbooks, reference works, and consumer guides, often published in successive editions. Currency is essential in maintaining medical collections used by practitioners. Click here to see an online exhibition of anatomical illustration in medical books of the 16th-18th centuries (Glasgow University Library, Special Collections). *See also*: American Medical Publishers Association and medical library.

medical library : A type of special library maintained by a university medical school, hospital, medical research institute, public health agency, or medical association to serve the information needs of students, researchers, and practitioners in the health sciences (medicine, nursing, dentistry, pharmacy, etc.), with collections that include print and online resources related to medicine and allied health. The largest medical library in the United States is the National Library of Medicine, located in Washington, D.C. Medical librarians are organized in the Medical Library Association (MLA). Synonymous with *health science library*. *See also*: hospital library.

Medical Library Association (MLA) : Founded in 1898, MLA has a membership of librarians and other individuals engaged in professional library or bibliographic work in medical libraries and allied scientific libraries. An affiliate of the American Library Association (ALA), MLA publishes the quarterly *Bulletin of the Medical Library Association (BMLA)*. Click here to connect to the MLA homepage.

mediumistic writing : A written work transmitted through a psychic medium who claims to have received it as a communication from the spirit of a dead person or entity. In libraries, such works are cataloged under the name of the medium with an added entry under the name of the purported author(s).

Microforms : A term used to describe documents that have been photographed or filmed. Microforms require the use of special reader machines. Common formats for microforms are microfilm, microfiche, and microcard.

microforms : These are materials which have been photographed or filmed and are not in their original printed formats. Jernigan Library has both microfilm and microfiche. They are in cabinets on the first floor at the West end of the library. Microfiche and microfilm reader printers can be found along the back wall of the library on the first floor. There is no viewing charge, but printouts cost 10 cents for each page.

microscopic printing : Printing done in a very small type size. Although the first works printed in Europe were in large type, early printers soon realized that with smaller typefaces more matter could be fitted on a page. By 1825, the French type-founder Henri Didot had cast type that produced 25 lines to the inch. Because the casting of extremely small type has physical limitations, most microscopic reduction is now done photographically. *See also*: miniature book.

military library : A library maintained by a unit of government responsible for national defense, maintaining collections for the use of military staff, but sometimes with a broader mandate that may include accessibility to the general public (*example*: Nimitz Library at the U.S. Naval Academy). *Military librarians* are organized in the Federal and Armed Forces Libraries Round Table (FAFLRT) of the American Library Association (ALA) and in the Military Librarians Division (MLD) of the Special Libraries Association (SLA). For more information on military libraries, please see the article "Mission: Access" in the February 2006 issue of *American Libraries*. Synonymous with *armed forces library*. Also, a privately funded library devoted to documenting military heritage, for example, the Pritzker Military Library in Chicago, Illinois, which aims to acquire and maintain a collection of materials and develop programs on the role of the citizen soldier in a democracy.

minute book : A blankbook or series of blankbooks in which are recorded the minutes of the meetings of a society, association, board, agency, court, etc., usually on a regular basis. Becuase the information recorded in minute books can be of considerable historical value, they are often archived. Click here to see examples, courtesy of the Royal College of Surgeons of Edinburgh, and here to read the minute books of the Order of Railway Conductors and Brakemen Local 160, 1884-1892.

missionary book : Publisher's slang for the first book published on a subject. To catalog such a work, a new class number and new subject heading may be required.

model book : A book in which a medieval artist recorded a repertoire of designs for decorated initials and other ornamental motifs (birds, animals, imaginary creatures, etc.) of the artist's own invention or collected from other sources, sometimes with notes concerning execution, for use in underdrawing. Click here to see miniatures from two different manuscripts based on the same model (*Medieval Manuscript Manual*). By the late Middle Ages, engravings were circulated for this purpose. Also refers to a book created by a master scribe and/or illuminator to instruct pupils wishing to learn the art of fine handwriting and manuscript painting. Click here to see an example created in 1561-1562 by Georg Bocskay, Croatian-born court secretary to the Holy Roman Emperor Ferdinand I, and illuminated thirty years later by Joris Hoefnagel (Getty Museum, MS 20) or browse the *Göttingen Model Book*, courtesy of the Göttingen State and University Library. Also spelled *modelbook*. Compare with pattern book.

Moving Image Collections (MIC) : Sponsored by the Association of Moving Image Archivists (AMIA), the Library of Congress, and the National Science Foundation (NSF), MIC is an integrated online union catalog of moving images held by a variety of organizations, including libraries, museums, archives, and television broadcasting companies, including films, videorecordings, and digital streaming video. MIC also includes a directory of archives and links to resources on moving images and moving image preservation. MIC is part of the National Science Digital Library (NSDL). Click here to connect to the MIC homepage.

Multicast Address : An address that identifies zero or multiple interfaces and is used to deliver packets from one source to many destinations. With the appropriate multicast routing topology, packets addressed to a multicast address are delivered to all interfaces identified by the address.

Multicast Listener Discovery (MLD) : A set of three ICMPv6 messages that hosts and routers use to manage multicast group membership on a subnet.

multidisciplinary journal : A scholarly periodical that publishes articles of interest to researchers in a wide range of academic disciplines (*examples*: **Nature** and **Science** in the sciences). Compare with interdisciplinary journal.

museum publisher : A museum or historical society that issues books, exhibition catalogs, and other publications under its own imprint or in cooperation with other publishers, for example, the Metropolitan Museum of Art in New York City. Museum publications are usually of fine quality, often issued in both hardcover and softcover editions to appeal to collectors and casual buyers.

music library : A library containing a collection of materials on music and musicians, including printed and manuscript music scores, music periodicals, recorded music (CDs, audiocassettes, phonograph records, etc.), books about music and musicians, program notes, discographies, and music reference materials. Music collections in public libraries are selected and maintained for lifelong learning and leisure pursuits. Academic and conservatory libraries provide resources for music study and research, including original source materials (*example*: Columbia University Music & Arts Library). National libraries offer unique and often rare musical heritage collections (*example*: The Aaron Copland Collection at the Library of Congress). *Music librarians* are organized in the Music Library Association (MLA). *See also*: International Association of Music Libraries, Archives and Documentation Centres.

Music Library Association (MLA) : Founded in 1931, MLA promotes the establishment, growth, and use of music libraries and collections of music, musical instruments, music literature, music recordings, and related materials in both print and nonprint format. An affiliate of the American Library Association (ALA), the organization also seeks to advance music librarianship, scholarship, and publishing. MLA publishes the monthly *Music Cataloging Bulletin*. Click here to connect to the MLA homepage. *See also*: Major Orchestra Librarians' Association.

MyDocumentDelivery : MyDocumentDelivery is a fee based electronic document delivery service offered by Cornell University Library. Faculty, staff and students may request copies of journal articles, book chapters and other materials located in the print collection of the Cornell University Libraries including the Library Annex. Documents will be scanned and made available on the web as pdf files.

Name Resolution : The process of resolving a name to an address.

name-title added entry : In *AACR2*, an added entry in the library catalog giving the name of a person (or corporate body) and the title of a work, for the purpose of identifying: (1) a work that is included in or the subject of the work being cataloged; (2) a larger work of which the work being cataloged is part; or (3) another work to which the work being cataloged is in some way related. Synonymous with *author-title added entry*.

narrow : The shape of a book in which the width of the cover is less than two-thirds its height, a format commonly used in the design of field guides and travel guides. Click here to see a diminutive 18th-century example (Bakken Library and Museum) and here to see a late 19th-century example (British Library). Compare with square. *See also*: oblong and portrait.

National Agricultural Library (NAL) : Established as a federal library in 1862 under legislation signed by President Abraham Lincoln, NAL is part of the Agricultural Research Service (ARS) of the U.S. Department of Agriculture (USDA). With a collection of over 3.3 million items, NAL is the primary source of agricultural information in the United States and the largest agricultural library in the world. Located in Beltsville, Maryland, NAL works closely with libraries at land-grant universities to improve access to, and utilization of, agricultural information by researchers, policymakers, educators, farmers, consumers of agricultural products, and the general public. Click here to connect to the NAL homepage.

National Archives and Records Administration (NARA) : The national archives of the United States, a federal agency established by Congress in 1934 to oversee the management of all federal records, including the public's right of access to documents and information not specifically exempted under the *Freedom of Information Act (FOIA)*. NARA's 33 facilities house approximately 21.5 million cubic feet of original textual materials collected from the executive, legislative, and judicial branches. Its collections also include nonprint materials, such as motion pictures, sound and videorecordings, maps and charts, aerial photographs, architectural drawings, computer data sets, posters, etc. NARA is administered by an Archivist of the United States appointed by the president with the approval of Congress and advised by a National Archives Council. Click here to connect to the NARA homepage. *See also*: National Association of Government Archives and Records Administrators and National Historical Publications and Records Commission.

National Awards for Museum and Library Service : Honorary awards made annually by the federal Institute of Museum and Library Services to outstanding institutions that make significant and exceptional contributions to their communities. To be selected, an institution must demonstrate extraordinary and innovative approaches to public service, exceeding the expected levels of community outreach and core programs generally associated with its services. The National Museum and Library Services Board reviews nominations and makes recommendations to the IMLS Director, who makes the final selection. Winners are announced in the fall of each year.

National Commission on Libraries and Information Science (NCLIS) : An independent agency within the executive branch of the U.S. federal government, established in 1970 to advise the president and Congress on national library and information policy, conduct studies of library and information needs, assess the adequacy of current resources and services, promote research, develop plans for meeting the nation's information needs, and help coordinate library-related activities at the federal, state, and local levels. Click here to connect to the NCLIS homepage.

National Historical Publications and Records Commission (NHPRC) : A 15-member statutory body established by Congress in 1934 and affiliated with the National Archives and Records Administration(NARA), NHPRC supports a wide range of activities to preserve, publish, and encourage the use of documentary sources created in every medium, from quill pen to computer, relating to the history of the United States. Chaired by the Archivist of the United States, its membership includes representatives of the three branches of the U.S. federal government as well as representatives of professional associations of archivists, historians, documentary editors, and records administrators. NHPRC grants are administered through the State Historical Records Advisory Boards (SHRABs) chaired by NHPRC-designated State Historical Records Coordinators. Click here to connect to the NHPRC homepage. *See also*: Council of State Archivists.

national library : A library designated and funded by a national government to serve the nation by maintaining a comprehensive collection of the published and unpublished literary output of the nation as a whole, including publications of the government itself. Most national libraries are also responsible for compiling a national bibliography, and some serve as the legal depository for works protected by copyright in the country. The national library of the United States is the Library of Congress, located in Washington, D.C. Three other libraries—the National Agricultural Library, the National Library of

Education, and the National Library of Medicine—contain national collections in specific subject areas. Click here to connect to the *Yahoo!* list of national libraries of the world, or try *National Library Catalogues Worldwide*, maintained by the University of Queensland, Australia. The national libraries of Europe are accessible via *The European Library*. Compare with national archives. *See also*: Bibliothèque Nationale de France, the British Library, Library and Archives Canada, and National Library of Australia.

National Library Legislative Day : An event cosponsored by the District of Columbia Library Association (DCLA) and the American Library Association (ALA) every year in May to bring librarians, library trustees, board members, and other friends of libraries to Washington, D.C., to talk with their representatives and senators about key issues of concern to the library community. Each year, the ALA's Washington Office prepares information on important legislative issues (copyright and intellectual property, Internet and telecommunications, access to government information, appropriations and funding for library programs, etc.) for discussion with Legislative Day participants in an all-day briefing. The following day, library advocates take their messages to their members of Congress. An annual public service award is given by FOLUSA on National Library Legislative Day to a member of Congress who provides leadership and demonstrates commitment to library priorities. In 2004, awards were presented to both Sen. Russ Feingold (D-WI) and Rep. Bernie Sanders (I-VT) for their commitment to modifying the *USA Patriot Act* to protect civil liberties. Click here to learn more about National Library Legislative Day.

National Library of Australia (NLA) : Established in 1901, the NLA moved from Melbourne to Canberra in 1927, following the opening of the Federal Parliament building, and in 1968 to its new and permanent home on the shore of Lake Burley Griffin, uniting collections formerly dispersed around Canberra. In addition to its Main Reading Room, the NLA has separate reading rooms for collections of Asian materials, manuscripts, maps, pictorial works, rare books, newspapers, oral history, music, and ephemera. The national library also has an active publishing program and is a member of the MARC Advisory Committee. Click here to connect to the NLA homepage.

National Library of Education (NLE) : The largest library in the world devoted solely to the collection, preservation, and effective use of research and other information in the field of education. Located in Washington, D.C., the NLE was established with the purchase of the private collection of Henry Barnard, the first U.S. Commissioner of Education following his resignation in 1870. Since then, its growth has been funded by the federal government. It serves the U.S. Department of Education, Congress, and the Office of the President, as well as the general public, and is the center of a national network of libraries, archives, and other information providers in education. Click here to connect to the NLE homepage.

National Library of Medicine (NLM) : The largest medical library in the United States, administered by the National Institutes of Health (NIH). Located in Bethesda, Maryland, NLM is home to over 7 million items, including one of the world's finest medical history collections of old and rare medical works. For the past 125 years, NLM has published the *Index Medicus*, a subject/author guide to articles published in 4,000 journals. It also provides public access to an online version of its *MEDLINE* bibliographic database at no charge under the title *PubMed*. A new service called *PubMed Central* provides open access to a central digital archive of full-text journal articles in the life sciences. Click here to connect to the NLM homepage.

National Library Service for the Blind and Physically Handicapped (NLS) : A national library program administered by the Library of Congress that produces and distributes Braille and recorded library materials at no charge to eligible borrowers through a national network of cooperating regional and local libraries. Established by Congress in 1931 to serve blind adults, NLS was expanded in 1952 to serve visually impaired children, in 1962 to provide music materials, and in 1966 to serve individuals with other physical impairments that prevent them from reading print of standard size. Click here to connect to the NLS homepage.

National Library Symbol : Originally designed by Ralph E. DeVore for the Western Maryland Public Libraries, the generic figure of a human being reading a book (see this example) was endorsed at the 1982 annual conference of the American Library Association (ALA) as the standard symbol representing all types of libraries in the United States to increase public awareness of libraries as an institution by its utilization on directional signs and promotional materials. In 1985, the symbol was accepted by the Federal Highway Administration for inclusion in the manual setting standards for highway signs. Click here to learn more about the symbol's history.

National Library Week (NLW) : Sponsored for the first time in 1958 by the National Book Committee and the American Library Association (ALA), National Library Week is an officially recognized seven-day period in the spring of each year during which special attention is given to promoting libraries of all types in the United States. Most public libraries celebrate the event by displaying posters and exhibits, issuing press releases, and sponsoring book talks and other promotional activities. In the United Kingdom, a similar event, National Libraries Week, is celebrated in the fall of each year. Click here to connect to the National Library Week Web site. *See also*: National Library Workers Day.

National Library Workers Day (NLWD) : A special day during National Library Week (NLW) reserved for formal recognition of the contributions of all library workers (librarians, support staff, and others), NLWD was established in 2003 by an ALA-APA Council resolution adopted at the annual conference of the American Library Association in Toronto.

National Science Digital Library (NSDL) : A digital library of collections and services funded by the National Science Foundation and intended to become a comprehensive, online source of digital resources for use in science, technology, engineering, and mathematics education. Click here to connect to the NSDL homepage.

Neighbour : A node that is connected to the same subnet as another node.

Neighbour Cache : A cache maintained by every IPv6 node that stores the IPv6 address of a neighbour and its corresponding MAC address. The neighbour cache is equivalent to the ARP cache in IPv4.

Neighbour Discovery (ND) : A set of ICMPv6 messages and processes that determine relationships between neighbouring nodes. Neighbour Discovery replaces ARP, ICMP router discovery, and the ICMP Redirect message used in IPv4.

NetBIOS : See Network Basic Input/Output System.

Network : Two or more subnets that are connected by routers. Another term for network is internetwork.

Network Address Translator (NAT) : An IPv4 router that translates addresses and ports when forwarding packets between a privately addressed network and the Internet.

Network Basic Input/Output System (NetBIOS) : A standard API for user applications to manage NetBIOS names and access NetBIOS datagram and session services.

neutral : Having a pH of 7; neither acid nor alkaline.

new library : An institutional library created from scratch or with the donation of one or more significant private collections. Most new libraries created in the United States are branch public libraries sited in areas of demographic growth, or academic libraries at newly created campuses. Core lists are helpful in collection-building. Also used synonymously with new construction.

new title notification : A free service offered by some book publishers and vendors, informing prospective buyers via e-mail of the availability of new publications on a prepublication or on-publication basis. Some sellers allow the customer to limit notifications to a specific interest profile (see this example). Click here to connect to the *AcqWeb* list of publishers and vendors providing new title notifications.

New York Public Library (NYPL) : The largest public library system in the United States, the New York Public Library was created in 1895 by the merger of the Astor Library, created in 1849 through the generosity of John Jacob Astor, with the Lenox Library, founded by James Lenox, and the assistance of a $2.4 million trust established by Samuel J. Tilden to "establish and maintain a free library and reading room in the city of New York." Librarian John Shaw Billings was named the first director. The jewel in the crown of the NYPL is the landmark building of beaux-arts design, located at 5th Avenue and 42nd Street in Manhattan on the site of the former Croton Reservoir. The largest marble structure ever attempted in the United States, the building was completed in 1911 at a cost of $9 million. While it was under construction, the NYPL established its circulating department after consolidating with the New York Free Circulating Library in February 1901. One month later, philanthropist Andrew Carnegie offered $5.2 million for construction of a system of branch libraries throughout New York City, if the City would agreed to supply the sites and fund operating expenses. Today, the NYPL is composed of four specialized Research Libraries supported largely by private funds and 85 neighborhood Branch Libraries serving the boroughs of Manhattan, the Bronx, and Staten Island, with collections totaling 6.6 million items, operated mainly from public funds allocated by the city and state of New York. The Library's facilities are used by more than 15 million people annually and it has 1.86 million registered cardholders. Click here to connect to the NYPL homepage.

Newberry Library : Located in Chicago, the Newberry Library is a privately funded independent research library devoted primarily to the humanities. Free and open to the public, it contains an extensive noncirculating collection of rare books, maps, manuscripts, and other materials related to the civilizations of western Europe and the Americas. The Library was established in the late 19th century at the bequest of the wealthy Chicago businessman and philanthropist Walter Loomis Newberry. Click here to connect to the homepage of the Newberry Library.

news library : A type of special library maintained in the offices of a newspaper publisher, or other news agency, that includes in its collection newspaper and magazine clippings, photo files (sometimes with negatives), maps, pamphlet files, microforms, reference materials, and online databases related to news and current events. Most are open to subscribers and librarians at the discretion of the *news librarian*, usually by appointment. News libraries are listed in *The International Directory of News Libraries*, a serial published in cooperation with the News Division of the Special Libraries Association (SLA).

Next-hop Determination : The process of determining the next-hop address and interface for sending or forwarding a packet, based on the contents of the routing table.

niche publishing : The activities of small presses and divisions within large publishing companies that limit their scope to a relatively narrow subject area (*example*: auto repair manuals or travel guides) or type of literature (genre fiction), producing publications intended to meet the needs of a specific market segment. Some niches are broader than others.

Node : Any device, including routers and hosts, which runs an implementation of IP.

North American Sport Library Network (NASLIN) : Founded in 1989, NASLIN is dedicated to facilitating communication and resource sharing among sports libraries, archives, and information services through conferences, educational programs, and other cooperative projects. Its members are librarians, archivists, and information specialists involved in the publication, acquisition, organization, retrieval, and dissemination of information related to all aspects of sports, physical education, and recreation. NASLIN publishes the semiannual newsletter *NASLINE*. Click here to connect to the NASLIN homepage.

Not Charged : If a library item is not checked-out, the online catalog will indicate that the status of the item is Not Charged. This means that the item is available in its call number location in the library.

nswer print : The first composite print of an edited motion picture on which each scene has been corrected in the laboratory for brightness and color, allowing the quality of production, printing, or preservation elements to be checked. Several answer prints may be necessary before release prints can be made. The final answer print is usually presented to the customer for approval. Synonymous with *approval print* and *trial print*.

Numeric Data : Numeric data files are those with significant numeric content, either statistical, coded, or graphically displayed. An example of numeric data found on the Library Gateway is the FAOSTAT Statistics Database.

OASIS : This is the name of our online catalog. Remember the old card catalogs? Well, now they are electronic. OASIS allows you to search for all of our cataloged material, including books, audio-visual materials, theses and dissertations, and journal titles. You can search the catalog for a specific title or author or call number, or you can use a keyword search or a subject search. OASIS can be accessed from the library's homepage, or, if you'd like to see the OASIS search options, click HERE.

OCLC holding library code : A four-character code, unique within an OCLC symbol, identifying one location or collection within an institution. A library may choose any combination of codes, but each code must begin with an alphabetic character A-Z, and the last three characters must be A-Z or 2-9. The holding library code determines some OCLC profile options and is exported in local OCLC field 049.

OCLC WorldCat : This database is an online catalog of the holdings of books, journals, and other materials held by thousands of OCLC member libraries. (OCLC is Online Computer Library Center.) Cornell researchers can identify and locate materials in other libraries and collections using WorldCat, and request these materials through interlibrary loan.

Office of Government Relations (OGR) : The executive office of the American Library Association charged with following and influencing legislation, policy, and regulation concerning issues of importance to libraries and library users. In cooperation with the Office for Information Technology Policy (OITP), OGR seeks to involve libraries in legislative and policy-making processes by (1) informing government of the needs and concerns of the library community; (2) providing library supporters with current information concerning government proposals and actions; (3) building coalitions with Washington-based representatives of groups with similar concerns; and (4) developing grassroots networks to lobby legislators and further library interests. At the direction of the ALA's Committee on Legislation, OGR monitors a broad range of issues, including copyright, appropriations, government information, and telecommunications. Click here to connect to the OGR homepage.

office of record : The unit within an organization responsible for systematically documenting an activity and preserving the resulting records for the normal period for which they are needed to conduct business or affairs, for example, a personnel office in the case current employment records. Synonymous with *agency of record*.

official publication : A document issued in multiple copies by an official body, such as a government agency or intergovernmental organization, under its legal name, often retained by libraries for reference purposes (*example*: Budget of the United States Government issued annually by the Office of Management and Budget). U.S. federal government documents fall into this category.

official records : The formal written documents in which the ongoing activities of a company, government, organization, or institution are recorded, usually retained in archives for their evidential, legal, informational, or historical value, in accordance with instructions contained in a disposition schedule (*example*: Congressional Record). *See also*: office of record.

on order : This is the designation in the CATALOG for an item that has been ordered from a book dealer but has not yet been received.

on-demand publishing : Production by a commercial service of single copies or small quantities of rare, out of print, or difficult to find publications in response to orders from individual customers, as opposed to supply from inventory. An example of such a service is *Dissertation Express* from ProQuest, which provides photocopy reproductions of Ph.D. dissertations made to order from microform masters for a fixed fee. On-demand publishing is expected to grow, especially to meet sci-tech and business needs, as digital archives expand. Synonymous with *demand publishing*.

one-person library (OPL) : A library or information service operated and managed by a single individual, usually with minimal assistance, more common in special libraries than in other types of libraries. In public library systems, small branch libraries are often run by a solo librarian or paraprofessional, sometimes with the help of volunteers from the community. Bookmobiles are nearly always operated by a single person.

online book club : A group of readers who select a book on a regular basis and exchange comments about it via an online mailing list or Web blog, for example, The Book Clique, operated successfully since 1999 by the Tippecanoe County Public Library (Indiana). The advantages are no set meeting times, relative anonymity, and accessibility to readers unable to travel. The disadvantages are lack of face-to-face interaction and slower communications. For more information, see the article "Online Book Clubbing Made Easy" by Neal Starkey in the September 2005 issue of *American Libraries*.

online bookstore : A commercial enterprise that markets and sells books and nonprint media (videos, CDs, DVDs, CD-ROMs, etc.) electronically over the Internet, with payment by credit card. Some online booksellers have retail outlets (*example*: Barnesandnoble.com); others do not (Amazon.com). Click here to connect to a list of links to online bookstores, maintained by Peter Scott of the University of Saskatchewan Library. *See also*: Amazon.com.

Online Catalog : An electronic or digitized version of a library's card catalog. The Cornell University Library's online catalog is called the CU Library Catalog. It is the database that contains records that refer to the many materials held by Cornell University Library.

online catalog : A library catalog consisting of a collection of bibliographic records in machine-readable format, maintained on a dedicated computer that provides uninterrupted interactive access via terminals or workstations in direct, continuous communication with the central computer. Although the software used in online catalogs is proprietary and not standardized, most online catalogs are searchable by author, title, subject heading, and keywords, and most public and academic libraries in the United States provide free public access, usually through a Web-based graphical user interface. Click here to log on to the online catalog of the Library of Congress in Washington, D.C. Synonymous with OPAC.

Online Computer Library Center (OCLC) : The largest bibliographic utility in the world, providing cataloging and acquisitions services, serials and circulation control, interlibrary loan support, and access to online databases. OCLC began as the Ohio College Library Center in 1967, changed its name in 1981 to reflect wider membership, and has since become a major source of cooperative cataloging data for libraries around the world. OCLC maintains *WorldCat*, the largest online bibliographic database in the world, containing over 50 million MARC records. Click here to connect to the OCLC homepage. *See also*: Auto-Graphics, Inc.

Online Information Exchange (ONIX) : A family of XML-based metadata schemes developed by publishers to communicate book trade information such as bibliographic data, pricing, and marketing and promotional information. Some library systems are developing the capacity to use ONIX data to enrich catalog records with tables of contents, author bios, dust jacket blurbs, and similar information. The standard is maintained by EDItEUR jointly with Book Industry Communication and the Book

Industry Study Group (BISG). ONIX for Serials is under development.

Online Programming for All Libraries (OPAL) : A collaborative effort by libraries of all types to provide cooperative Web-based programming and training for library users and library staff from any location, using Web conferencing software (synchronized browsing, text chatting, Voice Over Internet Protocol, etc.). OPAL public online programs include book discussions, interviews, memoir writing workshops, virtual tours of selected digital library collections, special events, and library training. OPAL is administered by the Alliance Library System, the Mid-Illinois Talking Book Center (MITBC), and the Illinois State Library Talking Book and Braille Service. Programs are free, with no registration required. The OPAL homepage provides access to a digital archive of past programs.

online renewal : Books can be renewed online using MY ACCOUNT. In order to renew a book online you must have a valid, current LIBRARY CARD, and the book cannot be over due, recalled for another user, or have reached its renewal limit.

OPAC : Acronym for Online Public Access Catalog. See Online Catalog.

OPAC : This acronym simply stands for Online Public Access Catalog. At our library, the OPAC is called OASIS. OPAC's are electronic card catalogs that provide you with information about materials held by the library.

Open Archival Information System (OAIS) : A reference model for digital archiving systems initially developed by the Consultative Committee for Space Data Systems and adopted by ISO as International Standard ISO 14721:2002. The OAIS model is widely used by libraries as a framework for the development of preservation archives for digital materials. Click here to learn more about OAIS.

Open Archives Initiative (OAI) : An organization funded by the Digital Library Federation, the Coalition for Networked Information, and the National Science Foundation to develop and promote interoperability standards as a means of facilitating the exchange of digital information content. Its program originated in the desire to advance scholarly communication by improving access to distributed repositories of e-prints, known as "archives." The main product of the OAI is a framework for harvesting and aggregating metadata from multiple repositories and a harvesting protocol known as the OAI Protocol for Metadata Harvesting (OAI-PMH). Click here to learn more about OAI. *See also*: open access and Scholarly Publishing and Academic Resources Coalition.

Open Shortest Path First (OSPF) : A link state-based routing protocol for use within a single autonomous system. An autonomous system is a portion of the network under the same administrative authority.

open source : A computer program for which the source code is made available without charge by the owner or licenser, usually via the Internet, to encourage the rapid development of a more useful and bug-free product through open peer review. The practice also allows the product to be customized by its users to suit local needs (*example*: **Linux** operating system). To be certified "open source" under the Open Source Initiative (OSI), software must meet certain established criteria that include no restrictions on access.

open systems : Computer systems (hardware and/or software) designed to operate using standards that are publicly available, allowing competition among vendors based on the features and performance of their products, as opposed to systems that use proprietary standards developed and controlled by a single company. One important advantage of open systems is that anyone can design add-ons; however, by making specifications public, a manufacturer allows others to copy its product. Because UNIX was designed to run on more types of computers than any other operating system, it was synonymous with open systems for many years. Since the mid-1990s, Linux and Java have been the leading models for open systems/open standards.

Open Systems Interconnection (OSI) : An ISO standard for network telecommunication developed in the 1980s to allow direct communication between computers of all types and sizes by defining a general framework for implementing communication protocols in seven layers. Apart from the X.400 e-mail and X.500 directory standards, OSI was never widely implemented and is now useful mainly as a framework or teaching model for other protocols. *See also*: Z39.50.

Oral History Deed of Gift : A legal document transferring ownership of a taped interview from the interviewee to The University of Texas at Arlington Libraries, Special Collections Division. The deed of gift must be signed and dated by both the donor (interviewee) and the interviewer and by a university representative. Restrictions may be placed by the donor on the use of the interview.

Original Order : The order in which records and archives were kept when in active use. The principle of original order requires that this order be preserved or reconstructed, unless it is clear that there was no order or that the records had been accumulated haphazardly.

orphan : In printing, an incomplete line of type, such as a heading or the first line of a paragraph, when it appears at the foot of a page or column of text. Skilled typographers consider such lines awkward and avoid setting them if possible, just as they avoid setting widows. Compare with club line. In indexing, a descriptor or subject heading that has no relation, hierarchic or associative, to any other term in the indexing language (*example*: **Chank**, the Library of Congress subject heading for a type of seashell used in Indian folklore and religion). Orphans are rare in indexing. *See also*: sibling.

orthophotograph : An aerial photograph of uniform scale on which horizontal distance can be accurately measured, the central perspective of the original conventional photograph having been converted to an orthogonal projection by a process of *rectification*, which removes displacement and distortions, giving the image the spatial attributes of a map. To see examples, try a keyword search on the term "orthphotograph" in *Google Image Search* or log on to the National Digital Orthophoto Program (NDOP) of the U.S. Geological Survey. When several orthophotos of uniform scale are combined to create a continuous image of a larger area, the result is an *orthophoto mosaic*. *See also*: digital orthophotograph and digital orthophoto quadrangle.

OSPF : See Open Shortest Path First (OSPF).

Other Operating Expenditures : Any expenditures other than those for materials, binding, and salaries and wages, from a library's budget during a given time period.

out of stock (OS) : A term used on a publisher's invoice to indicate that a publication cannot be supplied at the time the order is received because it is not in inventory. Also abbreviated *o.s.* The opposite of in stock. Compare with out of print. *See also*: temporarily out of stock.

outreach : Library programs and services designed to meet the information needs of users who are unserved or underserved, for example, those who are visually impaired, homebound, institutionalized, not fluent in the national language, illiterate, or marginalized in some other way. Large public libraries often have an *outreach librarian* who is responsible for providing such services. Compare with library extension. *See also*: *Americans with Disabilities Act* and Office for Literacy and Outreach Services.

over due : An item that has not been returned by the DUE DATE.

Packet : The protocol data unit (PDU) that exists at the Internet layer and comprises an IP header and payload.

page number : A number assigned in sequence to a page in a manuscript, book, pamphlet, periodical, etc., to facilitate reference. Page numbers are written or printed in the head or tail margin, usually centered or in the outer corner. Front matter is usually paginated in lowercase roman numerals, text and back matter in consecutive arabic numerals. Blank pages are left unnumbered. Compare with foliation. *See also*: blind page.

painted binding : A style of binding in which a design or picture is painted directly on one or both covers of a book. Because of its light color and smooth surface, vellum was the best covering material for this type of decoration before paper came into widespread use. To see examples, try a search on the keywords "painted and vellum" in the British Library's *Database of Bookbindings*. Click here to see a 16th-century calf binding by Christopher Plantin on which some of the tooled elements are painted in white, gray, black, green, and red (Koninklijke Bibliotheek). See also this 14th-century example in tempera on wood and this 18th-century lacquered example on papier-mâche, courtesy of the Metropolitan Museum of Art).

pamphlet binding : A self-cover or paper publisher's binding in which the leaves of a periodical or pamphlet are wire-stitched or stapled, rather than sewn or glued. Also refers to the rebinding of a pamphlet or its enclosure in a specially-made outer binding, usually for purposes of preservation (click here to see the processes illustrated, courtesy of the University of Illinois Library).

panel back : The spine of a hand-bound book on which the space between two or more of the bands has been enclosed in decorative tooling or panel-stamped with a similar design, in blind or gilt (see this example).

paper preferred : In acquisitions, an approval plan option specifying that the library is to receive the paperback edition in place of the cloth (hardcover) edition whenever the two are published simultaneously. The cost of rebinding the paperback is often less than the price difference between the two editions.

paper splitting : A conservation technique in which one or more paper leaves of a book or manuscript are strengthened by splitting the core of each leaf to allow a second sheet to be inserted between the two halves. Support sheets are first applied to both sides of the leaf to be split, using a gelatin adhesive. After the adhesive has set, but while the core of the paper is still moist, the support sheets are carefully pulled apart, splitting the core into two halves, which are then dried and reassembled with a sheet of Japanese paper sandwiched between them. The adhesive used to bind the Japanese paper to the two halves is soluble only in cold water. After it dries, the support sheets are removed in a bath of very hot water, dissolving the gelatin adhesive but not the core adhesive. Paper splitting is a delicate process that should be undertaken only by an experienced conservator. Click here to see the process illustrated.

pass-along : The likelihood that a copy of an issue of a newspaper or periodical will be read by more individuals than the person who actually purchases it at a newsstand or by subscription. Some publishers use this as a justification for charging libraries a substantially higher subscription price than the rate paid by individual subscribers, a practice known as differential pricing. Although pass-along is difficult to quantify, when combined with circulation it gives an approximate indication of total readership.

Path Vector : A routing protocol technology that exchanges sequences of hop information that indicate the path for a route. For example, BGP-4 exchanges sequences of autonomous system numbers.

Patron Info : A link available through the library catalog that allows Cornell patrons to view their library account information charged items, pending requests, and fines or fees owed. Accessing Patron Info requires the user to enter their Cornell ID number and last name. Patron Info is also accessible via the link View your account or renew a book on the Library Gateway.

patron record : A confidential record in a library circulation system containing data pertinent to a borrower account (full name, street address, telephone number, patron ID, patron type, items on loan, holds, unpaid fines, etc.). In electronic circulation systems, an authorized member of the library staff is permitted to access the patron record by scanning the barcode on the library card or by using a keyboard to enter the patron's name or library card number as input. Some online catalogs allow registered borrowers to view thir own patron records with proper authorization. Synonymous with *circulation record*. *See also*: blocked.

pattern heading : The principle incorporated into Library of Congress subject headings in 1974 that allows a full set of free-floating subdivisions to be established for one or a few representatives of a particular category of subject headings or name headings, which are appropriate for use under other main headings belonging to the same category. For example, the subdivision —**Biopsy** under the pattern heading **Heart** can be used under the heading **Breast** even though no specific authority record exists for the combination **Breast—Biopsy**. The rule does not apply when there is a conflict with a heading established in the subject authority file in another form. For example, the subdivision —**Dislocation** under the pattern heading **Foot** may not be applied to the heading **Joints** because the combination **Joints—Dislocation** is a UF (used for) reference under the heading **Dislocations** in the subject authority file.

pen-flourished initial : An initial letter in a medieval manuscript to which the scribe had added fine linear embellishment in the same color ink as the text or in a different color (usually red, blue, and/or green). Compare these examples in a 15th-century English manuscript (British Library, Arundel 112) with this gilt example in a 15th-century Italian manuscript (British Library, Arundel 271). Pen flourishes were also added to other decorative elements, such as borders, as in this leaf from a 15th-century Delft Book of Hours (Cleveland Museum of Art) and this English manuscript of the same century (British Library, Lansdowne 398). Compare with penwork initial. *See also*: filigree letter.

performing rights society : An association, corporation, or other entity responsible for licensing the public performance and broadcast of nondramatic musical works on behalf of the copyright holders and for collecting and distributing licensing fees to the owners. Examples include the American Society of Composers, Authors and

Publishers (ASCAP); Broadcast Music, Inc. (BMI); SESAC, Inc.; and the MCPS-PRS in the UK.

Periodical : Although the terms periodical, journal, serial, and magazine have slightly different definitions, they are often used interchangeably. They are published on a regular basis (weekly, monthly, annually, etc.) and contain articles written by various authors. A journal contains peer-reviewed articles written by scholars while a magazine contains more popular articles often written by journalists. The terms periodical and serial are more generic and refer to all types of these materials.

Periodical Index : A cumulative list of periodical articles in which the citations are entered by subject (or in classified arrangement) and sometimes under the author's last name. Periodical indexes may be general (*Reader's Guide to Periodical Literature*), devoted to a specific academic discipline (*Education Index*) or group of disciplines (*Humanities Index*), or limited to a particular type of publication (*Alternative Press Index*). In libraries, periodical indexes are available in print, as online electronic databases, or on CD-ROM. Some electronic indexes will provide full-text articles. Print indexes and some electronic indexes only provide citations to articles. The actual periodicals would have to be located for the full articles.

periphrasis : Saying something in a less direct, more roundabout way. Synonymous in this sense with *circumlocution*. Also refers to speech or writing that uses an excess of words to convey an idea or concept that could be expressed more succinctly. Compare with paraphrase.

Permanent/Durable Paper : A term generally applied to pH neutral papers.

Personal Papers : The documents accumulated by an individual or a family.

pharmacopoeia : A book or online resource that lists drugs, chemical compounds, and biological substances, providing information on molecular structure and properties, therapeutic uses, derivatives, and sometimes formulas for manufacture, with tests for establishing identity, purity, strength, etc. (*example*: The Merck Index or PDR: Physicians' Desk Reference). Most libraries keep the current edition of at least one modern pharmacopoeia in the reference section. Click here to read a 17th-century example, courtesy of the Whitney Medical Library at Yale University.

philatelic library : A library devoted to the history of postage stamps and stamp collecting, with a collection consisting of books and periodicals on philately, auction catalogs, government documents, maps, clippings, etc., for example, the American Philatelic Research Library in State College, Pennsylvania.

phonograph record : A thin, flat disk, usually made of vinyl, impressed on one or both sides with a continuous spiral groove in which audible sound is recorded (click here to see examples). As the disk revolves on a playback machine, called a *record player* (see this portable example), the groove causes a stylus to vibrate, producing electrical impulses in a cartridge that can be amplified as sound. The most common playing speed is 33 1/3 rpm (long-playing), but 45 and 78 rpm disks were also manufactured. Audio compact discs have superseded phonograph records in the retail market for sounds recordings, but there is still a market for secondhand records, some of which have become collectible. In libraries, "vinyl" is preserved primarily for its archival value. In *AACR2*, the term "sound disc" is used in the physical description area of the bibliographic record representing a phonograph record, with "analog" given as type of recording. Synonymous with *audiodisc* and *gramophone record*. *See also*: record album.

photogrammetry : The technique of using photographs and other remote sensing images to measure and obtain information about two-or three-dimensional objects. Aerial photogrammetry is mainly used to produce topographic and thematic maps and digital elevation models. Click here to learn more about photogrammetry, courtesy of the *Aerial Archive* maintained by the University of Vienna, or try *The Basics of Photogrammetry*, courtesy of Geodetic Services Inc. *See also*: aerial photograph.

physical processing : The activities carried out by the technical processing department of a library to prepare items for use. The specific techniques used in physical processing depend on the format of the item. A book is usually stamped with at least one ownership mark, labeled, jacketed, and barcoded. A magnetic strip may also be applied to the item to prevent theft. Items such as videocassettes, audiocassettes, CDs, and CD-ROMs may be given a protective container. Physical processing also includes mending, repair, and rebinding in libraries that have an in-house bindery. *See also*: preprocessing.

picture cycle : A series of illustrations in a medieval manuscript, usually appearing on the same page, on successive pages, or at major divisions in the text, forming a set because they are related in subject and often similar in treatment, for example, scenes of events in the life of the Virgin, traditionally associated with the canonical hours in a Book of Hours, or seasonal labors traditionally associated with the months of the year in calendars (see *Les très riches heures du Duc de Berry*, courtesy of WebMuseum, and the *Da Costa Hours*, courtesy of the Morgan Library, MS M.399). Click here and here and here to see scenes from the life of Christ in the *De Lisle Psalter* (British Library, Arundel 83 II). See also this series of historiated initials featuring King David in a 13th-century French psalter (Getty Museum, MS 66). When it introduces the main text, such a series is called a prefatory cycle.

picture library : A library collection consisting primarily of visual documents (prints, photographs, illustrations, posters, postcards, clippings, etc.), mounted or unmounted. The largest collections are maintained by national libraries and museums. Indexing is usually limited to a specific collection. Digitization has made picture collections more accessible. Click here to connect to the Prints & Photographs Reading Room at the Library of Congress, or browse the New York Public Library's *Picture Collection Online* or the Picture Library at the Natural

History Museum in London. For more information on picture libraries, see the entry by Hilary Evans in the *International Encyclopedia of Information and Library Science* (Routledge, 2003). The term is also used by commercial outlets that specialize in providing visual images (see the Mary Evans Picture Library in London).

place of publication : The city where the work is published.

plagiary : Work offered as original that has, in fact, been copied (plagiarized) from another source, usually without permission.

plain binding : A bookbinding made of ordinary materials, often in a neutral color, with little or no adornment, generally produced by a job binder (see this example). *See also*: law calf.

platinum print : A photograph printed on paper treated with iron (ferric) salts that are dissolved out in developing and replaced with platinum. Patented and introduced in 1873 under the name Platinotype by the Englishman William Willis, the process was popular through the 1920s until the price of platinum rose so high that it became too expensive for commercial photography. Platinum prints are valued for their wide range of delicate gray tones and their resistance to fading (permanence). The process has recently been revived in fine art photography and for "keepsake" commercial photographs, such as wedding portraits. Click here to see a selection of platinum prints (Getty Museum) and here to see examples exhibited by the Victoria & Albert Museum, London.

Polyester : A common name for the plastic polyethylene terephthalate. Its characteristics include transparency, colorlessness, and high tensile strength. Polyester is useful in preservation because it is chemically stable. Commonly used in sheet or roll form to make folders, encapsulations, and book jackets. Its thickness is measured in mils. Common trade names are Mylar by DuPont and Meliinex by ICI.

pornography : From the ancient Greek *porne* and *graphos*, meaning "writing about prostitutes." Works of no artistic value, depicting sexuality with the conscious intent to arouse sexual desire. The qualifiers *soft core* and *hard core* are often added to indicate degree of licentiousness. Ownership of print collections is generally limited to private individuals and the special collections of large libraries. Proliferation of pornographic Web sites has been a major impetus for advocates of Internet filtering. In the antiquarian and used book trade, pornographic works are often listed in catalogs under curiosa, erotica, or facetiae. Compare with obscenity. *See also*: banned book, censorship, cyberporn, and expurgated.

postdated : An item bearing a publication date *later* than the actual date of publication. In *AACR*, the date given on the item is used in cataloging even if it is known to be incorrect, and the correct date is added as an interpolation in square brackets (*example*: **1959 [1958]**), with an explanatory note if necessary. The opposite of *antedated*. Also spelled *post-dated*.

poster : A large single sheet of heavy paper or cardboard, usually printed on one side only, with or without illustration, to advertise a product/service or publicize a forthcoming event (meeting, concert, dramatic performance, etc.), intended for display on a bulletin board, kiosk, wall, or other suitable surface. Poster design is a branch of the graphic arts made famous by the 19th-century French artist Henri de Toulouse-Lautrec and his contemporaries. *Posters American Style* is an online exhibition provided by the Smithsonian American Art Museum. The Digital Collections of the University of Washington Libraries include a selection of War Posters. The American Library Association (ALA) publishes a series of celebrity READ posters. Synonymous with *placard*. Compare with handbill. *See also*: ephemera.

practicum : A limited period of hands-on work in a library or other information service agency structured to provide an opportunity for a novice to relate theory to practical experience, usually in the student's field(s) of specialization. Compare with internship.

Prefix Length Notation : The practice of expressing address prefixes as *StartingAddress/PrefixLength*, in which

PrefixLength is the number of high-order bits in the address that are fixed.

prelibrary binding : The binding of new books to meet a higher standard of durability than the normal hardcover publisher's binding. A graphic design similar to that of the original binding is usually preserved on the front cover. In public libraries, *prebinding* is used extensively for children's books, which must withstand heavy wear. Standards for prebinding, issued by the Library Binding Institute, include oversewn sections, a rounded and backed spine, and hinges made of cloth instead of paper. Directory information on prebinders is available in the annual reference serial *Literary Market Place*. Compare with library edition. *See also*: Bound to Stay Bound.

presentation miniature : A small stand-alone painting in an illuminated manuscript, representing the formal presentation of the book to the patron or donor who commissioned it, usually a wealthy aristocrat or ecclesiastic. Michelle Brown notes in *Understanding Illuminated Manuscripts* (Getty Museum/British Library, 1994) that this type of image was sometimes incorporated into subsequent copies where it is more appropriately termed a *dedication miniature*. The popularity of presentation miniatures reached its highest point in the 15th century (see this example in the 15th-century *Chroniques de Hainaut*, courtesy of the Getty Museum).

Preservation : Activities associated with maintaining library, archival, or museum materials for use, either in their original physical form or in some other format. Preservation is considered a broader term than conservation. See also conservation.

pressboard : A highly glazed form of paperboard used when strength and rigidity are required of comparatively thin board because it is very dense and tough. Made from rag or chemical wood pulp, it is less acidic than board made from mechanical wood pulp.

printer's copy : The manuscript version of a work used as the model for setting the type in a printed edition. Survival of such copies is rare, but when properly authenticated, they can be of considerable interest to scholars engaged in textual bibliography and criticism.

Private Addresses : IPv4 addresses that organizations use for private intranet addressing within one of the following address prefixes : 10.0.0.0/8, 172.16.0.0/12, 192.168.0.0/16.

Processing : The operations performed on materials to make a collection available for use.

promotional book : A profusely illustrated book on a popular subject, usually an out of print trade title reprinted in a less expensive edition specifically for sale as a bargain item in trade bookstores. Art, travel, cooking, gardening, and natural history are favorite subjects. In public libraries, a promotional book received in good condition as a gift may be added to the collection if demand exists for the subject. Abbreviated *promo book.*

Public Addresses : IPv4 addresses that are assigned by the ICANN and that are guaranteed to be globally unique and reachable on the IPv4 Internet.

Public Information Office (PIO) : The executive office of the American Library Association responsible for developing and implementing strategic plans for communicating ALA goals and priorities in the areas of media relations, advocacy, public education, and crisis communications. PIO creates targeted initiatives that communicate the position of the ALA on key action areas: 21st-century literacy, diversity, education and lifelong learning, intellectual freedom, and equity of access. The Office also provides public relations counsel and media training and support to ALA executive staff, officers, and members; coordinates national media relations efforts; organizes an advocacy network; and develops materials in support of efforts by librarians to promote local programs and services. Click here to connect to the PIO homepage.

Public Libraries International Network (PLIN) : Founded by a group of former members of the International Network of Public Libraries (INPL), a "think tank" for public librarians established in 1996 with support from the Bertelsmann Foundation to develop and nurture innovative practices, PLIN will begin accepting new members in 2005. The Bertelsmann Foundation is a 26-year-old nonprofit organization established by the multinational media publishing giant Bertelsmann AG. The INPL was created to facilitate cooperation and exchange of experience among public library experts across national boundaries. Click here to learn more about PLIN.

public library : A library or library system that provides unrestricted access to library resources and services free of charge to *all* the residents of a given community, district, or geographic region, supported wholly or in part by public funds. Because public libraries have a broader mandate than academic libraries and most special libraries, they must develop their collections to reflect diversity. The largest public library system in the United States is the New York Public Library. Click here to connect to the *Libweb* directory of U.S. public libraries, or try the *Public Library Locator* maintained by the National Center for Education Statistics (NCES). *See also*: Public Library Association.

Public Library Association (PLA) : A division of the American Library Association (ALA) since 1944, PLA has a membership of librarians, library trustees, and friends interested in the general improvement and expansion of public library services for readers of all ages. PLA publishes the bimonthly magazine *Public Libraries*. Click here to connect to the PLA homepage.

Public Library Geographic Database (PLGDB) : A demographic resource for public library planners and decision-makers developed by the GeoLib Program at Florida State University (FSU) and the Information Institute at the FSU School of Information Studies, with funding from the Institute of Museum and Library Services (IMLS), *PLGDB* uses geographic information systems (GIS) software to link key public library data sets to a national interactive digital base map of over 16,000 public library locations in the United States. The first key data set contains data on library use, staffing, and funding for each library or library system's central facility, collected by the Federal-State Cooperative System (FSCS) of the National Center for Educational Statistics (U.S. Department of Education). The second key data set includes U.S. Census data selected on the basis of relevance to public library use (age, education, income, and language spoken) provided at the block group level (about 1,000 persons). Block groups are aggregated to form census tracts (4,000 to 8,000 persons), which in turn make up counties. Click here to connect to *PLGDB*.

publisher : The person or company that prints and issues books and periodicals.

pyro-patron : A library patron who is (1) showing signs of combustability, (2) in imminent danger of igniting, or (3) already on fire, usually a test of the civility and self-control of the reference librarian. For possible responses, see John Herbert's "Pyro-Patron Policy" in *The Unabashed Librarian* (1998). Synonymous with *flaming patron* and *conflagrated patron*. *See also*: problem patron.

pyroxylin : A chemical substance (partially nitrated cellulose) used in the manufacture of lacquers, plastics, and artificial leathers. In bookbinding, it is used to coat or impregnate book cloth to enhance durability.

quad-centered photograph : The second exposure in a series of three consecutive aerial photographs taken of the area covered by a quadrangle used as a unit in mapping. The first exposure is taken directly above one of the boundaries of the quadrangle, the second directly above the center of the quad, and the third above the opposite boundary. The quad-centered exposure is made from an altitude that permits coverage of the entire area of the quad.

quadraphonic : Sound reproduced by an audio device simultaneously from four separate channels with four amplifiers or speakers. Quadraphonic sound separation produces a more realistic result than monaural or stereophonic sound recording.

quarter binding : A style of bookbinding in which the spine is bound in a different material than the sides, usually a more durable covering such as leather, often in a contrasting color, extending no more than one-eighth of the width of the boards. Click here to see a 19th-century example in quarter goatskin with marbled paper boards and here to see an example with the spine in cloth, courtesy of the British Library's *Database of Bookbindings*. Compare with full binding, half binding, and three-quarter binding. *See also*: quarter cloth and quarter leather.

quasi-synonym : A word or phrase not precisely the same in meaning as another term, which is nevertheless treated as synonymous in a given indexing language, for example, the term "Library science" used for (UF) "Librarianship" in the *Library of Congress Subject Headings* list. Synonymous with *near-synonym*.

quatern book : In hand-binding, the binder traditionally bound the thirteenth book at no charge, presumably as an incentive to place larger binding orders, but by the early 19th century, this custom was restricted in England to all the copies of a single title delivered to the bindery at the same time and was not carried over into machine binding.

quill pen : A writing implement made by cutting back the plume and shaping the thick end of one of the flight feathers of a large bird, such as a goose or swan, used prior to the invention of the dip fountain pen in the 18th century for writing documents and for copying manuscripts by hand. Using a quill pen was a two-handed operation in the Middle Ages, with a knife held in the spare hand for making corrections (see this illumination in a 12th-century Gospel book). A quill pen had to be sharpened repeatedly because the nib wears and often breaks with use. Click here and here to learn more about the cutting of quill pens.

rare book : A book so difficult to find that only a few copies are known to antiquarian booksellers. Those that do exist seldom appear on the market and are consequently coveted. Rare books are often valuable, but not all highly valuable books are rare. Most libraries keep their rare books in a secure location to which access is restricted (usually in special collections). Very rare books are sold at book auctions and by dealers serving collectors (see for example the Philadelphia Rare Books & Manuscripts Company). For a detailed discussion of the history of rare book libraries, see the entry by Daniel Traister in the *International Encyclopedia of Information and Library Science* (Routledge, 2003). Many libaries are digitizing images from their rare books collections (see this exhibition by the Missouri Botanical Garden Library). Rules for cataloging rare books are given in *Descriptive Cataloging of Rare Books*, 2nd edition (Library of Congress Cataloging Distribution Service, 1991). The Rare Book School at the University of Virginia is the only one if its kind in the United States. *See also*: first edition, incunabula, price guide, and Rare Books and Manuscripts Section.

Rare Books : Books that are valued for the significance of their contents, their scarcity, their imprint or date of publication, their physical characteristics or condition, or their associations (signed or annotated by a famous author, for instance). Cornell's primary collections of rare books are are located in the Rare Books & Manuscripts Collections in Kroch Library.

readership : The total number of people who read, or are estimated to read, a given publication, not necessarily equal to the number who purchase or subscribe to it. In periodical publishing, total readership equals base circulation plus pass-along. The term is also used to refer to a particular class of reader, for example, *educated readership* as opposed to *general readership.*

reading disability : Difficulty in learning to read, a serious obstacle to individual achievement in a literate society. The causes can be physical (e.g., dyslexia or ADHD), psychological (fear of failure), or cultural (lack of exposure to basic language skills in early childhood). In the public schools in the United States, reading failure is disproportionately prevalent among children living in poverty, but Dr. G. Reid Lyon of the Child Development and Behavior Branch of the National Institute of Child Health and Human Development (NICHD) of the National

Institutes of Health (NIH) has noted that through "systematic, explicit, and intensive instruction in phonemic awareness, phonics, reading fluency, vocabulary, and reading comprehension" the majority of kindergarten and elementary school children at risk of reading failure can learn to read at average or above levels. Research by NICHD reveals that failure to develop basic reading skills by age nine predicts a lifetime of illiteracy. The key to effective prevention is early identification and intervention.

reading matter : Anything that can be read, from the back of a cereal box to a philosophical treatise. Reading material need not be written or printed on paper, merely text-based, for example, a news article published at a Web site. Choice of reading material reflects a person's interests, tastes, education, and experience. *See also*: readers' advisory and reading preference.

rebacked : A book given a new spine and mended hinges, usually because the spine was cracked or the hinges weakened. Original materials are used where possible, but when new cover material is required, a close match is usually attempted by the binder. Rebacking is not as extensive as rebinding since some of the original binding (usually the boards) is retained. Click here to see the steps in the process. *See also*: backstrip.

rebinding : The complete rehabilitation of a book too worn to be mended or repair, a process that usually entails removing the cover or case, resewing the sections, and applying a new cover or case. In some instances, parts of an old binding can be incorporated into a new one. When this is impossible and the old binding is important, it should be kept as part of the book's history. The steps involved in preparing a book for rebinding are collectively known as pulling. Very large libraries are often equipped to perform rebinding in-house, but smaller libraries must rely on the services of a commercial bindery. Click here to see the process documented by the University of Washington Libraries. Compare with recased and recover. *See also*: covers bound in.

recall : To request that a book which has already been CHECKED OUT be returned to the library prior to the DUE DATE. You may ask for a recall by filling out a form at CIRCULATION. You will be notified when the book is returned.

receipt : A written document stating that something has been received, usually in exchange for payment of an amount noted in the acknowledgment. Sometimes found among personal and family papers, receipts may contain information of historical importance. Click here to see a receipt for tobacco purchased by Meriwether Lewis for the Lewis and Clark expedition to the West (National Archives and Records Administration). Also used synonymously with *recipe*, as in *receipt book*.

reciprocal borrowing privileges : Loan privileges granted by independent cooperating libraries to registered members of each other's user groups, sometimes for a modest fee. In September 2004, the Office of Research and Statistics (ORS) of the American Library Association (ALA) surveyed the state data coordinators of each state or territorial library agency concerning the presence of statewide reciprocal borrowing, reciprocal borrowing between similar libraries (public, academic, school, and special), multistate reciprocal borrowing, and whether the state had issued a statewide library card. The results were summarized in the January 2005 issue of *American Libraries*. Click here to read the results.

Record : A collection of related data fields organized and accessible as a single entity. Examples of data fields are author, title, publisher, abstract, call number, etc. In a periodical index, which is a collection of article citations, each citation is a record. In the CU Library Catalog, each reference retrieved per title is also a record.

record album : One or more paper sleeves designed to hold phonograph records, usually enclosed in a colorful pasteboard cover, often with a list of the contents and descriptive notes printed on the back or on the inside (see this example). The sleeves may have wide circles cut from the center, sometimes replaced with transparent material to allow the record labels to remain visible. Also used in reference to the recording itself.

record copy : In records management, the single copy of a document (handwritten, printed, photographic, or machine-readable), designated as the official copy or most important copy for purposes of reference and preservation, usually held by the creating office or another office of record, for example, the official transcript of a student's grades, usually held by the administrative offices of the educational institution at which the course work was undertaken. The record copy is often but not always the original. Convenience copies may be retained in other departments within the organization. Synonymous with *copy of record*, *official copy*, and *principal copy*.

Records : All recorded information, regardless of media or characteristics, made or received and maintained by an organization or institution in pursuance of it legal obligations or in the transaction of its business.

records management : The field of management devoted to achieving accuracy, efficiency, and economy in the systematic creation, retention, conservation, dissemination, use, and disposition of the official records of a company, government agency, organization, or institution, whether in physical or electronic form, usually undertaken by a professionally trained *records manager* on the basis of a comprehensive and thorough records survey. Security and disaster preparedness are essential elements of a good records management program.

recruitment : The process of attracting qualified personnel to work in a library or library system by posting a notice and position description in appropriate LIS journals and to library-related electronic mailing lists and by publicizing the vacancy at job fairs and word-of-mouth. Also refers to the efforts of library schools and professional library associations to attract promising students to careers in library and information science. *See also*: Office for Human Resources Development and Recruitment.

reference : The reference desk and the reference and collections department are located on level 2 of Tisch Library.

Librarians at the reference desk can help you with your research and with using library resources. The library keeps reference materials apart from the regular collection. Dictionaries, encyclopedias, and indexes are examples of reference materials. You cannot CHECK OUT reference materials.

reference collection : Books containing authoritative information not meant to be read cover to cover, such as dictionaries, handbooks, and encyclopedias, shelved together by call number in a special section of the library called the reference stacks. Reference books may not be checked out because they are needed by librarians to answer questions at the reference desk. Their location and circulation status is usually indicated by the symbol "R" or "Ref" preceding the call number in the catalog record and on the spine label. *See also*: ready reference.

Reference Desk : When a person has a question about how to find specific information or how to use library services and resources, assistance can be obtained from a reference librarian at the reference desk. Professional librarians and reference assistants staff reference desks to assist patrons with their questions.

Reference librarian : Reference librarians are specialists in the field of information retrieval. Generally they have a Masters degree in library science, and may have other graduate degrees as well. Reference librarians work in public services answering questions posed by library patrons at the reference desk, by telephone, via e-mail, or through an online chat session. They also provide instruction on the use of library resources and information technology.

RefWorks : RefWorks is a web-based tool for managing citations and bibliographies. Researchers can create their own personal database by importing references from online databases. They can use these references in writing their papers and automatically format the paper and the bibliography in seconds.

relative index : A subject index to a classification system indicating the classes under which subjects are listed, with their notations. In the Dewey Decimal Classification schedules, subjects are arranged by discipline. At the end of the schedules, an alphabetical index of subjects is provided (the Relative Index). Indented under each subject heading is an alphabetical list of the disciplines in which the subject is found, with corresponding class numbers. For example, the entry in the index for the subject "Books" directs the cataloger to the discipline "Bibliographies" with the notation **011** and also to "Publishing" (**070.5**), "Sociology" (**302.232**), and "Technology" (**686**).

remainders : Publisher's overstock (unsold copies of a book or other item) purchased by lot by a *remainder dealer* on the understanding that the items may be offered for sale at a substantially reduced price. Bound remainders may be marked to distinguish them from copies sold at list price. Unbound overstock may be bound in an inexpensive *remainder binding* or reduced to pulp if there is no market for the title. The author receives no royalty on remaindered copies. The fact that a book is *remaindered* does not necessarily reflect the quality of the work—the edition may have been too large, the published price too high, the subject matter esoteric or ephemeral, or the content revised and issued in a new edition. Abbreviated *rem*. Compare with job lot.

renew : To extend the DUE DATE for a book. This is taken care of at the CIRCULATION desk in person or by telephone, or by ONLINE RENEWAL.

Renewal : An extension of the loan period for charged library materials. Renewals may be handled in person at the circulation desk, by phone, or through the link "View your account or renew a book" on the Library Gateway.

repetitive stress injury (RSI) : Tissue damage resulting from the frequent performance of tasks requiring repeated movements of the hands, arms, legs, or torso, for example, the stamping of due dates on books and other items at the circulation desk. Effects include chronic nerve and joint pain and swelling, carpal tunnel syndrome, and damage to the spine. RSI has been cited as a justification for the use of radio frequency identification (RFID) technology in libraries. Preventive measures include regular rest breaks and changes in the ergonomic design of the workplace. Click here to learn more about RSI in *Wikipedia*. The Arthritis Society of Canada also provides Quick Facts on RSI. Synonymous with *musculoskeletal repetitive motion disorder* and *repetitive strain injury*.

representative fraction (RF) : In cartography, the relationship of scale between distance on a map or chart and the actual distance on the area of land or sea represented, given with the title or in the legends as a ratio or fraction understood to be in standard units of measurement (*example*: **1:1,000,000** or **1/1,000,000**). Click here to zoom in on an example printed on the lower-left-hand corner of a map of South America, courtesy of the Perry-Castañeda Library. Synonymous with *fractional scale* and *natural scale*. Compare with bar scale and statement of equivalency.

Request for Comments (RFC) : An official document that specifies the details for protocols included in the TCP/IP protocol suite. The Internet Engineering Task Force (IETF) creates and maintains RFCs for TCP/IP.

Research Libraries Group (RLG) : A not-for-profit membership corporation of over 120 libraries, archives, historical societies, museums and other institutions devoted to improving access to information that supports research and learning.

Research Libraries Information Network (RLIN) : Owned and operated by RLG, RLIN serves the information access and management needs of its member institutions as well as individuals worldwide. It contains over 55 million bibliographic records.

reserves : The "reserve lists" feature can be found in the CATALOG. Check here to find the call number(s) of the item(s) placed on reserve for your class. You may search by the name of the course or your professor's name. Printed materials "placed on reserve" may be requested at CIRCULATION. Media reserve items must be used in the MEDIA CENTER. You will need a valid LIBRARY CARD and your CALL NUMBER. Reserve materials are usually available for short LOAN PERIODS.

reshelving : The job of returning books and other items to the shelves of a library in correct call number sequence after they have been used, usually performed by a student assistant in an academic library or by a staff member called a page in a public library. The University of Illinois Library provides a brief online tutorial on *Proper Shelving Habits*. *See also*: reshelving cart and shelf reading.

retensioning : The unspooling of archival magnetic tape (audiotape and videotape) onto a take-up reel from which it is rewound at controlled tension and speed to redistribute stresses and keep the edges of the tape from touching the spool, a procedure preservationists recommend for audiovisual collections every three years. Retensioning is also recommended for optimal performance when using a new tape and after exposure to major temperature changes or other shock.

Retrospective Conversion : The process of converting bibliographic records from print to a machine-readable format.

reused number : In Dewey Decimal Classification (DDC), a class number assigned to a different subject than the one it represented in a previous edition. As a general rule, numbers are reused only in complete revisions or when the reused number has been vacant for at least two consecutive editions.

review journal : A scholarly journal devoted to the publication of articles providing analysis of trends in an academic field or summaries of the current state of research on topics of particular interest within the field (*example*: **Statistical Science: A Review Journal of the Institute of Mathematical Statistics**). Articles may be submitted at the editor's invitation. *See also*: annual review.

RFC : See Request for Comments (RFC).

RIP : See Routing Information Protocol (RIP).

RLIN (Eureka) : The Research Libraries Information Network (RLIN), is an information management and retrieval system used by hundreds of comprehensive research libraries, archival repositories, museums, academic, public, law, technical, and corporate libraries to build an international database of bibliographic information. The RLIN database indexes books, journals, and other materials held by full-member Research Library Group (RLG) libraries. Cornell researchers can identify and locate materials in other research libraries and collections using RLIN, and order these materials through interlibrary loan. As a member of RLG, records for many of the Cornell University Library's holdings will show up in this database. RLIN is available through the catalog and Find Databases.

role indicator : In indexing, a code used to indicate the syntactic relationship between two or more index terms (subject headings or descriptors) assigned to a document to facilitate retrieval by subject (adapted from the *ASIS Thesaurus of Information Science and Librarianship*, Information Today, 1998).

Route Determination Process : The process of determining which single route in the routing table to use for forwarding a packet.

Route Summarization : The practice of using address prefixes to summarize the address spaces of regions of a network, rather than using the routes for individual subnets.

Router : A node that can be a source and destination for IP traffic and can also forward IP packets that are not addressed to an IP address of the router. On an IPv6 network, a router also typically advertises its presence and host configuration information.

Router Advertisement : For IPv4, a message sent by a router that supports ICMP router discovery. For IPv6, an IPv6 Neighbour Discovery message sent by a router that typically contains at least one Prefix Information option, from which hosts create stateless autoconfigured unicast IPv6 addresses and routes.

Router Discovery : A Neighbour Discovery process in which a host discovers the local routers on an attached subnet.

Routing Information Protocol (RIP) : A distance vector-based routing protocol used in small and medium sized networks.

Routing Protocols : A series of periodic or on-demand messages that contain routing information that is exchanged between dynamic routers.

Routing Table : The set of routes used to determine the next-hop address and interface for IP traffic sent by a host or forwarded by a router.

rule interpretation (RI) : A formal explanation, clarification, or expansion of existing cataloging rules, usually resulting from a case that raises questions concerning the applicability of established policy and/or procedure. In the United States, the Library of Congress issues rule interpretations (*LCRI*) for *AACR2*, formulated as needed by the Cataloging Policy & Support Office, to reflect internal LC policy decisions. Distributed by the Cataloging Distribution Service, *LCRI* are followed by other libraries for the sake of consistency.

sacramentary : A liturgical book containing prayers recited by the celebrant during the consecration of the Eucharist at high Mass (other parts were contained in the evangelary, gradual, and epistolary). Michelle Brown notes in *Understanding Illuminated Manuscripts* (Getty Museum/British Library, 1994) that by the end of the 13th century the sacramentary had been superseded by the missal, a new book combining the various texts in a single volume, introduced during the Carolingian period to standardize Church ritual. Click here and here to view two leaves from a beautifully illuminated 9th-century Carolingian sacramentary (Bibliothèque Nationale de France, Lat. 2290) and here to page through an 11th-century Ottonian sacramentary (Getty Museum, MS Ludwig V 2).

Salaries and Wages : All monies paid in salaries and wages from the library's budget during a given period of time before deductions for all staff paid.

sample book : An album or other volume containing specimens, usually of a commercial product such as cloth, yarn, leather, wood, wallpaper, or paint, from which the customer may make a selection. Click here to see a 19th-century French example containing samples of dyed yarn (University of Delaware Library) and here to see a 20th-century example containing fabric samples, courtesy of Fabrics.net. Typefaces and printing papers are also displayed in sample books. Also, a book containing models of designs and lettering for the use of medieval scribes (see this example, courtesy of The Lilly Library at Indiana University).

schedule reduction : The elimination of some of the provisions made in a previous edition of a classification schedule, resulting in the discontinuation of certain class numbers, usually because the literature on the subject has dwindled significantly or because the class represents a distinction no longer recognized in the discipline or field.

school library edition : A special edition of a serial publication, issued specifically for distribution to school libraries. In August 2005, *American Libraries* reported that tobacco advertisements will be removed from school library editions of *Time, Newsweek, People,* and *Sports Illustrated* under an agreement between publishers, tobacco companies, and the state attorneys general. The action follows a similar agreement, reached in 2003, under which publishers provide classroom editions of magazines for schools, containing no tobacco advertising.

School Library Journal (SLJ) : Published by R.R. Bowker since 1961, *SLJ* is a monthly trade journal and review publication for school, children's, and young adult librarians. In addition to regular columns, feature articles, and news of interest to the profession, *SLJ* reviews approximately 4,000 new trade books for children and young adult readers each year and over 1,000 educational media titles, including CD-ROMs. The reviews are short but evaluative, written by and for librarians. Click here to log on to the homepage of *School Library Journal*. ISSN: 0362-8930. Previous title: *Junior Libraries*.

Science and Technology Section (STS) : Established in 1961, STS is the section of the Association of College and Research Libraries (ACRL) within the American Library Association (ALA) that provides a forum for librarians in scientific and technical fields to achieve and maintain awareness of the impact and range of information with which they work. STS also seeks to enhance the accessibility and active use of scientific and technical information. The section publishes the electronic journal *Issues in Science & Technology Librarianship (ISTL).* Click here to connect to the STS homepage.

scope note (SN) : A brief statement included in an entry in a list of subject headings or in a thesaurus of indexing terms to indicate the intended use or meaning of the term in the indexing language and any special rules for assigning it in indexing. Scope notes are usually added for clarification or to restrict the use of a term to one of several possible meanings. Not all terms require a scope note, but if one is given, it normally precedes any synonyms (UF), broader terms (BT), narrower terms (NT), or related terms (RT). Compare with parenthetical qualifier. In Dewey Decimal Classification (DDC), a note in the schedules indicating that the subject represented by a class number is broader or narrower than the heading implies.

scout : A person with experience in the book trade, employed by a publisher to seek out new writers and illustrators whose early works show promise and to explore with them possibilities for new books. In the motion picture industry, producers also employ such persons to locate books, manuscripts, etc., with potential for film adaptation. Compare with book scout.

scrapbook : A blankbook, usually of large size, containing unprinted leaves for mounting or inserting photographs, pictures, clippings, letters, invitations, and other memorabilia, usually to preserve them for sentimental reasons. Click here to see a 19th-century example (Metropolitan Museum of Art) and here to see an example of an online scrapbook, courtesy of the town of Auburn, Wisconsin. The Library of Congress provides the searchable *Lewis Carroll Scrapbook*. Click here for advice on how to make archival scrapbooks, courtesy of the Florida Bureau of Archives and Records Management. Compare with album. *See also*: memorabilia.

screen dump : The process of saving as a file, or sending to a printer, a copy of the image displayed on the monitor of a computer, usually to create a record that can be used to document and/or diagnose a malfunction. Synonymous with *screen capture*.

searchable : An electronic resource running on software designed to allow the user to type a word, phrase, or string of words or phrases as input to find all the records, entries, or text containing the search term(s). Most online catalogs and bibliographic databases can be searched by author, title, subject heading (descriptor), and keywords. Boolean logic and truncation are permitted in a keywords search in most library catalogs and databases; wildcard and proximity searching in some.

security audit : A thorough on-site inspection in which a person (or persons) trained and experienced in library security critically examines and analyzes all the existing security systems and procedures used in a library to ascertain current status, identify deficiencies or excesses, and make recommendations based on findings. A professional security audit may include the analysis of crime statistics, an assessment of insurance needs, and discussion of sensitive topics, such as internal theft and personal security issues.

selection criteria : The set of standards used by librarians to decide whether an item should be added to the collection, which normally includes a list of subjects or fields to be covered, levels of specialization, editions, currency, languages, and formats (large print, nonprint, abridgments, etc.). Selection criteria usually reflect the library's mission and the information needs of its clientele, but selection decisions are also influenced by budgetary constraints and qualitative evaluation in the form of reviews, recommended core lists, and other selection tools. *See also*: collection development policy.

Self-Check Station : Bar-code reading machines for patrons to check out materials themselves, rather than checking materials out at the circulation desk. Self-check stations are available at Olin and Hotel School libraries. A Cornell ID card is required to use self-check. A receipt is printed indicating when the materials are due back at the library.

Serial : Although the terms periodical, journal, serial, and magazine have slightly different definitions, they are often used interchangeably. They are published on a regular basis (weekly, monthly, annually, etc.) and contain articles written by various authors.

Series : File units or documents arranged in accordance with a filing system or maintained as a unit because they relate to a particular subject or function, result from the same activity, have a particular form, or because of some other relationship arising out of their creation, receipt, or use. Also known as a record series.

series statement : The area of bibliographic description reserved in library cataloging for information concerning the group of which a work issued as one of two or more separately published items is a member, including the title proper of the series, statements of responsibility concerning the series, ISSN, and number within the series (if the items are numbered). In the MARC record, series statements are entered in fields tagged 4XX.

service contract : An arrangement in which the supplier (or some other service provider) agrees to regularly maintain and repair one or more pieces of equipment after any warranties have expired, usually in exchange for payment of an annual or monthly fee. Libraries enter into such agreements to keep photocopiers, microform reader-printer machines, security devices, automation equipment, etc., in working order. Synonymous with *service agreement*.

SFX : Linking software that libraries use to link from one database to another.

shifting : The laborious process of moving an entire collection, or sections of a collection, from one location to another in the stacks of a library, usually to create shelf space in classifications that have become overcrowded.

shrink-wrap license : Licensing terms stated in a notice printed in or on the package containing a new software product, which the manufacturer considers the purchaser to have accepted by the act of removing the plastic wrapper from the container ("breaking the seal") and keeping the product. Such agreements often include provisions and restrictions that have not been uniformly enforced by the courts, because they give software publishers more rights than are permitted under federal copyright or patent law. The controversial *Uniform Computer Information Transactions Act (UCITA)* would allow software publishers to embed non-negotiable, enforceable contract terms in this type of mass-market license. Also spelled *shrinkwrap*. *See also*: click-on license.

signed : An entry in a reference work or an article in a periodical that includes the name of the author (or authors), usually given at the beginning or end of the text. Also refers to a copy of a limited edition bearing the signature of the author or illustrator in the statement of limitation. In a more general sense, any written document, such as a letter or legal instrument, that indicates the identity of the person who wrote it, usually by the presence of a signature. The opposite of unsigned. *See also*: byline.

sister library : A library that enters into a voluntary partnership with a library from another culture for the purpose of encouraging multicultural exchange and international understanding. In 1999, the National Commission on Libraries and Information Science (NCLIS) and Sister Cities International (SCI) embarked on a major initiative, Sister Libraries: A White House Millennium Council Project, chaired by First Lady Hillary Rodham Clinton, to pair public and school libraries in the United States with similar libraries worldwide, with focus on programs for children and adolescents. Many sister libraries are in locations already affiliated through SCI, an organization for sister city, county, and state programs in the United States (see this example). NCLIS support for the project ended in 2000. Click here to learn more about the sister libraries, courtesy of the American Library Assocaition.

Site-local Address : A local-use IPv6 address identified by the prefix FEC0::/10. The scope of a site-local address is a site. Site-local addresses are equivalent to the IPv4 private address space. Site-local addresses are not reachable from other sites, and routers must not forward site-local traffic outside the site.

sketchbook : A blankbook containing leaves of drawing paper for making sketches. Also, such a book when it is filled with drawings. Click here to see examples from the Smithsonian *Archives of American Art*.

solander : A box in the shape of a book, wide enough to stand upright, hinged to fold open at the front or side, with a clasp or spring catch, used for storing books, pamphlets, maps, plates, papers, and other documents. Named after Daniel C. Solander, the 18th-century Swedish botanist who designed it for storing specimens at The British Museum, this type of container is virtually dustproof and waterproof. Click here to see diagrams of two designs, courtesy of *Conservation OnLine*, and here to see a large example (Heritage Collections Council, Australia). Compare with pull-case and slipcase.

Solicited-node Multicast Address : An IPv6 multicast address that nodes use to resolve addresses. The solicited-node multicast address is constructed from the prefix FF02::1:FF00:0/104 and the last 24 bits of a unicast IPv6 address. The solicited-node multicast address acts as a pseudo-unicast address to efficiently resolve addresses on IPv6 links.

Sorting : The process by which manuscripts are physically divided into appropriate alphabetical, chronological, numerical, subject, or other groups. Less frequently used with archives, except when restoring them to their original or intended order.

Spatial Data : Spatial data is data pertaining to the location and spatial dimensions of geographical entities. Examples of spatial data files can be found within the Cornell University Geospatial Information Repository (CUGIR), accessible through the Library Gateway.

special appointment : An employee hired, usually full-time, for a period of specified length (often one or two years) without expectation of permanent employment. Special appointments are sometimes renewable, but usually not indefinitely. If the person accepting such employment subsequently applies for a permanent position at the same institution and is hired, the period of special appointment may be considered part of the probationary period.

special collections : A location that houses rare and unique materials that cannot be used outside of the library. Access to Special Collections is through Digital Collections and Archives, which is located on level G of Tisch Library.

specimen page : One of several sample pages submitted by the printer to the publisher to show the proposed typographic style for a prospective publication, usually *four* in number, including the first page of a chapter and at least one subhead to show display type. Also refers to a copy of a page from a book or other publication reproduced on any scale for use by the publisher in marketing or for purposes of display (see this example).

spell checker : A feature of most word processing software that automatically checks the spelling of words typed in a document against a built-in dictionary, alerting the user to any misspelled words and even correcting typos on the fly. Spell checkers are not infallible. A misspelling will not be flagged if it is itself a word ("their" for "there"). The option can usually be turned "off" by the user if not desired. Also spelled *spellchecker*.

spoilage : In book production, printed sheets or entire copies discarded because they contain imperfections or were damaged in printing or binding. Allowance for spoilage is included in the size of printing and binding orders.

spreadsheet : In computing, an application program designed to assist the user in creating and maintaining two-dimensional tables of numerical data and textual information, widely used in budgeting, financial and statistical analysis, and reports. Spreadsheet software allows the user to create mathematical formulas to compute row and column totals, variances, etc., automatically whenever new values are supplied. Most programs allow two or more spreadsheets to be linked by formulas, so that a change in one is automatically reflected in the others. Sophisticated spreadsheet applications support graphics features, enabling the user to manipulate data and display the results in charts and graphs. *Excel* and *Lotus 1-2-3* are the two most widely used spreadsheet packages. Also refers to the result of using such a program, in print or electronic format.

stacked advertising : Advertising that appears only in the front or back, or in the front *and* back, of a periodical and nowhere else in the issue (*example*: **National Geographic**). In custom binding of periodicals, unpaginated advertisements appearing in the front and/or back of each issue may be removed to reduce bulk.

Stacks : Stacks or stack area refer to the space in a library where the majority of library materials are shelved. Often the stacks are made up of multiple floors and contain many rows of shelving units.

standard number : The unique identification number assigned to an edition at the time of first publication, in accordance with an internationally standardized identification system, usually appearing somewhere on the item. In books published in hardcover, the International Standard Book Number (ISBN) is printed on the verso of the title page and usually on the front flap of the dust jacket. In paperback editions, it appears on the verso of the title page and on the back cover (usually in the lower-right-hand corner). In serials, the International Standard Serial Number (ISSN) appears in the masthead or with the table of contents of each issue or on the copyright page of each volume or part of a series. In printed music, the International Standard Music Number (ISMN) appears on the copyright page. In *AACR2*, the standard number is entered in the standard number and terms of availability area of the bibliographic description.

Static Routing : The use of manually configured routes in the routing tables of routers.

stationery binding : A general term for the bindings on volumes designed to be written in (blankbooks, ledgers, etc.), as distinct from those on books intended for reading, typically more sturdy than the usual publisher's binding. To see examples, try a keywords search on the phrase "Boorum & Pease" in *Google Image Search*. Stationery bindings may include a spring action in the binding that elevates the spine so that the leaves lie flat when the volume is opened. Synonymous with *accounts binding* and *ledger binding*.

status : (1) This message appears on the CATALOG screens and indicates whether or not a book has been CHECKED OUT. If the screen indicates AVAILABLE, the book should be on the shelf. However, the book may be in use in the library by some one else or it may be waiting to be reshelved. If you cannot find a book that should be on the shelves, go to CIRCULATION and ask them for a trace form. (2) Status refers to a person's standing as a library borrower, for example : student, staff, faculty, and community user.

stichometric note : A brief note in a manuscript indicating the number of lines in the text, often the basis for determining the amount to be paid for scribal work (see this example in a papyrus codex of the *Pauline Epistles*, courtesy of the University of Michigan Library).

storage orientation : The direction in which materials are placed in library or archival storage, relative to the surface of the earth. Because the force of gravity may affect the condition of materials over time, whether they are stored vertically or horizontally can make a difference in their preservation. For example, for long-term storage, films must be placed horizontally on a rack or shelf to distribute the weight of the film over the entire side surface of the pack and to maintain uniform wind tension throughout the pack. Click here to learn about the effects of downward pressure on film packs stored vertically (National Film and Sound Archive, Australia).

student publication : A newspaper or magazine published in print or online by students enrolled at a high school, college, or university, usually funded by student fees and edited by journalism majors or members of an interest group or club. Most student newspapers are issued daily (*Yale Daily News*) or weekly (*The Wooster Voice*). U.S. college and university newspapers available online are indexed by state in *Yahoo! See also*: yearbook.

Subject Headings : Words or phrases assigned to books and articles which are used to index these items by topic. The Cornell University Library uses Library of Congress subject headings.

subject specialist : A librarian qualified by virtue of specialized knowledge and experience to select materials and provide bibliographic instruction and reference services to users in a specific subject area or academic discipline (or subdiscipline). In academic libraries, subject specialists often hold a second master's degree in their field of specialization. Also refers to a librarian trained in subject analysis.

Subnet : One or more LAN segments that are bounded by routers and that use the same IP address prefix. Other terms for subnet are network segment and link.

Subnet Mask : The expression of the length of an address prefix for IPv4 address ranges in dotted decimal notation. For example, the address prefix 131.107.0.0/16 in subnet mask notation is 131.107.0.0, 255.255.0.0.

Subnetted Address Prefix : Either a new IPv4 address prefix that is the result of subnetting an IPv4 address prefix or a new IPv6 address prefix that is the result of subnetting an IPv6 address prefix.

Subnetting : The act of subdividing the address space of an IPv4 or IPv6 address prefix.

Subseries : An aggregate of file units within a record series readily separable in terms of physical class, type, form, subject, or filing arrangement.

suggestion box : Some libraries in the United States provide a means for patrons to suggest improvements in services, request the purchase of a specific item, or comment on library policies and practices in writing on a slip of paper deposited in a small box provided for the purpose near the circulation desk, reference desk, or main entrance (see this example). Some online catalogs and library Web pages allow users to post suggestions and comments electronically. The responses of library staff and administration may be posted on a public bulletin board or kiosk or in a special section of the library homepage.

Supernetting : The obsolete use of route summarization to assign blocks of Class C address prefixes on the Internet.

supplemental invoice : In acquisitions, an invoice sent by a publisher or vendor of books or serials for added charges not covered by prepayments, usually an unexpected price increase by the publisher, publication of additional volumes, or fluctuations in currency exchange rates.

synopsis : A concise written description of the plot of a long narrative work (novel, play, opera, epic poem, etc.) giving a quick, orderly overview of the whole, usually prepared by a person other than the author. As a general rule, academic libraries do not purchase reference works that specialize in providing *synopses* (*example*: **Masterplots**) because they are too easily used by students to avoid reading assignments. Synonymous with *plot summary*. Compare with abstract and summary.

synoptic chart : In cartography, a systematic representation of general conditions currently prevailing or predicted to prevail over a considerable geographic area at a designated time, for example, a chart used by meteorologists to forecast the weather. Click here to see examples used in forecasting weather over North America, courtesy of the University of Michigan.

systems librarian : A librarian whose primary responsibility is the development and maintenance of the hardware and software systems used in a library or library system, especially the online catalog and access to any bibliographic databases and other electronic resources. In some libraries, the systems librarian may also serve as Webmaster and be responsible for training staff members in the use of library systems. Systems librarians are organized in the Library and Information Technology Association (LITA), a division of the American Library Association (ALA).

table of contents (TOC) : A list of the contents of a printed publication in the order of their appearance, usually with page numbers as locators. In a book, the TOC lists the front matter, chapters or other major divisions of the work, and the back matter (see this example). In an anthology or collection, the TOC lists the titles of the works included by the editor(s) (stories, poems, plays, essays, etc.) in order of appearance. In books, the TOC is printed in the front matter on the first recto following the dedication or title page. In periodicals, the TOC appears near the front of each issue or on the back cover, listing the editorial content (articles, columns, reviews, etc.) but not any advertising. *See also*: current contents.

tawing : Preparation of an animal skin by treating it with alum and salts of iron or chromium, rendering it flexible and whitish in color. Tawed skins are very durable and more resistant to deterioration caused by atmospheric pollution than tanned leather. Geoffrey Glaister notes in *Encyclopedia of the Book* (Oak Knoll/British Library, 1996) that *alum-tawed* skins were used in bookbinding in England from the mid-12th to the mid-15th century and in Germany for panel-stamped bindings during the 16th century, sometimes dyed bright pink with *kermes*, a substance derived from the dried bodies of a scale insect that feeds on oak trees. Click here to see a 15th-century blind-tooled binding in alum-tawed pigskin (Cornell University Library). Synonymous with *whittawed*.

TCP : See Transmission Control Protocol.

TCP/IP : See Transmission Control Protocol/Internet Protocol (TCP/IP).

Telnet : On the Library Gateway, Telnet is an application that is sometimes used to access electronic databases. It is often thought of as access to databases in strictly textual format as opposed to access via the Web, which may provide images, search boxes, and "point and click" technology. Some people prefer using a database via Telnet when available since it can be faster and allow for more complex searching, but it is really a matter of personal preference.

temporarily out of print (TOP) : A term used on a publisher's invoice to indicate that the title ordered cannot be supplied because the last printing is sold out and to inform prospective purchasers that additional copies are expected from the printer in the near future. Compare with out of print at present. *See also*: out of print.

temporarily out of stock (TOS) : A term used on a publisher's invoice to indicate that the title ordered cannot be supplied because current inventory is exhausted but additional copies are expected, usually from the binder or manufacturer. Compare with out of stock. *See also*: in stock.

textbook pricing : According to the National Association of College Stores, the textbook market (including course packs) was a $6.77 billion industry in 2006, with the average cost of a college textbook slightly over $100. The relentless rise in textbook prices is one factor that threatens to make higher education unaffordable for students from low-to moderate-income families. The increases have sparked student resistance and forced college and university administrators, state legislatures, and even the U.S. Congress to address the issue. Various solutions have been suggested, including tax breaks, book rentals, and institutional licensing.

Textual Records : The term usually applied to manuscript or typescript, as distinct from cartographic, audiovisual, and machine-readable records and archives.

Thesaurus : A list of all the subject headings or descriptors used in a particular database, catalog, or index. The thesaurus for the Cornell Library Catalog is called *Library of Congress Subject Headings*.

thumbhole : One of a pair of semi-circular or triangular cuts in the sides of a slipcase, made at the mid-point of the fore-edge to facilitate removal of the enclosed volume.

According to Matt Roberts and Don Etherington (*Bookbinding and the Conservation of Books: A Dictionary of Descriptive Terminology*), the semi-circular cut is used in quality work, while the triangular cut, used primarily by library and edition binders in the United States, is more economical because it is usually made after the case has been covered.

title : The distinguishing name of a written, printed, or filmed work.

Total Library Expenditures (TLE) : The sum of expenditures for materials, binding, salaries and wages, and other operating expenditures during a given period of time.

toy book : A small, illustrated book for young children, published in 19th-century England and America, usually consisting of eight leaves of vivid, hand-colored pictures with very little text (alphabets and simple tales were popular). Originally issued in paper covers, later variations included cloth books printed on sturdy fabric, pop-up books, and flicker books. Toy books were often published in series to encourage gift buying and collecting. Click here to see an example illustrated by Walter Crane, courtesy of the British Library.

trace : A search by library staff for a book or periodical that the catalog indicates is on the shelf but you cannot find there. Request a trace for a book or other item at the circulation desk. Request a trace for a periodical at the microforms/ current periodicals desk. You will be notified when the item is found.

Transfer of Title : A legal document transferring ownership of a body of papers from one entity to another. The transfer of title must be signed and dated by the donor and by a university representative.

Transmission Control Protocol/Internet Protocol (TCP/IP) : A suite of networking protocols, including both IPv4 and IPv6, that are widely used on the Internet and that provide communication across interconnected networks of computers with diverse hardware architectures and various operating systems.

tribal library : A public library located on Native American tribal land (reservation, pueblo, etc.), usually staffed by a *tribal librarian* who speaks the native language. Funding for tribal libraries lags far behind that of libraries outside tribal lands in the United States. The Native American Access to Technology Program (NAATP) funded by the Bill and Melinda Gates Foundation from 1999-2003 helped to redress this inequity in American society. For more information, see the article *New Mexico Tribal Libraries: Bridging the Digital Divide* by Jessica Dorr and Richard Akeroyd in the October 2001 issue of *Computers in Libraries*. Lotsee Patterson of the School of Library and Information Studies at the University of Oklahoma maintains the *Directory of Native American Tribal Libraries*. *See also*: American Indian Library Association.

triennial : Issued every three years. Also refers to a serial publication issued every three years. *See also*: annual, biennial, quadrennial, quinquennial, sexennial, septennial, and decennial.

trilogy : A set of three narrative works related in theme or plot, which together form a larger work (*example*: the **Oresteia** of Aeschylus). Four similarly related works form a *tetrology* (**The Alexandria Quartet** by Lawrence Durrell). *See also*: prequel and sequel.

trimmed : A term used in the book trade to indicate that the leaves of a book have been cut down to a size smaller than the publication as originally issued. *See also*: trimming.

truncation : The dropping of characters and the addition of a symbol at the end, beginning, or within a word in a keywords search to retrieve variant forms. Truncation is particularly useful in retrieving the *singular* and *plural* forms of a word in the same search.

Truncation : Truncation is a symbol put at the end or in the middle of a word in order to catch all variant endings or spellings of that word when searching a database. For example, if conducting research on computers, entering comput? as a search term would yield records with the terms computer, computers, computing, computerized, etc. The truncation symbol is placed at the point in the word where various endings can begin to occur.

turnaway : In online systems, denial of access to an authenticated user when the allowable maximum number of simultaneous users is exceeded. Some database software includes an administrative feature designed to track and report turnaway statistics to the subscriber, for use in evaluating the need to upgrade the subscription.

typescript : An author's original typewritten copy of a work in the form in which it is submitted for publication, or a typewritten copy of the original commissioned by the author or publisher, as opposed to a manuscript written by hand. Click here to see a typescript of Philip Roth's *Patrimony* (1991) with holograph emendations, courtesy of the Library of Congress. Abbreviated *ts.* and *tss.* (plural).

typesetting : In printing, the setting of type from copy by hand or by machine, with attention to the aesthetic presentation of text, accomplished by a person called a *typesetter* (see these examples). To learn more about typesetting, try *Wikipedia*. *See also*: typography.

typographical error : A mistake in a printed work made by the typesetter. Also refers to a similar error made by a person using a keyboard to type a text. Most word processing software includes an automatic spell checker to alert writers to such errors. Abbreviated *typo*. Synonymous with *misprint*. *See also*: proofreading.

ultrafiche : A card-shaped transparent microform with a reduction ratio considerably greater than that of standard microfiche or superfiche (up to 3,000 frames per 4 x 6 inch sheet). A special ultrafiche reader-printer machine is required to view and make hard copies of documents stored in this medium.

ultraviolet (UV) : Electromagnetic radiation beyond the spectrum visible to humans as light, shorter in wavelength than violet light but longer than X-rays. The sun is the chief source of natural ultraviolet radiation. Because UV radiation can damage photographs and accelerate the deterioration of certain grades of paper, prolonged exposure of library and archival materials to direct sunlight should be avoided and incandescent lighting installed in storage areas where preservation is a high priority. Monitors can be used to measure UV exposure and filters installed to keep levels below the recommended 75 lux. Control is important because UV damage to books continues to a lesser extent even after the source is removed. The Heritage Collections Council of Australia provides information about the effects of ultraviolet radiation on library and museum collections. Click here to learn more about UV in *Wikipedia*.

unabridged : A version of a written work that has not been shortened and is therefore considered to be complete. The fact that an edition is unabridged is sometimes indicated on the title page of long works issued in paperback, but unless otherwise stated, a published work is assumed to be unabridged. An unabridged dictionary is the version containing the most words (*example*: **Webster's Third New International Dictionary**). Compare with abridgment.

unabridged dictionary : A dictionary that attempts to include *all* the words of a language. For the English language, there are only three, *Webster's Third New International Dictionary* (1961), *Random House Unabridged Dictionary* (1993), and the *Oxford English Dictionary* (1989). The latter is concerned more with etymology than with definition. First published in 1909, *Webster's Third* has about 450,000 entries (down from 600,000 in the second edition). The *Random House Unabridged Dictionary* has fewer words but more illustrations. Compare with desk dictionary.

uncoated paper : Paper to which no surface coating has been added to improve appearance and printability. In books consisting mostly of text, the text is usually printed on uncoated paper. Any illustrations printed separately from the text may be done on coated paper to permit greater detail in the graphic image.

uncorrected proof : A prepublication printing of a book, usually issued in plain colored wrappers, intended for editorial use or, in some cases, to be sent out for review. See this example or try a keywords search on the term in *Google Image Search*.

undergraduate library : A separate library established, supported, and maintained by a university to serve the information and research needs of its undergraduate students and the instructional requirements of the undergraduate curriculum (*example*: Odegaard Undergraduate Library and Learning Commons at the University of Washington). Sometimes administered as a branch library. Compare with graduate library. *See also*: college library.

undergraduate library : A separate library established, supported, and maintained by a university to serve the information and research needs of its undergraduate students and the instructional requirements of the undergraduate curriculum (*example*: Odegaard Undergraduate Library and Learning Commons at the University of Washington). Sometimes administered as a branch library. Compare with graduate library. *See also*: college library.

underground press : A publisher that issues printed publications unofficially or clandestinely, usually to members of a group or organization that opposes the policies of an established government or other authority, more common during periods of civil unrest than in times of peace and prosperity. Eventually, most underground presses either disband or become "above ground" publishing houses.

unexpurgated : A text or edition that includes passages omitted from other versions or editions, usually because the language or content was considered offensive to some readers. Compare with expurgated. *See also*: bowdlerize and censorship.

Unicast Address : An address that identifies a single interface and is used for delivering packets from one source to a single destination. With the appropriate unicast routing topology, packets addressed to a unicast address are delivered to a single interface.

Unified Medical Language System (UMLS) : A long-term research and development project undertaken in 1986 by a multi-disciplinary team at the National Library of Medicine to develop a metathesaurus, lexicon, and semantic network to overcome information retrieval problems caused by differences in biomedical terminology and the scattering of information across multiple databases. The purpose of UMLS is to facilitate the development of systems that enable health professionals and researchers to retrieve and integrate biomedical information from a variety of sources and make it easier for users to link disparate systems, including digital patient records, bibliographic databases, factual databases, and expert systems. NLM is employing UMLS in a wide variety of applications, including its *PubMed* database. Updated editions are distributed quarterly at no charge under a licensing agreement. Click here to learn more about UMLS.

Uniform Resource Locator (URL) : The unique address identifying a resource accessible at a particular location on the Internet for routing purposes. The same resource, or different versions of it, may be available simultaneously at other Internet addresses.

union case : A shallow, hinged box made to mount and protect an early light-sensitive photographic image by molding a compound of shellac and sawdust or wood flour, often into elaborate decorative patterns, using a thermoplastic process patented in 1854 by Samuel Peck. Most union cases are square or rectangular, but novel shapes are not uncommon (see this octagonal example). Click here to see the interior and exterior of a union case containing an ambrotype and here to see one made for a daguerreotype.

unit cost : The financial expenditure required of a library or library system to acquire and/or process an item, or to deliver a service that can be measured in discrete units, usually calculated as an average amount. For example, the Association of Research Libraries (ARL) includes in the unit cost of an interlibrary loan transaction the costs of staff time, network/communications, equipment, photocopying, supplies, delivery, and borrowing fees (*ARL Bimonthly Report* 230/231, October/December 2003). Economies of scale can be a factor in reducing unit cost.

United Kingdom Serials Group (UKSG) : An alliance of over 600 organizations concerned with the publication, distribution, and use of printed and electronic serials (and associated technology) and with their role in scholarly communication. UKSG publishes the electronic newsletter *Serials-eNews* and the journal *Serials* thrice yearly in print and online. Click here to connect to the UKSG homepage.

University Archives : University Archives, located in the Rare & Manuscripts Collections in Kroch Library, collects and preserves records of historical, legal, fiscal, or administrative value to Cornell University. Holdings include official records and reports of the university, its officers, and component parts; private papers of faculty, students, staff, and alumni; official and student publications; maps and architectural records; audiovisual materials including still photographs and negatives, motion picture film, oral history interviews, and audio and video tapes; and artifacts and ephemera documenting Cornell's history.

unlettered : A binding with neither the title nor the author's name displayed on the spine (or sides), making its content difficult to identify when placed upright alongside other volumes on the shelf. Prior to the 17th century, books were often marked by the owner with the title in ink on at least one edge of the sections to facilitate identification in a period when books were usually stored flat with one edge facing out. Compare with lettered.

unrecorded : A descriptive term used in the antiquarian book trade for a rare book or manuscript unnoticed by collectors and bibliographers (usually for centuries), whose discovery is of sufficient importance to merit recording an account of its existence.

unsophisticated : A term used in the antiquarian book trade to describe a book that has not undergone restoration or been altered with intent to deceive. Such a volume may, however, show definite signs of ownership and use.

Unspecified Address : For IPv4, the address 0.0.0.0. For IPv6, the address 0:0:0:0:0:0:0:0 (or::). The unspecified address indicates the absence of an address.

updating database : An electronic database in which the content is revised and/or augmented, usually on a regular basis, to provide current information or to add recently published sources. Most journal databases are updated on a regular basis as new issues are published and indexed.

Upper-layer Protocol : A protocol above IP that uses IP as its transport. Examples of upper-layer protocols include Internet layer protocols such as the Internet Control Message Protocol (ICMP) and Transport layer protocols such as the Transmission Control Protocol (TCP) and User Datagram Protocol (UDP).

Urban Libraries Council (ULC) : Founded in 1971, ULC is an association of approximately 150 public libraries located in metropolitan areas of the United States with 50,000 or more inhabitants, and the corporations that serve them, organized to solve common problems, take advantage of new opportunities, and foster applied research to improve professional practice. ULC is an affiliate of the American Library Association (ALA). Click here to connect to the ULC homepage.

URL : Uniform Resource Locator, or web address. Usually in the form of http://host.subdomain.domain Example : http://www.bls.gov

usability assessment : A variety of techniques for measuring or comparing the ease with which a computer system or interface, such as an online catalog or Web site, meets the needs of its users, including focus groups, surveys, direct observation of actual search behavior, exploratory activities in which volunteers are asked to organize categories of information or work with a prototype, comparison with existing guidelines and bench marks, and formal or informal testing. Without this process, librarians and technicians tend to design systems from a trained perspective, based on assumptions about information-seeking that may not reflect the behavior of actual users. A long-term usability assessment plan can become an ongoing component of library systems design. For more information, see *Usage and Usability Assessment: Library Practices and Concerns* (2002) by Denise Troll Covey, published by the Digital Library Federation and the Council on Library and Information Resources. Used synonymously with *usability testing*.

use life : The length of time or number of times an item can be used before it becomes so worn that it is no longer fit for use and has to be discarded. For books, use life depends on quality of paper, strength of binding, and actions taken to protect the cover, such as enclosing the dust jacket in a washable plastic sleeve.

User Datagram Protocol (UDP) : An unreliable, connectionless Transport layer protocol that runs on top of IP.

utility : A small program that expands the capability of a computer's operating system by enabling it to perform an additional task, usually something as routine as managing a disk drive, printer, scanner, or other peripheral device. Unlike the basic operating system, utilities can be added and removed as needed. A utility differs from an application program in being less complex, usually limited to a single function.

utopia : A term coined by Thomas More from the Greek *ou* ("no" or "not") and *topos* ("place"). A literary or artistic work in which the setting is an ideal society, usually existing in a future time or imaginary place (*example*: **Looking Backward** by Edward Bellamy). Utopian literature is created by authors who feel nostalgia for an idealized past or who wish to call attention to the need to reform existing social, political, or economic institutions. The opposite of *dystopia*. *See also*: fantasy.

UV Filter : A material used to filter the ultraviolet (UV) rays out of visible light. Ultraviolet radiation is potentially damaging to library, archival, and museum objects. More UV is present in sunlght and fluorescent light than in incandescent light. Removing UV radiation from storage, use, and exhibition spaces will reduce the rate of deterioration of library materials stored there.

Variable Length Subnet Masks (VLSMs) : The use of different subnet masks to produce subnets of different sizes.

Variable Length Subnetting : The practice of using variable length subnet masks.

Vertical File : A collection of materials such as pamphlets, newspaper clippings, brochures, or pictures, which because of their shape and often their ephemeral nature, are filed in drawers or cabinets for easy reference.

virtual reference : Reference Service conducted across the Internet in real time chat.

Volume : A physical unit of any printed, typewritten, handwritten, mimeographed, or processed work, contained in one binding or portfolio, hardbound or paperbound, which has been catalogued, classified, and made ready for use. (The study follows the definition used by ARL.)

Volumes Added Gross : The volumes catalogued by a library during a given period, usually a fiscal year. Not to be confused with acquisitions, although sometimes considered a surrogate for them.

wall shelving : Single-sided shelving placed against a wall and sometimes attached to it, as opposed to free-standing shelving (usually double-sided) designed to stand on its own away from a wall or other support. Shelving of both types is manufactured in sections to allow libraries to assemble ranges of varying length.

warehouse shelving : Library shelving with extra-deep shelves, capable of storing books 3 to 4 rows deep, used only in closed access collections to save space. According to Ruth Fraley and Carol Lee Anderson in *Library Space Planning* (Neal-Schuman, 1990), a section of warehouse shelving 30 inches deep and 36 inches wide with 7 shelves can store up to 63 linear feet of materials 3 rows deep and 84 linear feet 4 rows deep, compared with 42 linear feet for a double-faced section of standard library shelving, with the space gain outweighing additional floor space required. They note that although warehouse shelving is less attractive and not as flexible as standard shelving, it is the most efficient means of storing manuscripts.

warrant : A written document authorizing or certifying something, such as the payment or receipt of money. In law, a writ signed by the appropriate authority, authorizing a specific action, such as an arrest or search and seizure. In the United States, a warrant is presented to the person against whom legal action is to be taken. Because warrants often pertain to serious legal matters, they can be of considerable historical significance. Click here to see the warrant of James I, releasing Sir Walter Raleigh from the Tower on January 30, 1617 (Folger Shakespeare Library), and here to see the death warrant for the execution of John J. Kehoe on November 18, 1878, signed by Pennsylvania Governor John F. Hartranft and Secretary of the Commonwealth Matthew Quay (Pennsylvania State Archives). *See also*: literary warrant and user warrant.

water tear : Paper separated along a moistened line to give the tear a soft, uneven, feathered edge as the fibers gently pull apart without breaking, a technique used in making delicate paste repairs in books and other print materials.

waterstained : The condition of a book or other printed publication that has leaves or binding discolored by contact with water (see this example). *See also*: water-damaged.

Web browser : Client software that interprets the hypertext (HTML) code in which Web pages are written and allows documents and other data files available over the Internet to be viewed in graphical, as opposed to text-only, format. The appearance of a Web page may vary slightly depending on the type and version of browser used to view it. In the United States, the most widely used Web browsers are *Netscape Navigator* and Microsoft *Internet Explorer*. Netscape Communications is developing an open source Web browser called Mozilla.

welcome screen : The first screen a user encounters upon logging on to a database, Web site, or application program. A well-designed welcome screen gives the title, scope and coverage, name of author and/or producer, host, and a basic set of options, with instructions for using the system and a link to a more detailed help screen if needed. A well-designed interface includes a direct link back to the welcome screen on all subordinate screens.

wheel binding : A style of leather binding developed during the 18th century by Scottish binders in which the center of the cover is embellished with a circular design in the shape of a wheel, with spokes radiating from a central point. The style may have evolved from fan binding, popular throughout Europe during the 17th century. Click here to see an example with a foliate border (Glasgow University Library, Special Collections, Bm5-f.6). To view other examples, try a search on the keyword "wheel" in the British Library's *Database of Bookbindings*.

wildcard : In some bibliographic databases and search engines, the search software allows the user to insert a special character in the middle of a search term used in a keyword(s) search, to retrieve records or sites containing words with *any* character or *no* character in the position, useful for retrieving irregular plurals and variant spellings of a word. The wildcard symbol is not standardized. Users are advised to read the help screen(s) in an unfamiliar interface to see if wildcard is available and, if so, what symbol is used. *See also*: truncation.

Windows Sockets : A commonly used application programming interface (API) that Windows applications use to transfer data using TCP/IP.

wizard : An interactive utility available in some computer applications, usually in the form of a context-sensitive dialog box that provides step-by-step assistance in completing a complex task, as distinct from a general help menu accessible via the toolbar, from which the user may select as needed. Wizards can usually be turned "off" if found intrusive.

wood engraving : A relief process popularized as an illustration technique in the late 18th century by the British engraver Thomas Bewick, wood engraving differs from woodcut in the tools and materials used. The wood engraver applies the graver and the burin, tools associated with intaglio engraving, across the end-grain of a block of hardwood cut in cross section, rather than the plankside (side-grain) of softer wood, producing finer lines and wider tonal range than is possible in woodcut. In both wood engraving and woodcut, it is the uncut surface that takes the ink from which the image is printed, but in a wood engraving the impression is of dark lines on a light ground, the reverse of a woodcut. Click here to see examples of Bewick's work (Cornell University Library). For earlier examples, see *Teuerdank*, produced at Nuremberg in 1517 (Glasgow University Library, Hunterian At.1.10). Information on the *History of Wood Engraving* is provided by the University of North Texas Libraries and the Wood Engraver's Network.

workplace hazard : A substance or condition found in a place of employment, posing a real or potential threat to the safety and/or health of the employees exposed to it. Examples include asbestos, carbon monoxide, insecticides, mold and mildew, noise, radiation, repetitive movement, etc. In libraries, such hazards are typically encountered in preservation work and by employees whose duties require the routine use of toxic cleaning compounds. Click here to learn about workplace hazards involved in film preservation, courtesy of the National Film and Sound Archive of Australia. Because the identification and abatement of workplace hazards may involve substantial costs for the employer, success often hinges on the definition of "unacceptable risk" and "practical solutions." The Occupational Safety and Health Administration (OSHA) of the U.S. Department of Labor has established a Hazard Communication Standard (HCS).

works cited list : A kind of bibliography that appears at the end of a research paper. Only materials you quote in the body of the paper go on a works cited page.

workstation : An area within a workplace equipped with a personal computer and high-resolution monitor for accomplishing tasks that require the use of information in digital format (especially graphics), usually furnished with a desk, chair, and specially designed table to accommodate the PC and any peripheral equipment. If the microcomputer is networked, special wiring may be required. Also refers to a PC functioning as a client in a network. In this sense, compare with server.

World Wide Web : A graphical client-server information system that uses the Internet to access computers containing millions of hypertext documents.

xylograph : Text and/or image printed from a woodblock. The blockbooks of the 15th and 16th centuries are a prime example. Xylographic illustration was also used in manuscripts and press-printed books of the same period, sometimes hand-tinted. Click here to see woodcut illustration in a Book of Hours printed in 1503 (Cornell University Library). *See also*: chiro-xylographic.

xylography : Printing done from blocks of wood, especially by the early process of wood engraving, concurrent with the early development of printing from movable type. The results, known as *xylographica*, often contain more illustration than text. *See also*: blockbook and woodcut.

Yapp binding : A form of limp or semi-limp leather binding with rounded corners and bent-in edges that overlap the sections, sometimes by as much as half the thickness of the text block, named after William Yapp, the 19th-century bookseller who designed the style for pocket bibles sold in England. Geoffrey Glaister notes in *Encyclopedia of the Book* (Oak Knoll/British Library, 1996) that a similar style of binding with tooled edges was used in the mid-16th century. Synonymous wth *yapped binding*, *yapped edges*, and *Yapp edges*. Compare with circuit edges.

yellow pages : The portion of a telephone directory or trade directory following the white pages in which the names, phone numbers, and mailing addresses of commercial enterprises are listed, usually alphabetically by subject or in a classified arrangement, so named because the section is printed on yellow paper. Yellow pages are also available online (*example*: *SuperPages.com* from Verizon) and for specific professions (*Librarian's Yellow Pages*).

yellowback : An inexpensive popular novel bound in a shiny yellow paper or board cover with a picture printed on the front, usually a woodcut in three colors, a type of publication that originated in England in the 1850s and was used until the end of the century for inexpensive reprint editions. Click here to learn more about yellowbacks, courtesy of the British Library, and here to see them exhibited online (Monash University Library). Also spelled *yellow back*. Compare with dime novel.

zero-base budgeting (ZBB) : Financial planning that starts from zero at the beginning of each new budget cycle, with no assumptions carried over from previous experience, a method used in both the public and private sectors. In ZBB, every expense must be justified in each new cycle.

zig-zag book : A book made by folding a continuous strip of paper backward and forward accordion-style (see this example). When the pages are sewn at the back fold, the strip is printed on one side only. When both sides are printed, the folds are left unsewn to allow the volume to be opened to its full length. This form of book is called an orihon when made from a manuscript or printed document originally produced as a roll. Also spelled *zigzag book*. Compare with concertina.

zig-zag guard : In binding, a continuous single-piece guard produced by folding a sheet of strong paper or linen accordion-style, used in photograph albums and other guard books, in large blankbooks for sewing the folios, and in conservation bookbinding for resewing the sections. Also spelled *zigzag guard*. Synonymous with *continuous guard*.

zincograph : A print made from an engraving or etching done on a zinc plate. Click here and here to see two late-19th-century hand-colored examples by Alfred Jarry, inspired by devotional woodcuts (Spencer Museum of Art).

zip : To compress a data file using PKZIP software or some other utility capable of compressing data into PKZIP format. When such a file is restored to an uncompressed format, it is said to have been *unzipped*.

Zone ID : An integer that specifies the zone of the destination for IPv6 traffic. In the Ping, Tracert, and Pathping commands, the syntax for specifying a zone ID is *IPv6Address%ZoneID*. Typically, the *ZoneID* value for link-local addresses is equal to the interface index. For site-local addresses, *ZoneID* is equal to the site number. The *ZoneID* parameter is not needed when the destination is a global address or a Local address and when multiple sites are not being used.

zoom : In photography, to alter the size of an image from a stationary camera position without changing perspective by using a *zoom lens* to increase or decrease the focal length. In cinematography, this type of lens appears to make the camera advance toward the subject when *zooming in*, or retreat from it when *zooming out*. In word processing software, a feature that allows the user to enlarge or reduce the size of a page displayed on the screen, usually by a fixed percentage or in small increments. In Web browsers, a feature that allows the viewer to enlarge all or a portion of an image, sometimes in increments. Also, a feature on some photocopy machines that allows the user to specifiy the extent to which an original will be enlarged or reduced in size in copying.

zoomorphic initial : A figure initial in a medieval manuscript or early printed book composed wholly or in part of forms recognizable as animals or imaginary beasts. Zoomorphic initials are common in the *Book of Kells*. Click here to see a griffin in the the shape of an "S" in a 13th-century German psalter (Getty Museum, MS Ludwig VIII 2) and here to see an example in a 13th-century English Bible (Bodleian Library, MS Lat.bib.e.7). Click here and here and here and here to compare 11th-and 12th-century examples (courtesy of the British Library's *Digital Catalogue of Illuminated Manuscripts*) with this initial D in the 15th-century *Hours of Dionora of Urbino* (British Library, Yates Thompson 7) and this initial A in a 15th-century Italian antiphonal (Metropolitan Museum of Art). Zoomorphic motifs are also used in decorative line fillers, borders, and bas-de-page scenes. Compare with anthropomorphic initial and zoo-anthropomorphic initial.